THE TONY AWARD BOOK

FOUR DECADES OF GREAT AMERICAN THEATER

THE TONY AWARD BOOK

FOUR DECADES OF GREAT AMERICAN THEATER

LEE ALAN MORROW

ABBEVILLE PRESS · PUBLISHERS · NEW YORK

To Allison Burnett

JACKET PHOTOS (from top left): Richard Burton in *Camelot;* Len Cariou and Angela Lansbury in *Sweeney Todd;* George Hearn in *La Cage Aux Folles;* Terrence Mann in *Cats;* posters for *Brigadoon, The Gin Game, Big River,* and *The Mystery of Edwin Drood;* Julie Andrews and Rex Harrison in *My Fair Lady;* Jim Dale and Glenn Close in *Barnum;* Matthew Broderick and Randall Edwards in *Biloxi Blues;* scene from *A Chorus Line.*
Background: The Lunt-Fontanne Theatre, New York City (Christopher Little)

FRONTISPIECE: scene from *A Chorus Line.*
Photo credits follow Index on p. 274.

EDITOR: Alan Axelrod
ART DIRECTOR: James Wageman
DESIGNER: Renée Khatami
PRODUCTION SUPERVISOR: Hope Koturo
PICTURE RESEARCHER: Erroll Joseph Cantlin III

Library of Congress Cataloging-in-Publication Data

Morrow, Lee Alan.
　　The Tony Award book.

　　Bibliography: p.
　　Includes index.
　　1. Tony awards—History.　2. Performing arts—United States—History—20th century.　I. Title.
PN2270.A93M67　1987　792′.079　87-11501
ISBN 0-89659-771-7

First edition

CONTENTS

ACKNOWLEDGMENTS

During the months spent researching and writing this book a number of friends have offered their thoughts and suggestions, or have read parts of the manuscript, saving me from error. It is a pleasure to thank them: David Ascher, Wayne Koestenbaum, Glenn Ligon, William MacDuff, and especially, Frederick Q. Freyer.

The assistance of the librarians and staff of the Billy Rose Theatre Collection of the New York Public Library at Lincoln Center daily proved invaluable. In addition, Roger Puckett and the staff of Triton Gallery, and Martha Swope and her staff were exceedingly helpful.

The devotion of my research assistant, Erroll Joseph Cantlin III, to the enterprise has been my good fortune and has contributed immeasurably to this book.

My Abbeville Press editor, Alan Axelrod, and my agent, Eileen Fallon, have helped greatly through their patience, encouragement, and unerring sense of what this book should and should not be. The coagent on this project, Ruth Nathan, daughter of Jacob Wilk, a founding father of the Tony Awards, wishes that her contribution be dedicated to him.

But this book would not have been possible without the friendship and poetic vision of Allison Burnett. He has been, as always, my principal and most perceptive editor.

A NOTE ON DATES:
Unless otherwise noted, dates given for plays are those of the first Broadway production, not necessarily the date of composition or publication.

Mary Martin as Peter Pan (1954)

ROCCO LANDESMAN, WITH HEIDI LANDESMAN, RICK STEINER, M. ANTHONY FISHER AND DODGER PRODUCTIONS, PRESENTS "BIG RIVER: THE ADVENTURES OF HUCKLEBERRY FINN," A MUSICAL PLAY WITH MUSIC AND LYRICS BY ROGER MILLER, BOOK BY WILLIAM HAUPTMAN, ADAPTED FROM THE NOVEL BY MARK TWAIN, STAGED BY DES McANUFF.

BIG RIVER

THE ADVENTURES OF HUCKLEBERRY FINN

A NEW MUSICAL PLAY

THE BIG RIVER COMPANY: RENE AUBERJONOIS, EVALYN BARON, REATHEL BEAN, MICHAEL BRIAN, SUSAN BROWNING, RALPH BYERS, PATTI COHENOUR, GORDON CONNELL, CAROL DENNIS, ARAMIS ESTEVEZ, JOHN GOODMAN, BOB GUNTON, PEGGY HARMON, ANDI HENIG, ELMORE JAMES, DANIEL H. JENKINS, FRANZ JONES, RON RICHARDSON, JOHN SHORT, JENNIFER LEIGH WARREN AND WILLIAM YOUMANS. SCENERY BY HEIDI LANDESMAN, COSTUMES BY PATRICIA McGOURTY, LIGHTING BY RICHARD RIDDELL, SOUND BY OTTS MUNDERLOH, CHOREOGRAPHY BY JANET WATSON, STAGE MOVEMENT AND FIGHTS BY B.H. BARRY, CASTING BY STANLEY SOBLE/JASON LA PADURA, MUSICAL SUPERVISION BY DANNY TROOB, ORCHESTRATIONS BY STEVEN MARGOSHES AND DANNY TROOB, DANCE AND INCIDENTAL MUSIC BY JOHN RICHARD LEWIS, MUSICAL DIRECTION AND VOCAL ARRANGEMENTS BY LINDA TWINE, SOUND EFFECTS BY JOHN KILGORE, HAIR BY ANGELA GARI, PRODUCTION STAGE MANAGER: FRANK HARTENSTEIN, ASSOCIATE PRODUCERS: ARTHUR KATZ, EMILY LANDAU, FRED MAYERSON AND TM PRODUCTIONS, INC. GENERAL MANAGEMENT: DAVID STRONG WARNER, INC. "BIG RIVER" WAS ORIGINALLY PRODUCED BY THE AMERICAN REPERTORY THEATRE, CAMBRIDGE, MASS., ROBERT BRUSTEIN, ARTISTIC DIRECTOR AND SUBSEQUENTLY BY THE LAJOLLA PLAYHOUSE, LAJOLLA, CALIFORNIA, DES McANUFF, ARTISTIC DIRECTOR.

J EUGENE O'NEILL THEATRE, 230 West 49th Street

© 1985 DOUG JOHNSON

1 OVERTURE

On June 2, 1985, the Shubert Theatre was filled with Broadway's most famous for the thirty-ninth annual Tony Awards. The theater held eleven hundred, and the nationally televised production would be seen by millions. The previous month a musical version of Mark Twain's *Adventures of Huckleberry Finn* had arrived on Broadway. *Big River* did not get the rave reviews thought necessary to ensure a long run, and the ten Tony-nominated members of the *Big River* company—director, composer, author, designers, and actors—waited anxiously in their seats.

Big River had not come to Broadway with much going for it. The show had no stars, meager advance ticket sales, and only a so-so review by the all-important *New York Times* critic. Worse, it had originated in a regional theater and dealt with a rural theme, making it, perhaps, too provincial for a New York audience.

Winning a Tony Award often means the difference between success and failure on Broadway. The Tony identifies the winning show as a hit in the minds of potential audience members. The publicity bonanza of a Tony victory, a free, nationwide commercial, can negate bad reviews and almost serves as box-office insurance. Broadway audiences are human: they want to see and cheer "certified" winners. At the time of the first televised Tony Awards ceremony in 1967 Harold Pinter's *The Homecoming* was doing such poor business that a closing notice had already been posted backstage. The day after winning the Tony Award as Best Play, the box-office take for *The Homecoming* tripled, and the show ran for another seven months.

In recent years Broadway has played host either to stupendous hits (*Cats*: "Now and forever!") or one-night flops (*Harrigan 'n' Hart, The Three Musketeers*). The 1985 season in particular had not been a good one for Broadway musicals. Only seven had opened that year, and just three were still running on June 2. A month earlier, when the Tony nominations were being compiled, there had been talk that the award for best musical would not be given for lack of distinguished nominees. As it was, for the first time in Tony history, no awards were given for choreography or for leading actor and actress in a musical.

Just before the television cameras came to life, Alexander Cohen, producer of the telecast, walked onstage to deliver one last direction to the audience of potential winners: "I beg you to remember that acceptance speeches should be intelligent, witty, and brief. When you leave the stage, your award will be taken from you so that it can be engraved. If you take longer than thirty seconds to accept your award, it will be returned to you eventually, but your name will be misspelled."

Seven times that night a member of the *Big River* company went onstage to accept a Tony Award. Ten nominations, seven awards. The acceptance

Bob Gunton, Daniel H. Jenkins, and René Auberjonois in Big River *(1985)*

Ian Holm, Michael Craig, John Normington, and Paul Rogers in The Homecoming *(1967). Holm and Rogers won Tony Awards, as did the production's playwright, Harold Pinter, and director, Peter Hall.*

speeches were not those of jaded Broadway vets. Director Des McAnuff: ''I want to thank the Broadway community for being so good to us newcomers tonight.'' Composer Roger Miller: ''This is a hell of a deal. This is really exciting!''

The next day a line outside the *Big River* box office stretched down the block. The hopes and dreams of the *Big River* company, nursed through years of excitement and heartache, were at last realized. The Tony Awards had told millions that *Big River* was a hit, a must-see on their next trip to New York City.

Big River ran for 1,005 performances.

How did the Tony Award become the almost sovereign prescription for box-office success? Its origins are humble, its forty-year history glorious.

2 BEGINNINGS

Late in March 1917 playwright Rachel Crothers met with six other professional theater women to form an organization dedicated to helping those devastated by the war in Europe. Word was spread to women throughout the theatrical profession, and a mass meeting was held at the Hudson Theatre on April 13, 1917. The Stage Women's War Relief was founded.

Over the next three years this organization sold almost seven million dollars in Liberty Bonds at rallies, collected and donated to the Red Cross ten thousand cases of hospital supplies (including thousands of newly sewn and knitted garments), produced more than fourteen hundred stage shows for servicemen both here and abroad, and ran a servicemen's canteen in New York's Times Square.

A war relief committee theater men had formed was still in its infancy when the Armistice was signed. Rachel Crothers, on March 19, 1920, concluded the wartime venture of the Stage Women's War Relief more prophetically than she could have imagined: "At least we know this, that if we are needed again in a call which must supersede everything else in the world, we are here and ready—and if it comes after we ourselves are gone we should leave it in the annals of theatre that the trained imagination of the theatre can be used for serving humanity in more ways than entertaining."

In 1939 Rachel Crothers herself answered the call she had sounded two decades earlier. Joined by a group of illustrious theater women, including Vera Allen, Teresa Helburn, Josephine Hull, Gertrude Lawrence, and Antoinette Perry, she reawakened the quiescent Stage Women's War Relief and began again to aid America's allies. The organization became a branch of the British War Relief Society and was reconstituted as the American Theatre Wing War Service.

The Wing devoted itself at first to the same charitable duties it had performed throughout the First World War. During the American Theatre Wing's first year of service, two thousand newly gathered volunteers working out of space at Rockefeller Center sent to Britain six ambulances, three mobile feeding kitchens, clothing, blankets, cots, hospital equipment, money for the British Actors' Orphanage Fund, and four thousand pounds of coffee.

December 7, 1941, gave the Wing another nation's fighting men and their dependents to serve—its own. Some twenty-four years after the Stage Women's War Relief had first met in the Hudson Theatre, a second theatrical war relief meeting was held. Once again Rachel Crothers asked the profession for its collective help, declaring that their "unseen sponsor" was the United States government itself.

When America entered the war, the Wing announced its independence from the British War Relief Society in order to focus on American needs. While the Wing continued its donations of food, supplies, and clothing to all the Allies, under the new leadership of Antoinette Perry, it now moved vigorously into many other areas, eventually running fifty-three highly varied wartime activities.

Perhaps the most famous of all the organization's activities—or "projects," as Antoinette Perry liked to refer to them—was the Stage Door Canteen. Located in Washington, D.C., Newark, New Jersey, Philadelphia, Boston, New York, Cleveland, San Francisco, London, and Paris, the canteens welcomed millions of servicemen each year. Though no liquor was served, there were unlimited quantities of soft drinks, coffee, milk, sandwiches, doughnuts, and pie heaped on serving tables. The New York canteen opened March 2, 1942, with a bankroll of $300, to rousing renditions of "The Star-Spangled Banner," "God Save the King," "La Marseillaise," and the "Internationale." Located in a former speakeasy in the basement of the Shubert-owned 44th Street Theatre, the canteen welcomed more than one million servicemen a year—some three thousand daily—the queues often turning the corner and snaking down Eighth Avenue.

Forever memorialized by Irving Berlin in the song, "I Left My Heart at the Stage Door Canteen," the canteens were essentially sanitized nightclubs where off-duty servicemen could go to dance, relax, be entertained, and, perhaps, see a star or two. Without fail, the canteens would close each evening to a soldiers' sing-along of "Goodnight, Sweet Heart." During its four years of existence, one canteen wore out 120 copies of this record.

The scheduled entertainers, which included entire casts and orchestras of Broadway musicals, were joined each week by unannounced visitors like Alfred Lunt and Lynn Fontanne, Abbott and Costello, Gypsy Rose Lee, Harpo Marx, Jack Benny, Ed Wynn, Katherine Hepburn, Tallulah Bankhead, Shirley Booth, Katherine Cornell, Merle Oberon, Vincent Price, Rita Hayworth, Bette Davis, and Hedy LaMarr, all of whom pitched in as canteen workers.

While it was the presence of these stars that made the Stage Door Canteen famous, their visits were the exception rather than the rule. They were, in fact, rarely the main attraction. While most of the workers in the canteen were "names" only to their friends and relatives, the servicemen, if truth be told, were probably much too busy with the canteen hostesses to miss the stars. In a typically busy canteen, hostesses numbered over fifty per shift, nine hundred per week. The hostess corps included both black and foreign women, as the

RACHEL CROTHERS

The remarkable dramatic and social accomplishments of Rachel Crothers are now lost to memory. Most of her plays, which were written in the first three decades of this century, and her pioneering social work during and between the world wars are forgotten.

Beginning at age twelve, Crothers wrote plays for drawing-room performances, Sunday schools, and, while studying and later coaching at New York City's Wheatcroft School of Acting, for her fellow pupils and colleagues. In 1906 her short play *Nora* failed, and Crothers incurred heavy debts. The following year, John Golden produced her first full-length play, *The Three of Us*, which ran for over two hundred performances, astounding in those days.

After the success of *The Three of Us*, Crothers wrote twenty-eight Broadway dramas and social comedies, including *A Man's World, Ourselves, Myself, Bettina, Kiddies, As Husbands Go, A Lady's Virtue,* and *He and She,* in which Crothers herself starred. *Susan and God,* her most famous play, was chosen as the best play of the 1931 season by the Theatre Club and was similarly hailed in 1943 when it was revived with its original star, Gertrude Lawrence. Crothers wrote a number of screenplays for MGM, and several of her stage works were adapted for the screen. *When Ladies Meet* was filmed in 1932 with Ann Harding, Myrna Loy, and Robert Montgomery; it was remade in 1941 with Joan Crawford, Rita Hayworth, and Fredric March.

Rachel Crothers dramatized the conflicts between motherhood and career, the hollowness of marriage as refuge, and the unfairness of the male–female double standard. An early and ardent feminist who never married, Crothers mapped through her plays the step-by-step advances of women. "With few exceptions, every one of my plays has been reflective of a social attitude toward women at the moment I wrote it."

Crothers formed the Stage Women's War Relief during World War I, the United Theatre Relief during the Depression of the thirties, and the American Theatre Wing War Service, Inc. during World War II. By the time she died in 1958, at age eighty, her position as America's leading woman playwright had been usurped by Lillian Hellman, but Rachel Crothers's thirty years of work for those ravaged by war and economic hardship remained as a more enduring legacy.

Rachel Crothers in the World War I headquarters of the Stage Women's War Relief

Gracie Fields in the film The Stage Door Canteen *(1943)*

canteens were not only integrated but also open to all Allied soldiers. The job of a canteen hostess was to dance with the men ("Keep circulating!"), chat with the soldiers on safe, nonmilitary subjects ("Don't Talk! The Enemy Is Listening!"), and never surrender propriety: "No hostess is to leave the canteen at any time, under any circumstances, with a serviceman, or meet him outside in the vicinity of the canteen. Neither may she give out phone number or address. (Servicemen can write to the girls in care of the canteen.)"

"The Crossroads of the War," as the canteens were known, served as inspiration for a film and a radio series. The film, *The Stage Door Canteen,* featured a serviceman who falls in love with a canteen hostess. The forgettable story was really just a hook on which to hang the many cameo appearances of various stars. More important, 91.5 percent of the film's profits went to the Wing for support of the canteens.

"The Stage Door Canteen" radio show was broadcast on CBS from the 45th Street Playhouse, its proximity to the Times Square canteen enabling performers to move from canteen to broadcast studio and back. The opening show featured Helen Hayes and Selena Royle in a scene from *Mary of Scotland,* and comic relief was provided by George Burns and Gracie Allen.

Beginning with Katherine Cornell and Brian Aherne in *The Barretts of Wimpole Street,* the Wing, in conjunction with the USO, began to send the best of Broadway theater to the soldiers overseas. From Sicily to Iwo Jima, more than 350 shows toured. At first the Army shied away from the idea of sending touring productions into war zones. The huge casts and heavy props and scenery seemed a logistical nightmare. But, with the aid of many talented designers, directors, choreographers, and stage managers, the USO and the Wing endeavored to create Broadway spectacles in miniature. The musical *Mexican Hayride* was recreated with a touring cast of sixteen—on Broadway the same show used 107 singers and dancers. The prop case for the show came apart to form twin beds, reassembled into a tortilla stand, and, yet again, metamorphosed into park benches. Scenic drops were designed to fold into small satchels. Moss Hart took the entire production of *The Man Who Came to Dinner* to the Pacific in just two suitcases.

Such shows as *Three Men on a Horse, Panama Hattie, Oklahoma!, Anything Goes,* and even such classics as *Macbeth* toured to great acclaim. The shows went on even in active combat zones, with soldiers taking turns walking in from their foxholes.

Opera star Ernestine Schumann-Heink at a Liberty Bond rally organized by the Stage Women's War Relief. Madam Schumann-Heink just finished singing "The Star-Spangled Banner."

Maurice Evans and Judith Anderson in Macbeth *(1942)*

Also sent to entertain were concert, variety, and "Negro" shows, featuring such stars as Jascha Heifetz, Lily Pons, Jimmy Cagney, Bing Crosby, Fred Astaire, Ethel Waters, Bill Robinson, Cab Calloway, and, of course, even then, Bob Hope. None of the stars took salaries—such tours were a patriot's duty—and the chorus boys and girls accepted much lower wages than they would have earned if they had stayed at home.

Throughout the war the Wing used its primary resource, theater people, to head, staff, and maintain such additional wartime services as Mobile Libraries, Service Women's Tea Dances, the Ticket Committee (which distributed 1,500,000 free theater tickets), the Music War Committee (headed by Oscar Hammerstein II and charged "to find and exploit great war songs"), and the "Lunchtime Follies," short entertainments for use during war bond drives and for the lunch-hour relief of war-industry workers. Some of the Wing's 40,000 volunteers, in theaters ranging from the big Broadway houses to the smallest summer stock companies, gave intermission speeches from the stage and then passed the hat.

The Wing's Speakers Bureau sent specially trained actor-speakers, including members of Broadway road companies, barnstorming by taxi, subway, bus, railroad, and ferry to give bond-rally speeches and to perform informational sketches in stores and factories. Hundreds of speeches and performances a week made the Speakers Bureau the largest production organization in America. Such sketches as "You Give What You Got," on donating blood, and "I Didn't Know," on the necessity of keeping war information secret, "created a form of painless propaganda in which the factual is conveyed through pocket-dramas of genuine emotional appeal."

After the war, America moved to restore domestic stability. In 1946 the most celebrated symbol of the Wing's work, the Stage Door Canteen, closed. The Wing's charter was changed from its focus on war relief to service to the civilian population. Some of the wartime activities of the Wing continued, somewhat transformed, into the new peace. The Victory Players, who during the war presented educational dramas by famous authors intended to teach families how best to cope with their wounded—often helpless—sons, brothers, and husbands, now became the Community Plays—offering ten- and twenty-minute dramas to health and civic organizations. For example, "The Temperate Zone" demonstrated to parents techniques of teaching children discipline, and "The Room Upstairs" encouraged a lessening of tension between younger and older generations. Community Plays were not just public-spirited messages or casually produced skits, but good drama followed by expert speakers and discussions.

The vast number of wounded became the audience for the Wing's hospital shows, specially put together with help from physicians and psychiatrists. Many of the same performers who had entertained these soldiers overseas now toured among the military hospitals.

Having seen some of the finest actors, singers, and dancers, returning soldiers wanted to enter the field themselves, and the GI Bill became the means for theatrical training. In 1946 the American Theatre Wing founded its Professional Training School. That first year 1,650 former servicemen took courses in singing, fencing, directing, play analysis, acting for radio, television, and commercials, and writing for the musical theater. The program used the horse's mouth approach, with such teachers as Alfred Lunt, Sir Cedric Hardwicke, Margaret Webster, Eva Le Gallienne, Lee Strasberg, Ray Bolger, Martha Graham, Agnes de Mille, Kermit Bloomgarden, John Van Druten, Robert Anderson, Oscar Hammerstein II, Jo Mielziner, and Aline Bernstein. Producer/director Guthrie McClintic served as the artistic director of the drama division, while Jule Styne was the head of the musical theater division. Charleton Heston, Pat Hingle, Robert Horton, Gordon MacRae, Tony Randall, William Warfield, and James Whitmore were among the students who later rose to fame from these anonymous ranks. The program moved into a new home, and was rechristened the University of the Entertainment Arts. Workshops, seminars, and symposia joined the two-year planned courses, and a summer theater workshop, in Dennis, Massachusetts, was added. Even a "Winglet" program for the children of "Wingers" was developed. The Wing's "university" existed long enough to teach star-struck veterans returning from the war in Korea.

Today, the American Theatre Wing serves the American theater through such programs as Saturday Theatre for Children, which enables school-age children to see live theater—enriching the children's lives and encouraging the growth of future theater audiences—and through Working in the Theatre seminars, twice-yearly gatherings of talented and influential theater people who offer advice and guidance to newcomers and hopefuls in the audience. Continuing the tradition that started with the First World War, the American Theatre Wing still brings live theater to the hospitalized and institutionalized.

ANTOINETTE PERRY

Why, when I was 6, I didn't say as most children do, that I was going to become an actress. I felt that I was an actress and no one could have convinced me that I wasn't.

Antoinette "Tony" Perry did become a fine actress and also one of the most prolific and important female directors in America. But it is not for such achievements that she is remembered. Antoinette Perry's name and career are now honored but once a year, in the springtime, in association with Broadway's most prestigious theater prize, the Tony Award.

Born on June 27, 1888, in Denver, Colorado, Antoinette soon began giving performances of her own plays on the Perry front lawn—directing the other children—and studying voice and piano. The most important influence on Antoi-

Antoinette Perry

nette's choice of career was her uncle, George Wessel, who had acted with Edwin Booth in the late 1800s. Wessel, following the method of actor's training preferred in those days, schooled Antoinette to mimic Shakespearean parts as the famed stars of his day had declaimed them. This primitive training served well enough, and one day before her seventeenth birthday, Antoinette made her professional stage debut in Chicago as Dorothy in *Mrs. Temple's Telegram,* a play described as being "as full of complications as a door mat is of bristles."

On August 28, 1906, Antoinette Perry reached the New York stage. While the play, *Lady Jim,* was hailed by such reviews as "the most helpless mess . . . that has graced the metropolitan boards in a long day," Perry's New York debut garnered the personal reviews an actress dreams of: "Antoinette Perry, as little Miss Winifred, made about the sweetest, most piquant ingenue Broadway has seen for many long months; her personality is distinct, her acting clever, and her beauty is such as the poets apostrophize."

Perry's acting career blossomed, keeping her continually on Broadway and on the road. While she was playing opposite the great comedy star David Warfield in David Belasco's *A Grand Army Man,* she met Frank Wheatcroft Frueauff—cofounder of Cities Service Oil Company and, at his death, director of 141 corporations—and married him in November 1909.

Perry chose to retire from the stage to bear and raise the Frueauff children, Margaret and Elaine. Margaret became an actress (making her acting debut on Broadway in *Strictly Dishonorable* under her mother's direction) and married Burgess Meredith. Elaine began her theatrical career by understudying Ingrid Bergman in *Liliom* and stage managing the national tour of *The Barretts of Wimpole Street,* before developing into the producer/director of such Broadway shows as *King of Hearts* (with Jackie Cooper and Cloris Leachman). Elaine was also an active board member of the American Theatre Wing, serving for many years as Wing secretary.

Antoinette Perry

In 1922 Frueauff died. Perry, the two girls, and thirteen million dollars moved to England. Tiring of a socially prominent but prosaic existence, Perry returned to the United States and to the theater in 1924 in Zona Gale's *Mr. Pitt,* playing opposite Walter Huston at the 39th Street Theatre. Over the next few years Perry played in many forgettable comedies and melodramas, never quite matching her earlier success. She left the stage for the second time in 1928 and became a director, handling production staging for producer Brock Pemberton.

Pemberton had been the first to give Broadway productions to Sidney Howard (*Swords*), Maxwell Anderson (*White Desert*), and Paul Osborn (*Hotbed*), and Perry's association with him helped create one of Broadway's leading production teams. He would choose the plays and cast them, then hand script and cast to Perry, who would put the production together. During 1937 she simultaneously directed three major Broadway productions—*Now You've Done It, Chalked Out,* and *Red Harvest*—rehearsing in her living room segments of the three casts in rotation while she peeled peaches for preserves! Perry directed seventeen Broadway plays in fourteen years, a directing résumé rarely matched by man or woman.

Antoinette Perry was a pioneer. Except for costume design and, of course, acting, most of the theater was effectively off-limits to women in her day. Perry's initial directing work was received more as a curiosity than as a serious effort. Commenting on *Chalked Out,* for example, a violent prison drama by a New York State warden, *Daily News* critic Burns Mantle acknowledged Perry had done "a man's job." But she was soon appreciated as a force to be reckoned with. Her directing, always characterized by "brisk tempos, light touch, and delicate spirit," reached its apogee with her staging of Mary Chase's 1944 classic comedy, *Harvey.*

Antoinette Perry gave of herself not just to the commercial theater, but, as chair of the American Theatre Council's Committee of the Apprentice Theatre, she auditioned thousands of actors with the purpose of finding promising young performers, as yet unestablished in New York, and introducing them to leading producers, agents, and directors. In 1937 Perry became president of the National Experimental Theatre, Inc., an organization devoted to producing the work of new playwrights, which was jointly sponsored by the Dramatists Guild and Actors Equity. Each year Perry personally made up the company's operating deficit, until her increased preoccupation with the American Theatre Wing's war effort made it necessary for her to resign. Asked why she devoted so much of her time and personal fortune to such "thankless" activities, Perry replied, "I guess I'm just a fool about the theatre."

During the war, as Chairman of the Board and Secretary of the American Theatre Wing, Perry cut back on her own career in order to devote herself to the Wing's work. In fact, she was so often flying from one committee meeting to another that her mother once remarked, "You're not a person anymore. You're a Wing."

Perry's generosity was also directed toward her friends. Her associate, Brock Pemberton, remembered: "Once years ago, she wrote something and handed it to me. It was a promissory note from her to me for $25,000 I had never lent her. 'If anything should ever happen to me and you should be hard up,' she explained, 'just present this to my estate.'" Ironically, when she died of a heart attack in 1946, the day after her fifty-eighth birthday, her estate was worth $73,442 with debts of $376,265. Her production of *Harvey* was still running on Broadway, and would be for another five years.

THE TONY AWARDS

It was Jacob Wilk, a Warner Brothers executive, who first suggested, to Broadway producer John Golden the idea of an Antoinette Perry memorial. Since Perry had been chair of the American Theatre Wing board at the time of her death, Golden turned the matter over to the Wing, which asked Brock Pemberton to chair a special committee charged with finding a fitting tribute.

While many formal and informal suggestions for the memorial came in, "it was decided that any memorial for one so actively concerned with experimental effort and advancement in the theater should be, neither a building nor a monument, but a vital project to stimulate improvement in theatre arts." The Pemberton committee determined to begin "a living and self-renewing" memorial in the form of annual awards, by theater people for theater people. There had been some dissatisfaction in the theater community with the growing number of theater awards, including the Pulitzer Prize, which were given by "outsiders."

Following a professional rather than a critical policy, there were to be no "bests," but the awards were to be given for original contributions, innovations, and departures from the mean that were considered to further "good trends" in the theater and that "brought distinction" to it. The awards were to be for "outstanding" or "distinguished" work. It was felt, and rightly so, that no committee could ever hope to agree on the "best" performance, play, or collection of costume designs from an entire season's offerings. Anyone who has stood outside a theater as the audience is leaving knows from overhearing snatches of discussion that there is no possibility of agreement on the "best" from just that one performance.

The consequences of pitting one performer or production against another in some sort of contest, the winner chosen on perceived merit or popularity, discouraged the first Tony committee from publishing the nominations; only the people and productions finally recognized were to be made known to the public. The deliberations of the Tony committee were to remain forever secret. And it was not until 1956 that the Wing published a list of nominations. This was a move meant to heighten the suspense and popular appeal of the awards. Yet, to this day, the Tony is inscribed as an award for "distinguished" or "outstanding" achievement rather than for "the best" of a particular season—though the implication, as with other prizes of this nature, is inescapable. And while the nominees are now published, the process of their selection and the final voting remain shrouded in the traditional secrecy.

At the outset, the Tony committee announced no *permanent* categories of award. Rather, the categories were meant to be elastic, changing from year to year in order to acknowledge and encourage the new developments of value each season. The categories and the number of nominations in each category have remained in flux through the years. Tonys used to be given to Conductor–Musical Directors and to Stage Technicians. These categories were dropped in the sixties. In 1970 Tonys for Lighting Designers were instituted.

The Wing members who attended the special committee meeting and who chose by secret ballot the persons and productions to receive the first Antoinette Perry Memorial Awards—quickly known as the Tony Awards—included Vera

Allen, Jane Cowl, Helen Hayes, Brooks Atkinson, Kermit Bloomgarden, Burns Mantle, and Gilbert Miller. Before the meeting, a press release had been circulated in theater circles soliciting nominations, which would be considered by the committee, for the categories of Playwright, Scenic and Costume Designers, Dance Director, Stage Director, and Composer.

On Easter Sunday, April 6, 1947, the first annual Antoinette Perry Memorial Awards were presented in the Waldorf Astoria grand ballroom, which was decorated to resemble a wartime Stage Door Canteen. A Sunday night was chosen (and this continues to be the rule) because there were few if any Broadway

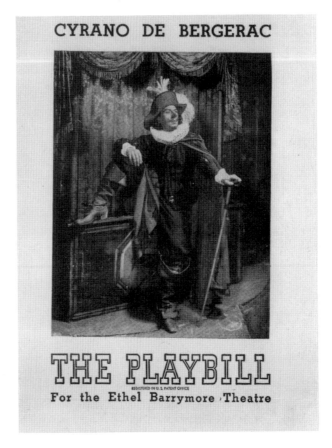

performances at that time, and members of casts and crews would be free to attend the festivities. As Antoinette Perry hated pomposity, there were no speakers or formal rhetoric that first ceremony. A nine o'clock supper, featuring breast of chicken Montmorency with black cherries and frozen soufflé Alaska with strawberry sauce, was followed by dancing and entertainment. At this, the first occasion on which the theater had ever given citations to its own, entertainment was drawn from current Broadway offerings. *The Chocolate Soldier, Street Scene, Brigadoon, Oklahoma!, Call Me Mister, Carousel,* and *Finian's Rainbow* were among the shows excerpted, in addition to such specialty performers as the Five DeMarco Sisters, the Golden Gate Quartette, Mata & Hari, Mickey Rooney, and Ethel Waters.

With tickets priced at $7.50 and the general public invited, more than 1,200 were present. (The public was to be welcome for many years: "All Theatre-Lovers are invited," began pre-event newspaper ads.)

At midnight the awards were made and broadcast over New York radio station WOR and the associated Mutual Network. Scrolls and sterling silver compacts for the women, and gold money clips for the men were awarded to the winners, who, it was said, would "not need an old family mantlepiece to harbor an 'oscar,' " as the Tonys were "useful articles." Before the design of the now-familiar Tony medallion—the product of a Stage Designer's Union competition won by Herman Rosse in 1950—other "useful articles," including watch fobs and bracelets, were presented.

It had been publicly hinted that, "in line with Tony Perry's lifetime effort to encourage young and new talent, preference will be given the youngsters," but a look at the winners of the first awards shows this was not necessarily true. While Patricia Neal and David Wayne were relative newcomers, the remaining winners were mostly seasoned veterans:

OUTSTANDING PERFORMANCE
    Ingrid Bergman, *Joan of Lorraine*
    Helen Hayes, *Happy Birthday*
    José Ferrer, *Cyrano de Bergerac*
    Fredric March, *Years Ago*

OUTSTANDING DEBUT PERFORMANCE
    Patricia Neal, *Another Part of the Forest*

OUTSTANDING MUSICAL PERFORMANCE
    David Wayne, *Finian's Rainbow*

OUTSTANDING SCORE
    Kurt Weill, *Street Scene*

OUTSTANDING PLAYWRIGHT
    Arthur Miller, *All My Sons*

OUTSTANDING DIRECTOR
    Elia Kazan, *All My Sons*

OUTSTANDING DANCE DIRECTION
    Agnes de Mille, *Brigadoon*
    Michael Kidd, *Finian's Rainbow*

OUTSTANDING SCENIC DESIGN
    David Ffolkes, *Henry VIII*

OUTSTANDING COSTUME DESIGN
    Lucinda Ballard, *Happy Birthday, Another Part of the Forest, Street Scene, John Loves Mary, The Chocolate Soldier*

SPECIAL AWARDS
    Dora Chamberlain—"For unfailing courtesy as treasurer of the Martin Beck Theatre."
    Mr. and Mrs. Ira Katzenberg—"For enthusiasm as inveterate first nighters."
    Jules Leventhal—"For the season's most prolific backer and producer."
    Burns Mantle—"For the annual publication of *The Ten Best Plays*."
    P. A. MacDonald—"For the intricate construction for the production of *If a Shoe Fits*."
    Vincent Sardi, Sr.—"For providing a transient home and comfort station for theatre folk at Sardi's for twenty years."

José Ferrer in Cyrano de Bergerac
(1946)

The special awards were handed out with an endearing charm, yet almost without discretion, and many of the newspaper accounts of the first ceremony devoted more space to the honors bestowed on personalities at the theater's periphery than to those awards acknowledging the genuine stars of the evening. In view of this, next year's ceremony did away with such appreciations and offered "special awards" only to insiders like Mary Martin and Joe E. Brown, for "bringing theatre to the regions while the original players remain on Broadway."

Probably the most telling acknowledgment of the first Tony Award ceremony was that reservations for the following year's ceremony, unannounced at the time, began to flow in during the dinner itself.

The first Antoinette Perry Memorial Awards were a success in every sense. The award acknowledged the contributions of both established and embryonic careers, recognized a season's most notable theatrical achievements, and, in a grand way, publicly honored careers spent on and about the stage. Throughout the next forty years, the vicissitudes and the glories of Broadway theater were to be mirrored in the Tony Awards.

3 ACTORS AND ACTRESSES

Hume Cronyn and Jessica Tandy in
The Gin Game *(1977)*

At the beginning of theater, thousands of years ago, there was the actor and the audience. Even today, with the elaborate intervention of such specialists as directors and designers, there is no theater without the actor. A playwright's text can be *read* by anyone, but an actor makes it *live*.

Actors fire an audience's imagination. People go to the theater to see the hit plays and musicals their neighbors have seen and are talking about. And they go to see stars. The name of a popular actor or actress on the marquee of a Broadway theater all but guarantees booming ticket sales. Indeed and unfortunately, most "straight" (nonmusical) plays enjoy healthy runs only when headed by a name actor.

Broadway stars whose presence guarantees ticket sales have "muscle"— muscle that not only boosts the box office but that encourages producers to invest in plays that interest the stars. Round and round it goes: a production can make a new star, and a star can make a production. And it all keeps the theater alive.

MUSCLE

Jason Robards has played more of Eugene O'Neill's heroes and has received more Tony Award nominations than any other actor. He is perhaps the finest American actor of the postwar generation.

Robards is the son of Jason Robards, Sr., a famed actor who, while never actively discouraging his son from going into the theater, always referred to the acting profession simply as "heartbreak, kid." While in the Navy (he was decorated for bravery at Pearl Harbor), the young Robards read O'Neill's *Strange Interlude*. That led him to begin acting studies at the American Academy of Dramatic Art after the war. His New York acting debut, in 1947, was as the rear end of a cow in a children's theater production of *Jack and the Beanstalk*.

In 1956 director José Quintero cast Robards in an Off-Broadway revival of O'Neill's *The Iceman Cometh*. His incisive portrait of Hickey, the dream mer-

Jason Robards—Jr. and Sr.—in The Disenchanted *(1958)*

chant, remained in Quintero's memory for many years: "The way he peeled away Hickey's cheerful front to get to the madness and guilt underneath was terrifying." The overwhelming success of the production convinced O'Neill's widow, Carlotta Monterey, to allow Quintero to stage *Long Day's Journey into Night,* a play O'Neill himself had not wanted performed until twenty-five years after his death. The production brought Tony Award nominations to Fredric March, Florence Eldridge, Quintero, and Robards, although only March, for his performance as the tortured James Tyrone, Sr., and the play itself, won.

Robards has performed in three other O'Neill plays on Broadway—*Hughie, A Moon for the Misbegotten,* and *A Touch of the Poet*—and in a revival of *The Iceman Cometh* in 1986. The first three of these performances were accorded Tony Award nominations. The foremost interpreter of O'Neill, Robards has much in common with the playwright. Both were sons of famous actors whose careers were overshadowed by one commercially popular play (O'Neill in *The Count of Monte Cristo* and Robards in *Lightnin'*); both had strained and intense relationships with a brother; and both fought long battles with depression and alcoholism.

The career of Jason Robards has not been limited to the plays of O'Neill. He received Tony Award nominations for his work in Lillian Hellman's *Toys in the Attic,* Arthur Miller's *After the Fall,* and Clifford Odets's *The Country Girl.* His only Tony Award win came in 1959 for his performance, opposite his father (their only performance together), in Budd Schulberg's *The Disenchanted.* Robards's stellar film career has included performances in Herb Gardner's *A Thousand Clowns* (in which Robards also played on Broadway), *Melvin and Howard, Julia,* and *All the President's Men.* These last two performances won Academy Awards.

★

The London stage debut of Rex Harrison, in *Getting George Married,* was greeted in 1930 with this review by James Agate: "Last night's play was a scratch affair, but it had one redeeming feature. A young man in it, whose name escapes me, seems to have a real talent for comedy." While at the start of his career he was barely noticed, his talent later made him perhaps the finest non-classical actor of his generation, a drawing-room comedian without peer.

Harrison's Broadway career reflects his growth as a man and an actor. In 1949, he won a Tony Award for his portrayal of the young and fiery Henry VIII in Maxwell Anderson's *Anne of the Thousand Days.* In 1957 Harrison's first performance in a musical, as Henry Higgins in *My Fair Lady*, was hailed both by Broadway audiences and Tony voters. In 1984 he was nominated for his performance as the ancient and sagacious Captain Shotover, in Bernard Shaw's masterpiece, *Heartbreak House.*

But it is as Professor Higgins that Harrison will be forever remembered. Actor and role came together in an inseparable blend of autobiography and fic-

Julie Andrews and Rex Harrison in
My Fair Lady *(1957)*

Barbara Cook and Robert Preston in The Music Man *(1958)*

tion. Harrison and Higgins: both reserved and somewhat diffident; both self-involved and uneasy in their relationships with women ("Sexy Rexy," as the tabloids called him, had—like King Henry—six wives); and both legends in theater history.

★ ▓▓▓

Look magazine once dubbed Robert Preston "America's answer to Rex Harrison." Preston also found himself inescapably linked to one role—that of a professor, albeit of a stripe rather different from Henry Higgins: "Professor" Harold Hill in Meredith Willson's *The Music Man.*

Preston began his career at the age of fifteen, touring with a stock company run by Tyrone Power's mother. Preston later joined California's Pasadena Playhouse, acting in forty-two productions over the next few years. Discovered there by a Hollywood scout, he was put under contract to Paramount and spent thirteen years making film after film, or, to be more exact, western after western.

Preston's Broadway debut came when he replaced José Ferrer in Hecht and MacArthur's *Twentieth Century.* The long years of preparation ensured that the opportunity was not wasted. Preston's success brought him more and more Broadway productions—*The Lion in Winter, The Male Animal, I Do! I Do!,* and *Mack and Mabel.* Though Richard Burton considered Preston's voice "golden thunder," like Rex Harrison, he was not a trained singer. Yet all Preston's Tony Award nominations have come for performances in musicals: *The Music Man, I Do! I Do!,* and *Mack and Mabel.* He died in 1987.

Robert Preston in The Music Man *(1958)*

Phil Silvers in the revival of A Funny Thing Happened on the Way to the Forum *(1972). His Tony Award for this performance was his second; twenty years earlier he received one for his work in the musical* Top Banana.

John Carradine, Jack Gilford, David Burns, and Zero Mostel in A Funny Thing Happened on the Way to the Forum *(1962)*

Zero Mostel considered painting his life's true career. Acting was only for the money to buy painting supplies. Because art-course offerings at New York's City College were limited, Mostel took freshman art eight times. He later taught art for the W.P.A. during the 1930s.

He began his entertainment career performing political satire in late-night clubs. His success at skewering the inflated pretensions of the day's political figures landed him on Broadway in the 1942 revue, *Keep 'Em Laughing*.

Mostel was endowed with a rubber face that could change from grin to grimace and from smile to smirk in an instant. He put that gift to work in Eugene Ionesco's absurdist farce *Rhinoceros* (1960). Using only face, voice, and body, he transformed himself from a mild-mannered man into a raging rhinoceros—hinting at the beast inside us all.

Two years later, in 1962, Mostel starred in his first Broadway musical, Stephen Sondheim's *A Funny Thing Happened on the Way to the Forum*. Playing Pseudolus, a slave willing to do anything in order to gain his freedom, he was perfectly suited to the show's inspired lunacy and won that year's Tony for Best Actor in a Musical. Ten years later, Phil Silvers, playing the same role in a Broadway revival, also won the Tony Award. Indeed, Silvers had been the original choice for the 1962 Pseudolus, but had turned down the role.

The son of a rabbi, Mostel—who didn't tell his father he had married a Catholic until his two children were nearing school age—was born to play Tevye, the woebegone dairyman in Bock and Harnick's *Fiddler on the Roof*. So close was the connection of actor to role, so strong the imprint of Mostel on the character, that all Tevyes are, to some degree, extensions of Mostel's creation. Mostel himself also realized the latitude that Tevye allowed an actor: "He's one of those characters who's bottomless. In the darkest moments, he has a lightness; in the lightest moments, a darkness."

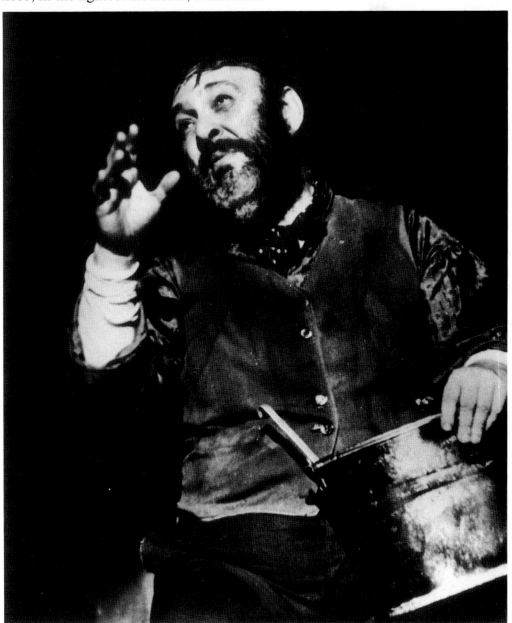

Zero Mostel in Fiddler on the Roof *(1964)*

The Fourposter (1951)

The American theater has been blessed with a number of distinguished husband and wife acting teams—Fredric March and Florence Eldridge, Eli Wallach and Anne Jackson, and the legendary Alfred Lunt and Lynn Fontanne. Beyond a doubt, the finest team of the Tony era is Jessica Tandy and Hume Cronyn.

During their forty-five years of marriage, Tandy and Cronyn have toured the world over, acting together and separately. Their work is marked by deft timing, subtle understanding, and an astonishing range of emotional color. The two have appeared together twelve times on Broadway, in everything from Albee and Beckett to Shakespeare and Tennessee Williams.

Jessica Tandy was born into poverty in London, in 1909. At the age of thirteen she began accompanying her widowed mother to Shakespeare-appreciation courses. Spurred by a love of the Bard, Tandy worked her way into and through the Ben Greet Academy of Acting. She started her career in small parts but soon made a London success in *Children in Uniform*, earning high praise from the not always generous Alexander Woollcott. After graduating to larger Shakespearean roles opposite John Gielgud and Laurence Olivier, Tandy moved to America.

Hollywood typed her as "English," and her career foundered. Tandy was anxious to continue to exercise her stagecraft, so her new husband, Hume Cronyn, directed her in a small showcase production of Tennesee Williams's one-act play *Portrait of a Madonna*. Williams happened to catch this performance, and it led to Tandy's engagement as Blanche DuBois in *A Streetcar Named Desire* (1947). The *New York Times* review by Brooks Atkinson dealt with Kim Hunter, Karl Malden, and Marlon Brando in just one sentence. The remainder of the review was devoted to Williams's poetical play and Tandy's unforgettable performance: "This must be one of the most perfect marriages of acting and playwriting," said Atkinson.

Born in 1911 into great wealth in London—Ontario, not England—Hume Cronyn studied law and art before beginning acting studies at the American Academy of Dramatic Arts in New York. He

was a character actor as interested in writing and directing as in performing. He spent much of his time in Hollywood as a writer of screenplays—most notably for Alfred Hitchcock, in whose films Cronyn also appeared as an actor. Cronyn continued writing; in 1983 his first Broadway play, *Foxfire* (cowritten with Susan Cooper), served as a starring vehicle for himself and Tandy.

Cronyn, whose acting is marked by an obsessive attention to detail, has given audiences perhaps the finest Polonius of this generation, and definitive performances in the title roles of Beckett's *Krapp's Last Tape*, and Molière's *The Miser*.

The radiant Tandy and the irascible Cronyn have each been nominated for five Tony Awards. Tandy has won three, and Cronyn one. From *The Fourposter* and *A Delicate Balance* to *The Gin Game* and *The Petition*, Jessica Tandy and Hume Cronyn have brought to the stage not only the wealth of their talents but the accumulated riches of their long life together.

Foxfire *(1983)*

If winning Tony Awards is used as a standard, then Julie Harris is Broadway's greatest actress. She has won five awards as Best Actress. A "very plain" child, Harris fantasized about becoming a star. At fourteen, after playing in a school production of *The Hunchback of Notre Dame,* she declared to her family: "Acting is my life."

Harris moved to New York, after studying at Yale, and made her Broadway debut in *It's a Gift* (1945) by Curt Goetz and Dorian Otvos. Five years later the twenty-four-year-old actress amazed Broadway audiences by playing the twelve-year-old motherless tomboy, Frankie Addams, in Carson McCullers's *The Member of the Wedding.* "That play," Harris once remarked, "was really the beginning of everything big for me."

Julie Harris is her generation's answer to Helen Hayes, the consummate character actress, perhaps most comfortable in historical roles. Hayes had made her mark playing Queen Victoria in *Victoria Regina,* and the title role in *Mary of Scotland.* Harris's major triumphs have been as Joan of Arc in Jean Anouilh's

Julie Harris in The Lark *(1955)*

The Lark (1955), Mary Todd Lincoln in James Prideaux's *The Last of Mrs. Lincoln* (1972), and as Emily Dickinson in a one-woman show by William Luce, *The Belle of Amherst* (1976).

The cardinal talent a character actress must possess is versatility. Harris has not only played historical figures—all painstakingly researched—but also a marathon dancer (*Marathon '33*; 1963), a chic divorcée (*Forty Carats*; 1968), and a flamboyant cabaret singer (*I Am a Camera*; 1952). Comedy or tragedy, classical or contemporary, Julie Harris year after year has proved herself one of acting's finest masters.

Peter Marshall and Julie Harris in Skyscraper *(1965). This was Harris's only musical.*

SHIRLEY BOOTH

At the age of twelve Thelma Booth Ford was forbidden by her father to pursue her dream of becoming an actress. She would not give up, and so her father, hoping she would quickly tire of the drudgery of theater, permitted her to play in various school and community productions. Thelma did not change her mind. Shirley Booth—her father refused her permission to act under the family name—left home at fourteen. She never spoke to him again.

Booth made her professional debut with a Hartford, Connecticut, stock company in *Mother Carey's Chickens*. She toured with the company for four years before making her Broadway bow in 1925, in *Hell's Bells*. The eighteen-year-old Booth was joined in the cast by another young actor, Humphrey Bogart. Booth followed *Hell's Bells* with *Laff That Off*, a flop that sent her back to stock for another decade. It was during these long years of touring that Booth learned the skills necessary to bring her dream of acting stardom to fruition. She learned to memorize fast and to bring variety to the many different roles in which she was cast. Touring, as Booth

remembered it, was night after night of "you get your cue and come out acting."

Booth returned to Broadway in 1935 in George Abbott's *Three Men on a Horse*, a hit farce in which she played for more than two years. After this came an almost unending succession of hits: *The Philadelphia Story*, *My Sister Eileen*, *Tomorrow the World*, and *Goodbye, My Fancy*, for which Booth won her first Tony Award.

In 1950 Booth opened in her greatest success, William Inge's *Come Back, Little Sheba*. She created a poignant portrayal as the deluded Lola, for whom the loss of beauty and the decline of her alcoholic husband's love threaten her world. Booth and her costar, Sidney Blackmer, won Tony Awards for their performances. Three years later Booth won an Academy Award for her recreation of Lola in the film version, which featured Burt Lancaster. That same year, 1953, she won yet another Tony, for *The Time of the Cuckoo*, becoming the first performer to win, in the same year, the highest honors for film and stage acting.

Come Back, Little Sheba *(1950)*

The Time of the Cuckoo *(1953)*

Shirley Booth spent five years during the sixties on television, winning Emmy after Emmy for her series, *Hazel,* the role (a housemaid) that forms most people's memories of Booth's acting. After quitting the still-popular series, Booth returned to stock, touring theaters in revivals of her biggest stage hits, *My Sister Eileen, The Time of the Cuckoo,* and *Come Back, Little Sheba.* She returned to Broadway to act in the musical *Look to the Lilies.*

Throughout Shirley Booth's long career she never received a bad review. Her performances—covering a vast range of characters—were always infused with a great wealth of warmth and humor. Her personal self-sufficiency served as the backbone for many of her characterizations. But the source of her continuing love affair with the theatrical community and her audiences was more basic. "I have the average woman appeal. I'm not terribly different. I symbolize the average woman with the same frailties; the audience can identify with me." And for more than fifty years, they did.

Colleen Dewhurst has tied Julie Harris with eight Tony nominations, but she has won only twice, for Tad Mosel's *All the Way Home* (1961) and O'Neill's *A Moon for the Misbegotten* (1974). Dewhurst was born in Montreal and trained at the American Academy of Dramatic Arts in New York.

Her performance as Kate in Shakespeare's *The Taming of the Shrew* for Joseph Papp brought the young actress to the attention of other New York producers. Although highly versatile, Dewhurst has spent much of her career using her husky voice, roaring laugh, and innate sexuality to play prostitutes and earth mothers. Many of these portrayals have been in the plays of Edward Albee— *The Ballad of the Sad Cafe* (adapted from the Carson McCullers short story) and *Who's Afraid of Virginia Woolf?*—and Eugene O'Neill—*More Stately Mansions, Mourning Becomes Electra,* and *A Moon for the Misbegotten.*

It was as Josie Hogan, the gigantic Irish farmgirl in *A Moon for the Misbegotten,* that Dewhurst achieved her biggest success. Her wrenching search for love and absolution was matched by the performance of her costar, Jason Robards, and the mastery of her director, José Quintero. This revival of *Moon* was entered into with few hopes: "When we decided to do this play, José, Jason and I, we were broke, with no place to go, and the most we hoped was that *Moon* would have a run in summer stock." It ran for 313 performances.

The biggest challenge to Mary Martin and Ethel Merman's domination of the musical came from an unexpected quarter. Gwen Verdon had neither Martin's winning personality nor Merman's mighty voice, but she could do what Martin and Merman couldn't do—dance.

Verdon began daily dancing lessons at the age of two as a knock-kneed child forced to wear corrective shoes (for which the other children nicknamed her "Boots"). Her mother, a former professional dancer with the Denishawn modern dance troupe, was her teacher. Dancing became Gwen Verdon's life. For Hollywood, she stood in as Rita Hayworth's feet and Marilyn Monroe's torso. She made her Broadway debut in *Alive and Kicking* (1950). Three years later her acrobatic "Apache Dance" stopped Cole Porter's *Can-Can.* Though this was her first major Broadway role, Verdon had already been dancing for twenty-five years.

In 1956 Verdon starred as the flirtatious and devilish Lola in *Damn Yankees,* choreographed by Bob Fosse, whom she later married, and who choreographed her next five Broadway shows.

Bob Merrill's musical adaptation of Eugene O'Neill's *Anna Christie, New Girl in Town,* followed *Damn Yankees* for the team of Fosse and Verdon. At that season's Tony Award ceremony (1958), Verdon and costar Thelma Ritter recorded the first tie ever, as both received leading musical actress awards. That Tony was Verdon's third in as many nominations.

Gwen Verdon in New Girl in Town *(1958)*

Stephen Douglass and Gwen Verdon in Damn Yankees *(1955)*

After the commercially less successful *Redhead* (which nevertheless garnered her yet another Tony Award), Verdon turned in her most famous performance, that of Charity Hope Valentine, in *Sweet Charity* (1966). Verdon's natural naiveté and vulnerability brought to vibrant life the ever-hopeful taxi dancer.

Broadway's greatest dancing star has begun passing on her command of the Fosse style by serving as dance supervisor and coach on Fosse's *Dancin'* (1978) and the 1986 revival of *Sweet Charity,* which starred Debbie Allen.

Like Gwen Verdon, Angela Lansbury has won four Tony Awards, although, unlike Verdon, Lansbury needed only four nominations. Her emergence as a musical star was a surprise to Broadway. Better known as an actress, Lansbury brought her dramatic skills to *Mame* (1966), *Dear World* (1969), *Gypsy* (1974), and, in her finest performance, to Stephen Sondheim's *Sweeney Todd* (1979).

Lansbury came to the United States from England at the age of fifteen, escaping the war in Europe. After a short stay in New York, Lansbury, the daughter of actress Monya MacGill, went to Hollywood in 1942. The week of her arrival she was cast in *The Picture of Dorian Gray* and *Gaslight* (receiving Oscar nominations for both).

Angela Lansbury in Dear World *(1969)*

Hollywood often cast Lansbury as a sexy bad girl. Her slapping Judy Garland in *The Harvey Girls* actually roused American filmgoers against Lansbury for a time. Later, she was frequently cast as a mother, but when she played the predatory mother in *The Manchurian Candidate,* she was only three years older than Laurence Harvey, who played her son.

Despite the rewards of Hollywood, Lansbury's first love was the theater, and she always alternated stage appearances with her film roles. It was her performance in Jerry Herman's *Mame* that proved to be her stage breakthrough. Whipping through twenty costume changes, and joining slapstick with sentiment, Lansbury dazzled Broadway.

After her next show, Herman's *Dear World* (a musical adaptation of Giraudoux's *The Madwoman of Chaillot*), Lansbury retired with her family to an isolated estate in Ireland. Her son had fallen into trouble in Hollywood, and the move in 1971 to Ireland was a chance for him to recover.

Two years later she restarted her career in London, playing Queen Gertrude to Albert Finney's Hamlet. There she also played in *Gypsy,* with which she later traveled to Broadway and toured the United States. *Gypsy* reminded Broadway of her stardom. Although she was not the overpowering presence that Ethel Merman had been in the original production, Lansbury created a Mama Rose that was a slow-gathering storm, bursting at the emotionally wrenching finale, "Rose's Turn."

Bernadette Peters is today's leading musical actress and one of the few contemporaries with the muscle to keep a show running. Both Sondheim's *Sunday in the Park with George* and Andrew Lloyd Webber's *Song & Dance* owe much of their popularity to Peters. It is something of a tradition with Peters: her performances are often the most acclaimed part of a production.

At the age of three Bernadette Peters began taking tap-dancing lessons. Two years later, in 1953, she was featured on television's "Horn and Hardart Hour." At thirteen Peters (with her stage-struck mother as chaperone) played Baby June in a road company of *Gypsy.* Her first New York hit was the Off-Broadway production of *Dames at Sea* (1968), a spoof of Busby Berkeley musicals that was a perfect showcase for the actress.

Peters's career foundered in the late sixties and early seventies through failures (*On the Town* and *La Strada*) and near-misses (*George M!* and *Mack and Mabel*), but her ability to turn in wonderful performances even in lackluster shows meant that she was highly valued by Broadway producers.

Peters's vulnerability brought humanity and warmth to *Sunday in the Park with George* and earned her a Tony nomination. Her tour-de-force performance in *Song & Dance,* with its one-hour, one-woman, all-singing first act, anointed Peters as Broadway's finest singing actress since Mary Martin and Ethel Merman.

CAMERON MACKINTOSH Inc.
THE SHUBERT ORGANIZATION
F.W.M. PRODUCING GROUP
by arrangement with
THE REALLY USEFUL COMPANY LTD
present

BERNADETTE PETERS
in
Andrew Lloyd Webber's
SONG & DANCE

also starring
CHRISTOPHER d'AMBOISE
with
CHARLOTTE d'AMBOISE
DENISE FAYE
GEN HORIUCHI
GREGORY MITCHELL
CYNTHIA ONRUBIA
MARY ELLEN STUART
SCOTT WISE
and
GREGG BURGE

Music by ANDREW LLOYD WEBBER Lyrics by DON BLACK
Orchestrations by ANDREW LLOYD WEBBER and DAVID CULLEN
Production musical advisor DAVID CADDICK Musical Supervision & direction by JOHN MAUCERI
Executive producers R. TYLER GATCHELL JR. & PETER NEUFELD
Casting by JOHNSON-LIFF ASSOCIATES Sound by MARTIN LEVAN
Settings by ROBIN WAGNER Costumes by WILLA KIM Lighting by JULES FISHER
Choreographed by PETER MARTINS
American adaptation,additional lyrics & direction by RICHARD MALTBY JR.
Entire production supervised by
RICHARD MALTBY JR. & PETER MARTINS

ROYALE THEATRE
45th STREET, WEST OF BROADWAY

45 ★

Ethel Merman in the film Stage Door Canteen *(1943)*

On May 15, 1977, to the accompaniment of "Send in the Clowns," a Navy nurse in an oversize sailor's uniform and a stage-struck mother dressed in a ratty coat and hat burst onto the Broadway Theatre stage. Mary Martin and Ethel Merman were appearing on Broadway together for the first, and only, time. Their special one-night benefit performance reprised and highlighted the careers of these two luminaries of the American musical theater.

While Ethel Merman was playing *Annie Get Your Gun* on Broadway, Mary Martin was playing it on the road. While Martin was playing *Hello, Dolly!* in London, Merman was closing the show in New York. But apart from these two shows, they represented very different strains of musical theater—Merman at her best with the jazzy syncopations of Cole Porter and Irving Berlin, Martin at home with the simpler joys of Rodgers and Hammerstein.

Born Ethel Agnes Zimmerman, Merman made her debut at the age of five singing for the Astoria (New York) Republican Club. Though determined to make it as a

Call Me Madam *(1950)*

singer, the pragmatic Merman went to a four-year business school to learn typing and shorthand just in case her vocal career failed to materialize. (Merman helped her career along by leaving one secretarial position for another when she heard that the new boss had important friends in show biz.)

Singing in nightclubs brought her an agent and her first role, as Kate Fothergill in George Gershwin's *Girl Crazy* (1930). The show's star, Ginger Rogers, worked to get Merman's part cut down drastically, but Merman didn't need dialogue when she had such songs as "Sam and Delilah," "Boy, What Love Has Done to Me," and "I Got Rhythm." Merman's trumpeting of a high C for an entire sixteen-bar chorus of the latter song—while the orchestra continued playing—made her an instant star.

A self-taught singer, Ethel Merman wowed Broadway with her clarion voice— "I just stand up and holler and hope my voice holds out." Composers soon learned that this force of nature walloped their songs clearly to the backs of the balconies. Cole Porter realized, "When you write lyrics for Ethel Merman they'd better be good because everyone's going to hear them."

Merman, who starred in more hit musicals than any other performer, began her string of five Cole Porter shows with *Anything Goes* (a show Merman wouldn't accept until Porter played the score for her parents and they approved; two songs were rejected). Merman went on to stun Broadway with her singing in *Red, Hot and Blue!* ("It's De-Lovely"), *Dubarry Was a Lady* ("Friendship"), *Something for the Boys* ("By the Mis-iss-iss-iss-iss-iss-iss-iss-iss-inewa"), and *Call Me Madam,* in which she played a role blatantly based on society hostess Perle Mesta ("The Hostess with the Mostes' on

the Ball"). The program lamely cautioned: "Neither the character of Miss Sally Adams nor Miss Ethel Merman resembles any person living or dead."

In 1946 Irving Berlin and Ethel Merman had their biggest success in *Annie Get Your Gun.* At first *Annie Get Your Gun* was meant to be a Jerome Kern musical, but Berlin was brought in after Kern's death. Unsure of his ability to write about the Wild West, the composer wrote ten songs in eight days for the approval of his star and producers, Rodgers and Hammerstein. Berlin's songs could have found no better interpreter than Ethel Merman. The brassy but naive Merman delivered "Anything You Can Do, I Can Do Better," and "There's No Business Like Show Business" like no one else. This combination of writer, role, and performer proved a sure-fire hit.

Thirteen years after *Annie Get Your Gun* Merman showed Broadway that she was more than just a pair of lungs. The ease with which Merman handled the drama of *Gypsy* proved her worth as an actress (yet she lost the Tony that year to Mary Martin's performance in *The Sound of Music*). Storming up the theater's aisle crying, "Sing out, Louise!," Merman's Mama Rose was her last new role and the first role in which she toured. It was as Mama Rose, her favorite role, that Merman came onto the Broadway Theatre stage for *Ethel Merman and Mary Martin: Together on Broadway.*

"The Merm" privately suffered the drug-related death of her daughter, Ethel, Jr., and the breakups of her four marriages (including one to Ernest Borgnine, which lasted just over a month). Her most fitting epitaph, typical of the unpretentious and outspoken Merman, was, "Broadway's been very good to me—but then, I've been very good to Broadway."

Mary Martin in her South Pacific *dressing room (1949)*

The only musical star to equal the stature of The Merm was Mary Martin. Martin is in many ways the opposite of what Merman was—rural Texan, fond of touring, ever cheerful.

Martin began as a child performer in Weatherford, Texas, church socials. Later, she supported her young son (Larry Hagman, who became famous as J.R. on television's *Dallas*) by giving dancing lessons. Finding that she was barely able to stay ahead of her pupils, Martin went to Hollywood for a summer's worth of lessons herself. One day she wandered into an audition, sang "So Red the Rose," and won the opportunity to serve as backup singer for her dance school's performances. Once back in Weatherford it wasn't long before her little Hollywood success propelled her to New York.

The success of Martin's Broadway debut was as instantaneous as Merman's. Dressed in a mink and little else, she cooed "My Heart Belongs to Daddy" in Cole Porter's *Leave It to Me!* (1938). Kurt Weill's *One Touch of Venus* (1943), Martin's first starring role, set her in Broadway's mind as the irrepressible innocent.

Martin had turned down *Oklahoma!* in order to do the Weill show. Martin's ability to choose winning projects was not always infallible. In later years, she turned down *Kiss Me, Kate; My Fair Lady;* and *Mame.* When Rodgers and Hammerstein approached Martin about starring in *South Pacific,* she was uncertain. The thought of singing with the famed operatic basso Ezio Pinza terrified and puzzled her ("Why on earth do you want two basses?"). Assuring her that she would never have to sing "in competition" with Pinza, Rodgers created a score for Martin in which the only duet consists of monologues sung alternately. Mary Martin spent over three years in *South Pacific* "not singing" with five different Emile de Becques.

Martin followed *South Pacific* with *Peter Pan* and forever etched her all-

American style into the memory of a generation. Her joy in performance was hurled across the footlights in handfuls of fairy dust. During the decade of the fifties, Martin performed—almost nonstop—in only three Broadway musicals, *South Pacific*, *Peter Pan*, and *The Sound of Music*. All three brought her Tony Awards. (Merman won only one Tony, in 1951, for *Call Me Madam*.)

Coproduced by her husband, Richard Halliday, *The Sound of Music* brought Martin back to Broadway with another stage full of children. Playing Maria Von Trapp, with whom she studied for the part, Martin was the quintessential Rodgers and Hammerstein heroine: self-sufficient, energetic, and deeply romantic.

Early in her career Martin received some advice from Alfred Lunt: "If you intend to make the theater your life, you must tour. You build your career, get the experience, create your own audiences, on the road." Martin took this to heart, touring with her hit shows across this country and throughout the world, and, of course, taking *Peter Pan* on an electronic tour—in televised form.

Peter Pan *(1954)*

How Do You Support a Star?

As far as the Tony Award is concerned, a leading actor is one whose name appears above the title of the play. The name of a "supporting" or "featured" actor (the terms are used interchangeably) is printed below the title, and, generally speaking, the supporting actor's part is smaller or less important to the play than the star's.

Supporting performers are a varied lot. While every actor wants to be adored, some appreciate the position of supporting actor—and others are simply willing momentarily to forego stardom to have a job. Not every actor possesses the temperament needed to withstand the pressures of being a star, although many supporting actors later graduate to starring roles.

Supporting performers are unsung heroes. They tend to stay with a production for many, many months, if not years, adjusting to dozens of cast replacements. Jerry Orbach played in *42nd Street* for four and a half years, 1,929 performances. Actors like Orbach provide the backbone that allows a show to continue without a loss of performance quality.

The names that recur most frequently in supporting actor and actress nominations are those of musical performers. Musicals tend to be more formulaic than comedies or dramas, and a performer who is successful as an ingenue's irascible father in one show will often be hired to play the ingenue's befuddled father in another.

For many years the grand old man of supporting actors was David Burns. Born in 1902 in New York's Chinatown, the son of a policeman, Burns would have followed in his father's footsteps had he not seen a sign on his high school's bulletin board offering twenty dollars a week for theatrical extras. He became an actor, making his Broadway debut in 1923, then left for London, where work was more abundant.

Burns returned to Broadway in 1939 to play in Kaufman and Hart's *The Man Who Came to Dinner* and then began a series of long-running engagements. He spent three-and-a-half years touring with *Oklahoma!,* two years on the road with *South Pacific,* and stayed on Broadway three years as Horace Vandergelder, the half-a-millionaire, in *Hello, Dolly!* ("What's the point of going around looking for jobs? I wouldn't know a better show if I read it.").

Playing the ineffectual Mayor Shinn in *The Music Man* brought Burns his first Tony Award in 1958. During yet another long run, he received his second Tony five years later playing an impotent lecher in *A Funny Thing Happened on the Way to the Forum.* Set to play the pivotal role of the secondhand furniture dealer in Arthur Miller's *The Price* (1968), he fell ill just four days before opening night. His understudy went on, but Burns returned several weeks later, and his performance was widely and critically acclaimed.

In 1971, while performing in the Philadelphia tryout of Kander and Ebb's *70*

Girls 70, David Burns died of a stroke. The show never made it to New York. A willing servant to the plays in which he appeared, the actor had earlier spoken his own epitaph, the creed of all supporting players: "I'm the best-known unknown actor around."

George Rose has a Broadway reputation as one of the stage's most dependable actors. He always turns in superior performances, staying with productions for long runs. Of his five Tony nominations, only one is in the supporting category, but Rose most often plays in ensemble pieces, where the play is more important than the individual performance.

Rose was a music student in college (he was disciplined after being caught playing "I'm in the Mood for Love" on the chapel organ) and started his theatrical career serving as an off-stage singer for Tyrone Guthrie's Old Vic production of *Peer Gynt* (1944). Rose left his music studies behind when Guthrie began using him for walk-ons and other small parts.

Rose first came to Broadway's attention when he played the Common Man (a collection of eight parts) with Paul Scofield's Thomas More in Robert Bolt's *A Man for All Seasons* (1961). He later played in Richard Burton's *Hamlet* (1964), winning high praise as Shakespeare's comic gravedigger.

Rose's performances as the "very model of a modern Major General" in Gilbert and Sullivan's *The Pirates of Penzance* (1981), as the bumptious Alfred P. Doolittle in *My Fair Lady* (1976), and as the music-hall master of ceremonies in *The Mystery of Edwin Drood* (1985) were all favorites with both critics and audiences. The last two performances won Tony Awards.

Rose was joined in *The Pirates of Penzance* by the consummate and versatile Kevin Kline, whose Pirate King was a bumbling swashbuckler more apt to stab himself than his enemies. Like many of his generation's actors, Kline alternates stage with film work—*Sophie's Choice* followed by *Henry V*; *The Big Chill* followed by *Hamlet.* The presence of numerous Shakespearean roles on Kline's résumé is explained by the fact that he was trained at Juilliard and was a founding member of the Acting Company, a touring group made up of Juilliard graduates and directed by John Houseman. Kline toured with the Acting Company for four years before settling in New York.

Working Off-Broadway, on soap operas, and in commercials sustained Kline until he landed the role of Bruce Granit in the musical *On the Twentieth Century* (1978). His Tony-winning performance as the narcissistic gigolo more in love with himself than his girl catapulted Kline into Broadway stardom and cleared his entry into Hollywood.

A fellow Juilliard alumnus, Mandy Patinkin, has also successfully combined film and stage careers. The intense Patinkin made his Broadway debut as Ché

Guevara in Andrew Lloyd Webber's *Evita* (1979). His passion brought him film roles in *Ragtime* and *Yentl,* and his sweet tenor brought Broadway's acclaim in *Sunday in the Park with George* (1984).

A native of Chicago, Patinkin dropped out of Juilliard after two years, finding the unceasing schedule of classes, rehearsals, and performances unbearable. Soon he was working regularly for Joseph Papp at the Public Theatre, playing in *Trelawny of the "Wells," Hamlet,* and *Rebel Women.* The Pulitzer Prize–winning *Shadow Box* served as Patinkin's 1977 Broadway debut.

Although he had sung in a synagogue choir as a boy, Patinkin had no formal vocal training. Indeed, his appearance in *Evita* was the first singing he'd done since high school. Nevertheless, his charismatic performance earned him a Tony Award.

George Hearn, in contrast, is a classically trained singer who once studied opera at the Aspen Music Festival. The Memphis-born Hearn won a talent competition at the age of twelve, singing ''Ol' Man River.'' He later majored in philosophy at his hometown's Southwestern University.

Hearn's voice proved the necessary tool for steady work in the New York theater. His performances in the musicals *I Remember Mama* (1979) and *A Doll's Life* (1982) transcended the less than inspiring material. His work in *The Changing Room* (1973) and *Watch on the Rhine* (1980) (for which he received a Tony nomination) strengthened him as a dramatic actor.

Hearn won a Tony Award in 1984 for his transvestite performance in *La Cage Aux Folles,* bringing both dignity and warm vulnerability to Albin, the nightclub entertainer. Hearn is one of those performers willing to let the production itself have center stage. Many performers were unwilling to play in drag in *La Cage,* but, as Hearn put it, ''I didn't have any trepidation playing a homosexual. Major actors do, because major actors are image conscious, but I'm not a major actor and I had no particular image to tarnish.''

George Hearn in La Cage Aux Folles *(1983)*

Joel Grey in Cabaret *(1966)*

Joel Grey started in show business in the mid-forties performing with his father, Mickey Katz, in Yiddish vaudeville's *Borscht Capades*. He was spotted by Eddie Cantor and began making television appearances. By the age of nineteen, he was headlining in top nightclubs.

After acting studies at New York's Neighborhood Playhouse, the diminutive (five-foot-two) Grey made a career of replacing performers in long-run shows. He spent three years in the sixties going from *Stop the World, I Want to Get Off* to *Half a Sixpence* to *Come Blow Your Horn* to *The Roar of the Greasepaint/The Smell of the Crowd*.

The first Broadway role Grey originated was as the decadent Master of Ceremonies in *Cabaret* (1966). The role was not in the original source material, Christopher Isherwood's *Goodbye to Berlin* and its dramatization, John Van Druten's *I Am a Camera,* but had been created by the book writer, Joe Masteroff, and the show's director, Harold Prince. Grey went far beyond his previous song-and-dance performances to create a characterization that was haunting and magical. He received a 1967 Supporting Actor Tony, and, recreating the role in the 1972 movie, won an Oscar as well.

Not many dancers become Broadway stars; there's usually much more opportunity in a show for a singer or actor. But Hinton Battle came to Broadway at the age of seventeen playing the Scarecrow in *The Wiz* (1975). While that show didn't make him a star, it started the process.

Battle, a former student at the School of American Ballet, made Broadway sit up and take notice with his stand-out tap dancing in *Sophisticated Ladies* (1981). For this, his first tap dancing ever, he was given a Supporting Actor Tony Award. As he put it, "Tap is about the feet—playing with sound, catching people off guard with a syncopated rhythm and then making it all look simple."

Battle's second Tony Award came three years later, in 1984, for his performance in *The Tap Dance Kid,* a show built around Battle's considerable talents.

Chita Rivera, who has often performed valiantly in less-than-successful shows, is another of Broadway's top dancers. Her mother put her into dancing classes at age eleven as a way of letting her use up excess energy. At sixteen,

Chita Rivera in Bye, Bye Birdie *(1960)*

Tammy Grimes in The Unsinkable
Molly Brown *(1961)*

Rivera entered the School of the American Ballet; in 1952, on a friend's dare, she auditioned for the chorus of *Call Me Madam.* She was cast, and, as the name Dolores Conchita Figueroa del Rivero couldn't fit into the program, after three days as Chita O'Hara, Chita Rivera was born.

Rivera danced in *Can-Can* (1953) and was Gwen Verdon's understudy in that musical. Four years later, she brought her bold, explosive dancing to the role of Anita in *West Side Story* (1957). For the first time her singing and acting talents were also showcased, and Rivera set a personal stamp on the role. In later years, she began performing in nonmusical roles and developed into a popular nightclub entertainer.

Rivera performed a song in her nightclub act that made joking reference to her many Tony losses. Finally, after four nominations—*Bye, Bye Birdie,* its sequel, *Bring Back Birdie, Chicago,* and *Merlin*—Chita Rivera won the 1984 Tony for the Kander and Ebb musical, *The Rink.*

When Tammy Grimes was sixteen she played Sabina in a school production of Thornton Wilder's *The Skin of Our Teeth.* The playwright saw this performance and, invidiously comparing it to the original Broadway production, said, ''Young lady, even Tallulah Bankhead didn't do the things you did to the role.''

Grimes continued to make impressions on playwrights. Her Broadway debut, *Look After Lulu,* was written by Noel Coward, who personally chose Grimes for the leading role after seeing her perform in a nightclub. While *Lulu* was not a success, Grimes's career was launched.

In 1961, Meredith Willson's musical about an indomitable survivor of the *Titanic* sinking, *The Unsinkable Molly Brown,* made Tammy Grimes a Broadway star. Her husky voice and offbeat personality kept the show running for more than five hundred performances. But for nine years after *Molly Brown*—and the Tony Award she won for that performance—Grimes's career was filled with many forgettable productions. A 1969 revival of Noel Coward's *Private Lives* finally resurrected her in the minds of Broadway audiences. And she won a Tony Award for her performance.

Grimes has often said that the role of Amanda in *Private Lives* is her favorite, and she gave that name to her actress-daughter by ex-husband Christopher Plummer. Besides Grimes's own two Tony Awards, this family boasts two others: Christopher's for *Cyrano* in 1974, and Amanda's Supporting Actress Award for *Agnes of God* in 1982. That same year Amanda was also nominated for her leading performance in *A Taste of Honey.*

In 1942, at the age of seventeen, Maureen Stapleton traveled by bus from Troy, New York, to New York City with one hundred dollars. Stapleton had spent years watching movies and fantasizing not only about Joel McCrea, her favorite, but also about her own dreams of movie stardom. While Stapleton was

nominated for an Oscar for her first film, *Miss Lonelyhearts* (1959), she didn't win that award until 1982 for her performance as the revolutionary Emma Goldman in *Reds*.

Stapleton got into films through her stunning stage portrayal in 1951 of Serafina delle Rose, the Sicilian widow in Tennessee Williams's *The Rose Tattoo*. This Broadway debut was rewarded with a Tony for Supporting Actress. Stapleton's unaffected Actors Studio approach was well-suited to Williams's plays. She later played in his *27 Wagons Full of Cotton*, *Orpheus Descending*, and a Broadway revival of *The Glass Menagerie*.

Stapleton has leavened her dramatic career with performances in numerous comedies, including Neil Simon's *Plaza Suite* (with George C. Scott) and *The Gingerbread Lady*—for which she won her second Tony Award.

★▨▨

The two-year-old Zoe Caldwell won a dancing contest in 1935 in her native Australia; at eleven she had her own radio interview program. At eighteen she

Zoe Caldwell, Kate Reid, and Margaret Leighton in Slapstick Tragedy *(1968)*

Zoe Caldwell and Amy Taubin in The Prime of Miss Jean Brodie *(1968)*

was a scholarship student at England's Stratford-on-Avon. There Caldwell took as her model Dame Edith Evans, who, according to Caldwell, "used all her senses all the time." Caldwell has brought this same concentration to her roles, and, also like Evans, she has a talent that triumphs over rather plain looks. Indeed, one of Caldwell's greatest successes was playing Shakespeare's temptress Cleopatra.

"Give me a girl at an impressionable age, and she is mine for life," rings the cry of the romantic, neurotic Miss Jean Brodie. Caldwell so perfectly captured the myopic passion of the Edinburgh schoolmistress that this combination of role and performer has gone down in Broadway history as one of the closest matches ever. Caldwell won a 1968 Tony for her performance.

Caldwell, while driven to strive for perfection, is not equally driven to perform. Often content to leave her career quiet for long periods of time, she chooses productions carefully. In 1982 she and her husband, producer-director Robert Whitehead, brought the Robinson Jeffers version of *Medea* back to Broadway. Judith Anderson had played the title role in the 1948 premiere. In the Caldwell production, Dame Judith returned, this time in the secondary role of the Nurse. The two productions had much in common. The Anderson production had been produced by Whitehead; the Caldwell was produced as well as directed by Whitehead. Ben Edwards served as scenic designer for both productions. And both Anderson and Caldwell received Tony Awards for their portrayals of the title role.

Zoe Caldwell as Medea and Judith Anderson as the Nurse in the 1982 production of Medea; *Anderson, pictured on a* Playbill *cover, played the title role in 1948*

Swoosie Kurtz and Judith Ivey: owing to frequent paternal job moves, both women attended fifteen or more schools during their childhood, forcing them, as perpetual outsiders, to practice changing and adapting swiftly to new surroundings. Both women have brought warmth and sympathy to rather strange characters—a pill-popping copper heiress cum rock singer (*The Fifth of July*), a woman who not only is, but is named, Bananas (*The House of Blue Leaves*), a naked Cockney tart (*Steaming*), and a vulnerable stripper (*Hurlyburly*). Kurtz and Ivey have each won two Supporting Actress Tonys.

Kurtz, the only child of the most-decorated flier in World War II, was named after his B-17, "The Swoose"—half swan, half goose. After studies at the London Academy of Music and Dramatic Art, Kurtz returned to New York and made her first appearance of note Off-Broadway in Wendy Wasserstein's *Uncommon Women and Others* and soon followed with a Tony-nominated performance on Broadway in *Tartuffe,* opposite John Wood and Tammy Grimes. Kurtz won her two Tony Awards in 1981 and 1986 for her performances in Lanford Wilson's *The Fifth of July* and the Broadway revival of John Guare's 1970 Off-Broadway hit, *The House of Blue Leaves.*

Judith Ivey was born in Texas and later moved to Illinois, where she attended Illinois State University. After graduation, she became part of Chicago's expanding theater scene before moving to New York. Playing matinees as Piaf, in the play of the same name, brought Ivey to the attention of the American producers of the British import by Nell Dunn, *Steaming,* Ivey's 1983 Broadway debut. She won her first Tony for that performance and won again two years later for her work in David Rabe's *Hurlyburly.*

Kurtz appeared in a short-lived television situation comedy series opposite Tony Randall, and both she and Ivey have made excursions into films, but they remain devoted to the stage. As two of America's finest young actresses, they are commonly expected to be the highlights of many Broadway shows in the future.

From Broadway to Hollywood

When talking movies replaced silents, stage-trained actors were rushed to Hollywood. They've been welcomed ever since. The Broadway star of a play would often be featured in the film version—but, just as often, he wouldn't. Henry Fonda was Mr. Roberts on Broadway and in film, and Geraldine Page and Paul Newman brought *Sweet Bird of Youth* from Broadway to Hollywood. Arthur Hill and Uta Hagen, Tony Award–winning stars of Edward Albee's *Who's Afraid of Virginia Woolf?*, were replaced on film by Richard Burton and Elizabeth Taylor, and Julie Andrews was moved aside for Audrey Hepburn (and the overdubbed voice of Marni Nixon) in *My Fair Lady.*

Many actors have had early success on Broadway only to retire almost

Paul Muni in Inherit the Wind *(1955). Muni received his only Tony Award for this performance, beating out Ben Gazzara* (A Hatful of Rain), *Boris Karloff* (The Lark), *Michael Redgrave* (Tiger at the Gates), *and Edward G. Robinson* (The Middle of the Night).

INHERIT THE WIND

Roy Poole and Meryl Streep in 27 Wagons Full of Cotton *(1976)*

Barbara Bel Geddes in Cat on a Hot Tin Roof *(1955)*

exclusively to film and television work—Tom Bosley, from the musical *Fiorello!* to *Happy Days*, and Barbara Bel Geddes, from *Cat on a Hot Tin Roof* to *Dallas*. And actors more accustomed to working in front of the camera have tried their luck on stage, many with success—Jackie Gleason in Bob Merrill's musical, *Take Me Along,* Dick Van Dyke in the Strouse–Adams musical *Bye, Bye Birdie,* Audrey Hepburn in Jean Giraudoux's *Ondine,* and Vivien Leigh in Robert E. Sherwood's *Tovarich.*

Today's actors move with ease between the stage and film, and the distinctions between stage and film actors have blurred. The versatility common among today's actors would have amazed earlier generations of performers. Filming a movie during the day and performing on Broadway at night is now an everyday occurrence.

★ ▓

"My mother and grandmother never let me out of the house until I was seven. I guess it was because I was very sensitive and they were afraid of what might happen to me." Al Pacino's childhood entertainment was almost exclusively a combination of attending movies with his divorced mother on weekends, and acting out those movies for his grandmother on weekdays. This youthful attachment to the fantasy of film served Pacino, as it did so many other actors, as the seed of a career.

Pacino attended New York's High School for the Performing Arts, though he dropped out before graduation. He began classes at the Actors Studio after working as a messenger, usher, and apartment building superintendent.

It was as the brutal hoodlum Murphy in Israel Horowitz's one-act, *The Indian Wants the Bronx,* that Pacino made his mark as a stage actor. After winning an Obie Award for his portrayal, Pacino made his Broadway debut in 1969, in a similar role in Don Petersen's *Does a Tiger Wear a Necktie?* He received that year's Tony for Supporting Actor. In 1979 he played the title role in Shakespeare's *Richard III.*

Pacino's film career, which includes the likes of *The Godfather* (parts one and two) and *Dog Day Afternoon,* has featured a series of characters whose barely controlled anger fuels their actions. His roles in *Serpico* and *Scarface* are first cousins of his work in David Mamet's *American Buffalo* and David Rabe's *The Basic Training of Pavlo Hummel.* This last role won Pacino a Tony for Best Actor in 1977.

★ ▓

In 1929 Henry Fonda made his Broadway debut in a walk-on role in *A Game of Love and Death*. He had come to New York from the Omaha (Nebraska) Community Playhouse, where he had spent three years growing from student to amateur to professional actor.

In 1934 Fonda parlayed his flat midwestern voice and disarmingly honest face into Broadway stardom as the farm-boy lead in *The Farmer Takes a Wife.*

After a thirteen-week run in New York, Fonda traveled to Hollywood, where he made the film version of Marc Connelly's play. He remained in Hollywood, forging his identity as film's man of integrity, most notably through his timeless performance as Tom Joad in *The Grapes of Wrath* and the title role in *Young Mr. Lincoln*.

In 1948 Fonda, as Lt. (j.g.) Douglas Roberts, began a three-year tour of duty aboard the naval supply ship *Reluctant* in *Mister Roberts* by Thomas Heggen and Joshua Logan. Fonda's performance as the officer adored by his crew but yearning for battle-front adventure won him a Tony for Best Actor (beating out Marlon Brando in *A Streetcar Named Desire*). Fonda played 1,700 performances, without missing a single show, even on the day after his estranged wife's suicide.

Fonda was only the third choice to play Roberts on film. Hollywood wanted either William Holden or Marlon Brando, but director John Ford held out for Fonda. The portrayal has gone down as a classic.

For the next quarter-century Fonda continued to return to Broadway between films. *The Caine Mutiny Court Martial, Two for the Seesaw,* and his one-man performance in *Clarence Darrow* alternated with such films as *Twelve Angry Men, The Ox-Bow Incident,* and his farewell role in *On Golden Pond*.

Henry Fonda, the shy star, cohosted the 1979 Tony Award ceremonies televised from the Shubert Theatre. His daughter Jane—herself a Tony nominee for *There Was a Little Girl* in 1960—was there on the pretext that she would join Fonda in presenting an award to his old friend Joshua Logan. She surprised Fonda by actually presenting to him the special Tony Award for "lifelong achievement." Fonda, after first protesting that "This isn't in my script," made a humble speech declaring his everlasting devotion to the theater.

Unlike Henry Fonda, Walter Matthau has not returned to Broadway since his early stage success but has chosen to remain in Hollywood. Rather like Fonda, it was Matthau's guy-next-door looks that served as his passport to movies: "Anybody with a big nose, little lips, and beady eyes looks like me." His father, a former priest, left home when Matthau was only three. While his Jewish mother toiled in a sweatshop, Matthau got his acting start in religious plays performed at the Daughters of Israel Day Nursery. At age eleven, Matthau began playing bit parts—for fifty cents a performance—in Yiddish theaters. When not onstage he ran the theaters' concession stands.

After serving in the army, Matthau used the G.I. Bill to study acting in New York with famed German director Erwin Piscator and made his Broadway debut as a candlebearer in the Rex Harrison production of Maxwell Anderson's *Anne of the Thousand Days* (1948). It was as Nathan Detroit in a 1955 revival of *Guys and Dolls* that Matthau first gained Broadway's attention. That same year he made his first film, *The Kentuckian,* with Burt Lancaster.

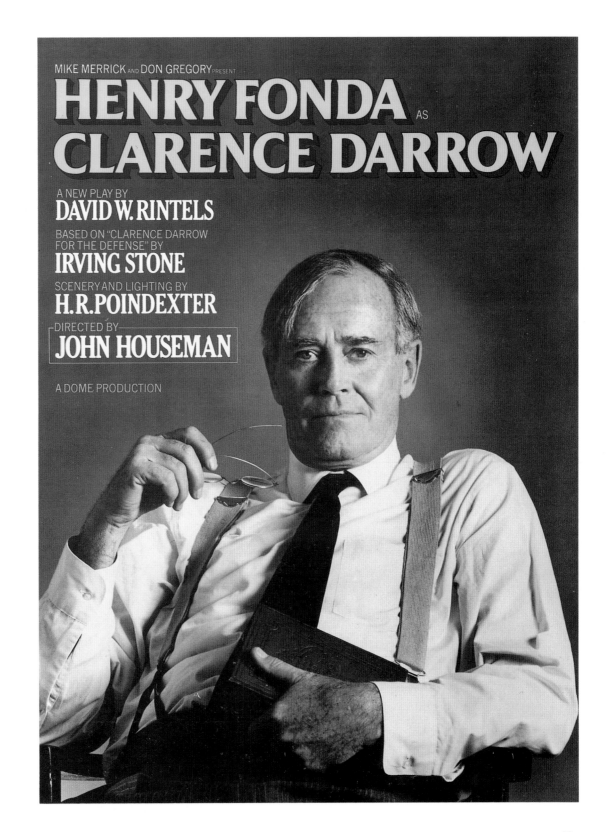

MIKE MERRICK AND DON GREGORY PRESENT

HENRY FONDA AS
CLARENCE DARROW

A NEW PLAY BY
DAVID W. RINTELS
BASED ON "CLARENCE DARROW
FOR THE DEFENSE" BY
IRVING STONE
SCENERY AND LIGHTING BY
H. R. POINDEXTER
DIRECTED BY
JOHN HOUSEMAN

A DOME PRODUCTION

Ten years later Matthau won the Best Actor Tony for *The Odd Couple* (1965). As the bearish grouch, Oscar Madison, Matthau shone, prompting Neil Simon (who had written the role with Matthau in mind) to declare him "the greatest instinctive actor around." Matthau later starred in the film version of the play, with Jack Lemmon, who replaced Broadway's Felix, Art Carney.

Matthau's great abilities as a comedian have not been seen on Broadway for more than twenty years—*The Odd Couple* was his last Broadway performance.

Anne Bancroft was a stage name chosen by Anne Italiano from a list provided by Darryl F. Zanuck, president of Twentieth-Century Fox. The young actress had come to Hollywood after a series of minor television roles. Her screen test won her a contract with Fox, and during the next six years she played in fifteen films, most of them quite forgettable.

Returning to her native New York, where she had studied at the American Academy of Dramatic Art, Bancroft achieved Broadway success in 1958 in William Gibson's *Two for the Seesaw*. She played Gittel Mosca, a Greenwich Village bohemian, opposite Henry Fonda's Omaha lawyer. Her spontaneous performance won a Tony for Supporting Actress.

Two years later Bancroft and Patty Duke took Broadway by storm playing Annie Sullivan and Helen Keller in Gibson's *The Miracle Worker*. Bancroft's fiercely committed acting style (a "female Marlon Brando," chirped one critic) earned for her a second Tony Award. She and Duke repeated their roles on film, for which they both won Academy Awards.

Hollywood success opposite Dustin Hoffman in *The Graduate* and in other films kept Bancroft from regular returns to Broadway until 1978, when she appeared as Golda Meir in *Golda*—yet another play by William Gibson. Gibson's script and Bancroft's performance were constantly being changed to accommodate Golda Meir herself. And Bancroft's health suffered from the chain smoking that she, a nonsmoker, had to make a part of her portrayal. The failure of this project elicited from Bancroft a vow never again to act on the stage.

Geraldine Page left her job modeling in a negligee factory to play Alma Winemiller in Tennessee Williams's *Summer and Smoke* (1952). Page had spent

Sidney Blackmer and Geraldine Page in Sweet Bird of Youth *(1959)*

a number of years in New York without much success as an actress. Her performance as the repressed spinster brought crowds and critics downtown to the small Off-Broadway theater where *Summer and Smoke* played.

Page reaffirmed her mastery of Williams's self-deluding dreamers with her portrayal of the drunken has-been actress, The Princess, in *Sweet Bird of Youth* (1959). Her sexually charged toying with her young lover, Paul Newman, was subsequently captured on film. But Page's film career had actually begun after her success in *Summer and Smoke,* with an Oscar-nominated performance opposite John Wayne in *Hondo* (1954). Then Joe McCarthy trained his sights on Hollywood "communists," and the actress was blacklisted for seven years: she had studied acting with Uta Hagen, a close friend and colleague of Paul Robeson, the uncompromising black singer and actor who had been branded a "Russian sympathizer." When Hollywood's blacklist died of its own absurdity, Page returned to film and scored a record seven Oscar nominations without a single win. Finally, in 1985, after nominations for such films as *The Pope of Greenwich Village* and *Interiors,* Page won for *The Trip to Bountiful,* playing an elderly woman desperately wanting to visit her hometown one last time.

From the start, Page was a character actress. Her small voice and signature mannerisms have been put variously in the service of a drunken wife in Alan Ayckbourn's *Absurd Person Singular,* the possessive and powerful Mother Superior in John Pielmeier's *Agnes of God,* and Off-Broadway in the Sam Shepard drama *A Lie of the Mind.* Even Page herself realizes, "It's no matter what part I play, instead of just sitting there saying lines, I use my hands, I wiggle around, and do a lot of stuff."

Two women who today move easily from film to stage and back again are Jane Alexander and Glenn Close. Both honed their skills in regional theater, moving to Broadway in supporting roles that later led to stardom.

Jane Alexander was born in Boston and went from Sarah Lawrence College, to the University of Edinburgh, to New York City's secretarial pools. She tried a novel approach to getting on Broadway, going from theater to theater, simply introducing herself to the stage managers, hoping that she would be remembered when it came time to hire replacements for the cast. The scheme worked. Alexander was hired as Sandy Dennis's standby for *A Thousand Clowns.* Alexander played the part several times and gained some notice.

Leaving New York often proves to be the means by which one returns to New York a star. Alexander's portrayal of Eleanor Bachman opposite James Earl Jones in *The Great White Hope* was brought in 1968 from Washington's Arena Stage, where the show originated, to Broadway. The show was later filmed with Alexander and Jones retaining their roles. On Broadway both won Tonys for their work.

Alexander has used her dramatic talents on Broadway in *Find Your Way Home* and *First Monday in October,* in films such as *Testament* and *Kramer vs. Kramer,* and on television as Eleanor Roosevelt, in *Eleanor and Franklin.*

Glenn Close was born in Greenwich, Connecticut, a town her ancestors helped found. She later moved to Africa, where her father was surgeon at a clinic in the Belgian Congo. At William and Mary College she majored in both drama and anthropology.

Choosing drama as a career, Close began working in regional theater. Her first success came with the New Phoenix Repertory in New York. At a final dress preview performance of a Broadway revival of William Congreve's *Love for Love,* Close was chosen to replace the leading actress, whose memory was failing. Close's performance led to roles in such shows as *Uncommon Women and Others,* the Richard Rodgers musical *Rex,* and Paul Giovanni's *The Crucifer of Blood.*

While playing the role of P. T. Barnum's feisty wife, Charity, in the musical *Barnum,* she was seen by film director George Roy Hill. Close made her film debut in Hill's *The World According to Garp,* which was followed by her leading role in *The Big Chill.* Both performances were honored with Oscar nominations. Though heartily embraced by Hollywood, Close has not forgotten Broadway. Her work in Michael Frayn's *Benefactors* and Tom Stoppard's *The Real Thing* was acclaimed, and her intelligent and sexually inflected performance in the latter won her a Tony as Best Actress.

THE BRITISH

Practically every major British performer has appeared on Broadway. The names read like the listing of great dynasties: Scofield, McCowen, Guinness, Jackson, Redgrave. Even among these giants, the British theater has been dominated for over sixty years by three actors: Laurence Olivier, John Gielgud, and Ralph Richardson. Their every visit to Broadway was greeted with respect, even adoration. But with Richardson dead, and Olivier and Gielgud restricting themselves to films, Broadway shall not see them again.

Olivier, the first actor to be named a lord by a British monarch, first appeared on Broadway in the 1929 flop, *Murder on the Second Floor.* The following year he returned in the famous production of Noel Coward's *Private Lives,* which also starred the author and Gertrude Lawrence. In 1957, for *The Entertainer,* Olivier received his only Tony Award nomination. His performance as Archie Rice, the seedy music-hall comic, was highly lauded and later preserved in a film version. Olivier's last Broadway performance was in 1961 as Henry II in *Becket.* Interestingly—perhaps ironically—the British theater's version of the Tony Award is named after Olivier, who never won the American prize.

John Gielgud has also failed to win a Tony for his acting. But in 1961 his direction of Jason Robards, Hume Cronyn, and George Grizzard in *Big Fish, Little Fish* did earn him a Tony. Gielgud's Broadway acting career began in 1928 with *The Patriot.* The 1936–37 Broadway season was graced by his Hamlet—hailed as the best of this century—which broke by one John Barrymore's record one hundred performances as the Danish prince. Twice Gielgud played Broadway and toured America with *The Ages of Man,* his one-man show devoted to Shakespeare. The first visit was awarded a special Tony; the second was televised nationwide.

In 1970 and 1976 Gielgud played on Broadway with Ralph Richardson. The

Laurence Olivier in The Entertainer *(1958)*

George Relph, Laurence Olivier, and Joan Plowright in The Entertainer *(1958). All three were nominated for Tony Awards; none won.*

first production was David Storey's *Home,* the two actor-knights playing inmates of an old-age asylum. The second production was Harold Pinter's enigmatic *No Man's Land,* where, as Gielgud put it, "We both felt we were paddling dangerously in uncharted seas."

If Olivier was the daring, athletic actor, and Gielgud was the poetically sensitive actor, Richardson was Everyman. Olivier and Gielgud made their reputations playing the great Shakespearean heroes Romeo, Hamlet, and Lear. Richardson's career was based on Falstaff, Bottom, and such non-Shakespearean roles as Cyrano and Peer Gynt. His common touch and eccentric nature

Ralph Richardson and John Gielgud in No Man's Land *(1976)*

endeared him to audiences throughout the world. Even late into his seventies, Richardson could still be seen racing through London on his motorbike, accompanied by his pet ferret or José, his Spanish-speaking parrot. Like Olivier and Gielgud, Richardson never won a Tony Award, though he was nominated three times—for *The Waltz of the Toreadors, Home,* and *No Man's Land,* the Broadway farewell for both Richardson and Gielgud.

Ian McKellan has been hailed as Olivier's successor, the great classical actor of his generation. He made his opening Broadway bow in 1967 in Aleksei Arbuzov's *The Promise.* For thirteen years the twenty-three-performance run of that show was the sum of McKellan's Broadway career. In 1980 he returned in grand style, as Antonio Salieri in Peter Shaffer's *Amadeus*. His histrionic performance, artfully switching between the elderly and the youthful Salieri, earned a Tony. Three years later he again played Broadway in *Ian McKellan Acting Shakespeare,* where his line-by-line textual analysis of the ''Tomorrow'' speech from the final act of *Macbeth* was a remarkable feature of both the stage production and its later television broadcast.

McKellan's comic counterpart is Jim Dale, who was born in a region of England without much theater. ''But when I was nine, I went to a show at the

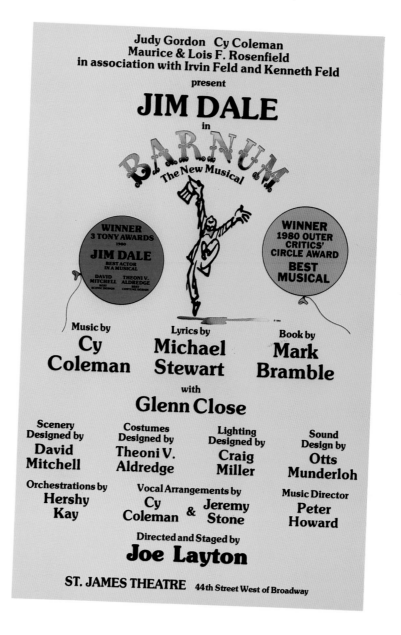

Margaret Leighton in Separate Tables
(1957)

Victoria Palace in London and saw a comic named Lupino Lane. I was surrounded by 2,000 people and when I heard the roar of the laughter. . . . Do you
know what a cat looks like when the hair goes up on its back? That was the way
I felt.'' He spent many years as a comic tumbler with traveling vaudeville
troupes, in music halls, on television, and in films, before he brought his physical comedy to the legitimate theater.

Dale played Shakespearean clowns in *A Winter's Tale, A Midsummer
Night's Dream,* and *The Taming of the Shrew* before he made his Broadway
debut in *Scapino!*—a play he and director Frank Dunlop adapted from a Molière
original. For his performance as the spaghetti-tossing scamp, Dale received a
Tony Award nomination. Five years later, in 1980, he won the award for his

tightrope-walking performance as P. T. Barnum, "The Prince of Humbug," in the musical *Barnum*. He has since begun playing dramatic roles and was nominated in 1985 for *Joe Egg,* playing the father of a severely retarded girl.

★ ▟

Margaret Leighton, Irene Worth, and Rosemary Harris have fourteen Tony Award nominations among them. But for Leighton's untimely death from multiple sclerosis at the age of fifty-three in 1976, the count would be higher.

Leighton first played on Broadway in 1946 with the visiting Old Vic company in *Henry IV, Part 1* and *Uncle Vanya*. In 1957 she won her first Tony Award playing two women—one sophisticated and the other mousy—in Terrence Rattigan's evening of one-acts, *Separate Tables*. Leighton spent most of the 1960s on Broadway in *Much Ado About Nothing, Night of the Iguana* (another Tony Award), *Tchin-Tchin,* and *The Chinese Prime Minister*. Even her disease could not stop her from performing. Leighton's final performance, in a London production of *A Family and a Fortune* with Alec Guinness, was played in a wheelchair.

Irene Worth was born in Nebraska but received most of her training in England. After her Broadway debut in 1943 in *The Two Mrs. Carrolls,* acting with the encouragement of the production's star, Elizabeth Bergner, Worth moved the following year to London for study. Two years later she made her London debut in William Saroyan's *The Time of Your Life* (1946). She returned to Broadway in T. S. Eliot's *The Cocktail Party* (1950), later replacing Margaret Leighton in the London production. Worth's growing expertise as a classical actress—blessed with one of the theater's most beautiful voices—prompted Tyrone Guthrie to engage her as the leading actress for his new theater at Stratford, Ontario.

In 1960 Worth received her first Tony nomination for her performance opposite Maureen Stapleton and Jason Robards in Lillian Hellman's *Toys in the Attic*. She won the award in 1965 and in 1976 for her performances in Edward Albee's *Tiny Alice* and a revival of Tennessee Williams's *Sweet Bird of Youth*.

Rosemary Harris was born in England but spent most of her youth in India, where her father was stationed with the R.A.F. Back in England, she spent time acting with stock companies before training with the Royal Academy of Dramatic Art. She made her Broadway debut in 1952, playing in *The Climate of Eden,* after having been seen in London by the play's director, Moss Hart.

In 1959 Harris and her then-husband, Ellis Rabb, formed the Association of Producing Artists (APA), a theater company that brought new plays and important revivals to Broadway and to regional theaters. For seven years she was one of the company's leading actresses, until she left to play Broadway with Robert Preston in *The Lion in Winter* (1966). That performance won her her first Tony Award. Harris has been nominated five more times, including three years in a row: *Heartbreak House* (1984), *Pack of Lies* (1985), and *Hay Fever* (1986).

ELLIOT MARTIN AND LESTER OSTERMAN PRODUCTIONS

present

JASON   COLLEEN
ROBARDS   DEWHURST

in EUGENE O'NEILL'S
A Moon For The Misbegotten

with
ED FLANDERS

Scenery & Lighting by   Costumes by
BEN EDWARDS   JANE GREENWOOD

LESTER OSTERMAN PRODUCTIONS
LESTER OSTERMAN—RICHARD HORNER

Directed by
JOSE QUINTERO

LIMITED ENGAGEMENT
MOROSCO THEATRE
45th St. West of Broadway   Evgs. at 7:30 · Mats. Wed. & Sat. at 2

AN AMICRAFT POSTER

4 PLAYS AND PLAYWRIGHTS

The novelist and critic William Dean Howells once observed that "What the American public always wants is a tragedy with a happy ending." To judge from those plays that have received Tony Awards as the outstanding dramatic work of a season, Howells was right. Broadway has embraced *The Crucible, The Miracle Worker,* and *That Championship Season,* all dramas dealing with serious situations, yet concluding with optimistic, if not quite "happy," endings.

Tony voters, like Broadway audiences, prefer attending comedies or "happy tragedies," but almost always vote at Tony Award time for the most serious play nominated. There is a prejudice against comedy as being not quite as worthwhile as tragedy. Such emotionally powerful plays as *Death of a Salesman, Long Day's Journey into Night,* and *Who's Afraid of Virginia Woolf?* will always be Tony Award winners. It is a rare comedy—*Mister Roberts, Rosenkrantz and Guildenstern Are Dead, Travesties*—that comes out on top at the Tony Award ceremony. And certainly all three comedies have "serious" content—Mister Roberts dies and *Rosenkrantz* and *Travesties* are philosophically quite formidable.

Virtually no nonmusical plays show up on lists of Broadway's longest runs. Usually the product of a single playwright's imagination, a play is necessarily more individual than a musical, almost always the joint creation of a composer, lyricist, and book writer. Also directors and choreographers tend to have a much stronger influence on shaping a musical than does the director of a drama.

What the Tony Award for Outstanding Play celebrates is the ability of a playwright to seduce audiences with a story and characters that are usually more enlightening, and certainly as entertaining, as the tunes and spectacle of that season's musicals.

MAKE 'EM LAUGH

The first four plays to win Tony Awards as Outstanding Play set a pattern that has carried through the entire forty-year history of the awards: 1948, *Mister Roberts,* a dramatization of the Thomas Heggen comic novel by the same name;

The Life and Adventures of Nicholas Nickleby *(1981)*

1949, *Death of a Salesman,* Arthur Miller's tragedy about a quintessentially American man; 1950, *The Cocktail Party,* a comedy in verse by T. S. Eliot; and, 1951, *The Fourposter,* a sketch by Jan de Hartog about the foibles of marriage.

The most recent winners as Outstanding Play have included the dramatization of a novel *(The Life and Adventures of Nicholas Nickleby),* an extended sketch about old age *(I'm Not Rappaport),* and several comedies *(Biloxi Blues, The Real Thing,* and *Torch Song Trilogy).* Though both *The Real Thing* and *Torch Song Trilogy* contained serious moments and themes, the truly serious American drama in recent years has been recognized only in nominations. The last serious drama by an American to win the Tony Award was *Children of a Lesser God* in 1980.

The reliance of Broadway on comedies, comic sketches, and dramatizations of popular material, whether novels or the lives of kings and saints, says more about Broadway's audiences than about the men and women who make their careers in the professional theater. Few contemporary nonmusical plays have run more than a thousand performances. Musicals command the top four positions on the list of longest-running Broadway productions. (The plays *Life with Father* and *Tobacco Road*—numbers five and six—are followed on the long-run list by more musicals.) And, as everyone knows, it is the critics first, and the audience ultimately, who determine which productions run and which quickly close.

Although comedies are second only to musicals in terms of Broadway popularity, it is the serious dramatic play that has dominated the overall forty-year history of Tony Awards in the category of Outstanding Play. Plays that grapple with the universal or the unknown maintain great appeal for Tony voters, and until recently, very few comedies have won as Outstanding Play. For instance, Neil Simon, whose comedies have entertained more audiences and employed more actors than any other modern playwright's work, had to wait through eight nominations before finally winning the Tony for Outstanding Play, in 1985, for *Biloxi Blues*—a play that is only partly comic at that.

Court Miller and Harvey Fierstein in Fierstein's Torch Song Trilogy *(1982). Fierstein won Tony Awards for both his acting and his writing.*

Ireland can boast of some of the finest playwrights of the twentieth century —Yeats, Synge, Shaw, O'Casey, and Beckett. The lilt and rhythm of Irish speech, coupled with the Irishman's sense of drama (brought on, perhaps, by his having been born into a divided, conflicted nation), has made Ireland a fertile ground for writers.

Two contemporary Irish playwrights, Brian Friel and Hugh Leonard, have brought a number of comedies to Broadway that are not only entertaining but also gentle evocations of other worlds. These "comedies" are generally enriched by strains of exultation and despair—Friel believes that Irish drama exists in a world that is "half threnody, half paean."

Short stories published in America became Brian Friel's release from having to follow in his father's footsteps as a teacher. After trying his hand at writing plays, Friel spent four months at the Guthrie Theatre in Minneapolis, during its first season, studying theater seriously. His invitation came from Tyrone Guthrie himself, Friel's next-door neighbor in County Tyrone, Ireland. Friel later remarked that the finest advice Guthrie gave him was that "the playwright's task is first to entertain, to have audiences enjoy themselves, to move them emotionally, make them laugh and cry and gasp and hold their breath and sit on the edge of their seats."

Friel's fourth play, and the first to be done in America, was *Philadelphia, Here I Come!* The play's most innovative feature was the casting of two actors in the role of protagonist: one played the public Gareth O'Donnell, the person "people see, talk to, talk about," and another played the private Gareth, the "unseen man, the man within, the conscience, the alter ego, the secret thoughts, the id." *Philadelphia, Here I Come!* was nominated for a Tony Award as Outstanding Play in 1966.

Three years later Friel received another nomination for *Lovers*. Again, the play featured a unique structure. Two separate one-act plays, *Winners* and *Losers,* featured a comic and a serious look at unconsummated love, and each of the acts embodied a narrator or omniscient presence to whom the play's action was indebted.

Friel's other plays produced either on or off Broadway—*The Loves of Cass McGuire, The Freedom of the City, Translations, The Faith Healer*—are also infused with the Irish spirit and remain true to Friel's roots.

Hugh Leonard is also an Irish playwright, but his work is more independent of Ireland. John Keyes Byrne christened himself "Hugh Leonard" after the hero of an early rejected playscript. Though he "loathes" his *nom de plume,* he has kept it, superstitious of losing his good luck in the theater.

The prolific Leonard began writing in the 1950s, working in the theater, television, and radio. His dramatization of two James Joyce novels, *Stephen D,*

Donal Donnelly and Patrick Bedford in Philadelphia, Here I Come! *(1966)*

was performed Off-Broadway in 1967. In 1974 he hit Broadway with *The Au Pair Man,* a comic allegory about Irish-English relations. Elizabeth Rogers, living in a ramshackle mansion whose doorbell plays "God Save the Queen," faces down, and finally seduces, an Irish debt collector. With Julie Harris as the Tony-nominated lead, the play enjoyed a healthy run.

Four years later Leonard won a Tony himself for his play *Da,* a drama of fathers and sons. Unabashedly autobiographical, *Da* told of a writer returning home for the funeral of his adoptive father. In the course of ordering the papers of his da (an Irish diminutive for "dad"), the writer is joined by his ghost, other family members, and himself as a child. The play was special to Leonard, and his sentiments carried over to his audiences. "I wrote the play to pay off a debt to my father. But the play made me successful as a writer and since I couldn't have written it without my father, the debt's now greater than ever."

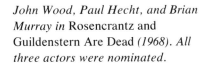

Tom Stoppard is the only comic playwright to have won three Tony Awards for Outstanding Play. He burst onto Broadway in 1968 with *Rosencrantz and Guildenstern Are Dead,* a brilliant farce that considers Shakespeare's *Hamlet* from the point of view of two minor characters, while the troubled Danish prince is reduced to a mere walk-on. This witty entertainment is filled with delightful puns, non sequiturs, double entendres, and variations on Shakespeare's original.

Stoppard's joy in the English language comes perhaps from the fact that it is

John Wood, Paul Hecht, and Brian Murray in Rosencrantz and Guildenstern Are Dead *(1968). All three actors were nominated.*

his second tongue. As director Peter Wood put it, "You have to be foreign to write English with [his] kind of hypnotized brilliance." Stoppard was born in 1937 in Czechoslovakia, traveled with his family to Singapore as the Nazi menace grew, and, when the Japanese occupied Singapore, left for England.

Stoppard's second Tony came in 1976 for *Travesties,* a play that considers the fact that Lenin, James Joyce, and Tristan Tzara, founder of the dada movement, were all in Zurich during World War I. This conceit, and the intense theatricality with which the playwright forms it, took Broadway by storm. There was always the question of what is real, based on fact, and what is poetic license. As Stoppard put it, "Ambushing the audience is what the theatre is about."

Stoppard received his third Tony for *The Real Thing* (1984), a play that also took on the question of what is real and what illusory. For instance, the first scene of *The Real Thing* turns out to be, in reality, the last scene of a play written by the leading character in *The Real Thing*—in and of itself another play. In *The Real Thing* Stoppard did not move away from his genius with word play, but he did invest his characters with a new capacity for genuine emotion. This growth as a writer is founded in his continuing work to bring worldwide attention to the plight of artists living under totalitarian regimes in Eastern Europe. Plays such as *Every Good Boy Deserves Favour* (written with André Previn) and *Dogg's Hamlet/Cahout's Macbeth* have succeeded in doing just that.

Neil Simon is a playwright in the strictest sense of the word: his plays are *wrought.* They are crafted, built joke upon joke, situation by situation. In his twenty-four years on Broadway, Simon has written twenty-two plays and musicals. And of them, only one has been a true flop (*Fools,* 1981). He has also adapted many of these plays and musicals for the screen and has written a number of original screenplays.

Simon was born in the Bronx, and, encouraged by his older brother, Danny, he dreamed of becoming "the greatest comedy writer in America." After leaving the Army in 1946 he wrote for radio before joining television during its golden age of the fifties. Simon wrote for all the major television comedians, including Sid Caesar, Phil Silvers, Jackie Gleason, and Carl Reiner. Television taught Simon how to write, and rewrite, fast and funny.

In 1961, after three years in the writing, Simon's first play, *Come Blow Your Horn,* was produced on Broadway. Critics hailed him as a new comic voice. From then on, at an almost unstoppable rate of one play a year, Simon has ruled Broadway. In 1964 he received his first Tony nomination, for *Barefoot in the Park.* Two years later *Barefoot* was still running and had been joined by three others—*The Odd Couple, The Star Spangled Girl,* and *Sweet Charity. The Odd Couple* had been nominated for a Tony, and, while it did not win (*The Subject Was Roses* by Frank Gilroy did), Simon won as "Outstanding Author"—a category never again awarded.

Neil Simon, Maureen Stapleton, George C. Scott, and Mike Nichols backstage at a rehearsal for Plaza Suite *(1968). Simon, Stapleton, and Nichols were nominated for Tony Awards; Nichols won.*

Elizabeth Ashley and Robert Redford in Barefoot in the Park *(1964)*

Matthew Broderick and Željko Ivanek in Brighton Beach Memoirs *(1983). Both actors were nominated for Featured Actor Tony Awards; Broderick won.*

Simon created and then perfected his own subgenre of comedy. As originally conceived, the "Neil Simon comedy" had a serious subject—alcoholism, death, adultery, God—treated in a succession of jokes parceled out to characters indiscriminately. The carefully mechanized plots were centered on two characters, usually men, around whom the plays revolve. And the plays were pictures of contemporary big-city life. *Plaza Suite, Last of the Red Hot Lovers, The Prisoner of Second Avenue,* and *The Sunshine Boys* all pleased Broadway audiences—and displeased Broadway critics.

The creation of the character of Eugene Morris Jerome in the 1983 *Brighton Beach Memoirs* signaled a new beginning for the plays of Neil Simon. Every play he writes is drawn from the material of his own life: *Barefoot in the Park* chronicled Simon's early married years; *The Odd Couple* told of his divorced brother and his brother's roommate; *Chapter Two* dealt with the death of Simon's first wife. But *Brighton Beach* took real people and situations (Simon's childhood in Far Rockaway, New York) and reconstituted them into a mature comedic expression in which characters develop and conflicts deepen. *Brighton Beach* has an ensemble cast, and the characters' stories unfold simultaneously

Bill Sadler, Geoffrey Sharp, Barry Miller, Matt Mulhern, Matthew Broderick, Brian Tarantina, and Alan Ruck in Biloxi Blues *(1985). Miller won a Featured Actor Tony for his performance.*

with no one story more prominent than any other. In addition, the warmth and charm with which Simon tells his tale are far removed from the atmosphere of his farces. In fact, only one character, Simon's alter ego, Eugene, is given funny lines. As the author put it, "Take him out and you have a straight play."

Brighton Beach Memoirs was not nominated for a Tony Award, an oversight corrected by the New York Drama Critics Circle, which gave their highest award to Simon. Amazingly, it was Simon's first major theatrical award. (The Nederlander Organization, a leading owner of Broadway theaters, that year honored Simon by renaming one of their theaters after him—the only living playwright so honored.) Two years after *Brighton Beach,* a second play about Eugene, *Biloxi Blues,* arrived on Broadway. Depicting Eugene's Army stint, it showed his further development and growth. For this, finally, after so many plays over the course of a quarter-century, Neil Simon won a Tony Award for Best Play. As befits Broadway's most prolific and successful playwright, Simon had the last word: "I've always dreamed of winning a Tony, but I didn't think I'd have to dream through twenty-two plays to get it."

Four years after his death in 1953, Eugene O'Neill won a Tony Award for Outstanding Play. That play, *Long Day's Journey into Night,* was supposed to have been hidden for another two decades. It was O'Neill's wish that the play, which mercilessly chronicled his family's internecine battles, would remain unseen and unperformed until twenty-five years after his death. After viewing the brilliant Jason Robards–José Quintero revival of *The Iceman Cometh* in 1954, O'Neill's widow, Carlotta Monterey, presented them with the opportunity of a lifetime: *Long Day's Journey,* a play "written in sorrow and tears," was resurrected and firmly fixed the reputation of O'Neill as America's greatest dramatist.

Eugene Gladstone O'Neill was born in 1888 in a hotel at the corner of Broadway and 43rd Street in New York City. He was the second son of the renowned actor James O'Neill, who had made his fame and fortune playing the title role in *The Count of Monte Cristo*—over 6,000 times. Eugene tried his hand at acting, gold prospecting, and journalism before tuberculosis landed him in a sanitarium. It was there that he began to read plays, notably those of August Strindberg, and to write plays, through which O'Neill tried "to evaluate the impressions of many past years in which one experience had crowded on another with never a second's reflection." In 1916 O'Neill, while on Cape Cod, fell in with a theater group called The Provincetown Players. It was there that he had his first production, a one-act play of the sea entitled *Bound East for Cardiff.*

O'Neill came to the American stage during a period of great change. The artificial, actor-dominated theater of the elder O'Neill was giving way to more realistic, playwright-dominated work. While his plays took many of their structural ideas from the European avant-garde, the powerful emotion contained in them was something entirely new to the drama. The human tragedies of murder, suicide, and insanity were common events in O'Neill's plays.

During the two decades after *Bound East for Cardiff,* O'Neill presented the American theater with such plays as *Desire Under the Elms, The Hairy Ape, Anna Christie, Strange Interlude,* and *Mourning Becomes Electra.* Sinclair Lewis declared that O'Neill "has done nothing much in American drama save to transform it utterly, in ten or twelve years, from a false world of neat and competent trickery to a world of splendor and fear and greatness."

Between *Days Without End* in 1934 and *The Iceman Cometh* in 1946, Broadway was without new work by O'Neill. Parkinson's disease had begun to destroy his ability to write. Accustomed to composing in pencil on paper, the ailing O'Neill could write only for short periods of time. Physically, his last plays took long to write; emotionally, they had taken a lifetime.

The Iceman Cometh, A Moon for the Misbegotten, A Touch of the Poet, and *Long Day's Journey into Night:* gone were the experimental structures and the sometimes overwrought melodrama. All that remained was the realistic revelation of his characters' destinies. Yet under all the despair remained the glimmer of life.

After the Broadway premiere of *Beyond the Horizon* in 1920, James O'Neill remarked to his son, "Are you trying to send the audience home to commit suicide?" O'Neill, the first and only American dramatist to win the Nobel Prize for Literature, was not a hopeless pessimist, but rather a clear-eyed realist: "I don't love life because it is pretty. I am a truer lover than that. I love it naked. There is beauty to me even in its ugliness."

Florence Eldridge and Fredric March in Long Day's Journey into Night *(1956). Eldridge and March were real-life husband and wife*

SOB STORIES

During the 1940s two American playwrights emerged from the shadow of Eugene O'Neill. Both Arthur Miller and Tennessee Williams produced plays that not only captured the imagination of their day but have remained at the forefront of the American drama. Where would the theater be without *Death of a Salesman, The Crucible, The Glass Menagerie, A Streetcar Named Desire,* and *Cat on a Hot Tin Roof*?

Miller and Williams were opposites, as men and as writers, yet there was between them a common bond. Critic Kenneth Tynan put it this way: "Miller's plays are hard, patrist, athletic, concerned mostly with men. Tennessee Williams's are soft, matrist, sickly, concerned mostly with women. What links them is the love for the bruised individual soul and its life of quiet desperation."

The playwrights' own words offer a similar testimony. Miller's "I am not a dime a dozen! I am Willy Loman and you are Biff Loman" is straightforward, a declarative statement by a committed man. Williams's "Whoever you are—I have always depended on the kindness of strangers" is the gentle defense of a helpless creature.

Arthur Miller was born in 1915 in Manhattan and later moved with his family to Brooklyn. After several years working in an auto-parts warehouse during the early years of the Depression, he entered the University of Michigan, where he began to write plays. His first, *Honors at Dawn,* won the school's Avery Hopwood Drama Award in 1936. Miller again won that honor the following year with *They Too Arise.*

After graduation Miller worked for the Federal Theatre Project and had his first professional production. *The Man Who Had All the Luck* ran four performances on Broadway in 1944. Miller wrote a novel, *Focus,* and then wrote his first Broadway hit, *All My Sons.* The play's story is of an aircraft-engine manufacturer whose moral myopia leads him to allow faulty engine parts to be delivered to the front lines. *All My Sons* was eligible during the first year of the Tony Awards, and Miller won as "Outstanding Playwright"—the award category for Outstanding Play did not come into existence until the following year.

Two years later, in 1949, Miller's finest play appeared on Broadway. *Death of a Salesman,* a tragedy of a common man, was a hit. Willy Loman, caught up in the illusions of the "American Dream" of success through personality—through being "well liked"—was forced by his delusions to retreat first into his dreams and then into death. *Salesman* ran for 742 performances and was awarded the Pulitzer Prize in addition to a Tony.

Miller's morality and his social conscience led him to indict the men and mores of America's McCarthy era. *The Crucible* was set during the Salem, Massachusetts, witchcraft trials of the 1600s. The prosecutors' fanatical zeal overwhelmed their common sense with such vehemence that innocents were sacrificed without cause or compunction. Clearly, it was an allegory of America

Mildred Dunnock, Lee J. Cobb, Arthur Kennedy, and Cameron Mitchell in Death of a Salesman *(1949). Only Kennedy received a Tony Award for his performance.*

All My Sons *(1947)*

Marlon Brando and Jessica Tandy in A Streetcar Named Desire *(1947). Only Tandy won a Tony Award for her performance.*

in the 1950s. Miller won his third Tony Award for this play. But after *The Crucible,* Miller was called to testify before the House Un-American Activities Committee. For refusing to answer their questions, he was found in contempt of Congress, a ruling later overturned by the Supreme Court.

Miller's later years have seen him roundly honored as a great man of letters whose well-made plays have captured Americans and their dreams. The last play of Miller's to be nominated for a Tony Award was *The Price* in 1968. This simple, quiet play about the meeting of two estranged brothers after sixteen years was yet another reminder of Miller's masterly command of the stage.

Tennessee Williams did not write well-made plays; nor did he write plays that tackled the social issues of contemporary man. He wrote poetic plays constructed of image, rhythm, and nuance, which tenderly bared the frailty of lost souls, the futility of the helpless in a brutal world, and the failure not only of the American Dream, but of every hopeful dream.

Thomas Lanier Williams was born in 1911 in Mississippi. A bout with diphtheria at age five left him in tenuous health. His mother protected him from a hard-drinking father who taunted him with the nickname "Miss Nancy." Williams, Sr., later abandoned the family, and Tennessee began working in a shoe factory, using his spare time to jot down stories and poetry on shoe boxes. Some of these early writing efforts were published under his real name. In 1939, feeling that that name had been "compromised," Williams adopted the nickname Tennessee—after his father's home state.

Through a web of memory, Williams looked at his life, his family, and his escape from them, and put it all on the stage. In 1944 (after his first play, *Battle of Angels,* folded in Boston in 1940), *The Glass Menagerie* was produced on Broadway. It introduced a new voice to the American theater. Williams captured the rituals of the decaying and self-deceived in this play about his mother, whose determination to ignore reality was as strong as reality itself. The woman, Amanda, was born through the acting talents of Laurette Taylor, whose performance set for all time the combination of lyricism and violence, repulsion and attraction that have come to define Williams's style.

In 1947 *A Streetcar Named Desire* arrived on Broadway with a stupendous cast—Jessica Tandy, Kim Hunter, Marlon Brando, and Karl Malden—directed by Elia Kazan in a setting by Jo Mielziner. The brutalization of Blanche Dubois by a raw, carnivorous Stanley Kowalski was greeted by a stunned silence: Williams had sent Broadway reeling. The sexuality branded him as a playwright of obsession, and the language marked him as a poet. The play won that year's Pulitzer Prize, but no Tony.

In 1951 Williams won his only Tony Award, for *The Rose Tattoo.* Five years later he was nominated for *Cat on a Hot Tin Roof,* which did win him another Pulitzer. In 1962 Williams had his last Broadway hit, *Night of the Iguana.*

Bette Davis in Night of the Iguana *(1961). Margaret Leighton (background at left) won a Tony Award for her performance; Davis was not nominated.*

During the final twenty years of his life, Williams wrote new plays and rewrote his old ones. He wrote revealing memoirs about his career, his homosexuality, and his abuse of drugs and alcohol. In 1983 Williams died, asphyxiated by the plastic cap from a bottle of nasal spray.

His work has influenced playwrights around the world and echoes hauntingly throughout the modern imagination. It constantly reaffirms the genius of this young Mississippi drifter.

★ ▩

For a period of six years, 1956–62, the Tony Awards for Outstanding Play were dominated by plays of ideas, great ideas made immediate and intimate by powerful heroes and heroines. Anne Frank, Thomas Becket, Thomas More, and the Bible's Job taught Broadway audiences lessons in integrity, for they were mere mortals caught in by their times—and in the onrush of sainthood.

"It's an odd idea for someone like me to keep a diary, . . . It seems to me that neither I—nor, for that matter, anyone else—will be interested in the unbosomings of a 13-year-old schoolgirl." With that entry, Anne Frank began the diary that would not only make her immortal but would serve as testimony to the unconquerable human spirit that prevails through even the most adverse conditions.

Days after receiving notices of deportation to Germany from Nazi-occupied Amsterdam, the Frank family, joined by five others, hid themselves in a secret attic space in Otto Frank's spice warehouse. For 657 days they remained in

hiding. Food was smuggled in through the entrance/bookcase by the few friends entrusted with the hideaway's secret.

Life for the nine was grim—little light came through the boarded-up windows, clothes wore out, and, as rationing became more stringent, food was less plentiful and palatable. Yet there were some simple joys. Anne put above her bed pictures of her favorite movie stars, which she tore from magazines. One doorway was lined with pencil marks showing the heights of the children as they grew. The men had a map of Europe dotted with pins showing the locations of the troops based on information they gathered from radio broadcasts.

On July 7, 1944, Allied forces invaded Europe at Normandy. On August 1 Anne recorded her final diary entry. Three days later, acting on information bought for the equivalent of twelve dollars, the Gestapo broke into the attic hideaway. Anne Frank and the others were just days from salvation: Amsterdam was liberated on September 4. Only Otto, Anne's father, survived the concentration camps. Anne died of typhus at Bergen-Belsen, aged fifteen.

Anne's diary was left behind by the Gestapo, and a family friend discovered and saved it. *The Diary of a Young Girl* was published in 1947; in 1956 the husband-and-wife writing team of Albert Hackett and Frances Goodrich dramatized the diary as *The Diary of Anne Frank* (though one-quarter of their royalties were ordered given to playwright Meyer Levin, who had sued for plagiarism). The story of two families struggling for survival won both the Tony Award and the Pulitzer Prize, and it made forever famous Anne Frank's philosophy that, "In spite of everything, I still believe that people are really good at heart."

★ ▩

The years 1961 and 1962 brought plays to Broadway that explored the struggles of two English saints to hold Church above King. *Becket, or the Honor of God* by Jean Anouilh and *A Man for All Seasons* by Robert Bolt told tales of great, uncompromising men who were martyred by the state. Both plays were presented with Tony Awards.

Becket begins with the naked Henry II being flogged as penance at the tomb of the assassinated Archbishop of Canterbury, Thomas Becket. Through a flashback that lasts the remainder of the play—except for the final scene, depicting Henry after his penance—the audience sees Becket and Henry share women and power. Henry named Becket England's chancellor and then, in an effort to gain control of the Church, named him Archbishop. But the passion of the unruly Henry was met head-on by the rigid principles of Becket, who knew he could not serve two masters. His choice led to his death. He was slaughtered by the King's henchmen on the cathedral altar.

Anouilh, who had begun writing plays at twelve, had earlier received Tony nominations for *The Waltz of the Toreadors* and *Time Remembered*.

Sir Thomas More was, in the words of Samuel Johnson, "the person of greatest virtue these islands ever produced." He was a product of the English

Renaissance: a lawyer, member of Parliament at age twenty-six, and author of *Utopia,* about the search for the best of all possible governments.

Henry VIII named More to succeed Cardinal Wolsey as lord chancellor, but More resigned only three years later when Henry declared himself the head of the Church in England after having been refused by the pope the right to divorce Catharine of Aragon to marry Anne Boleyn. More would not deny the supremacy of the pope, was imprisoned in the Tower of London, tried, and beheaded—his head exhibited on London Bridge. Four hundred years later More was beatified by the Catholic Church.

Robert Bolt's 1960 play about Sir Thomas More, *A Man for All Seasons,* employs a highly theatrical device—a narrator—which enables the melodrama to remain comfortably short of sentimentality. "The Common Man" is a combination of narrator and seven other characters ranging from servant to executioner. The Broadway production won a Tony in 1962. Ten years later Bolt was again nominated for his historical play *Vivat! Vivat Regina,* about the reign of Elizabeth I.

Anne Frank, Thomas Becket, and Thomas More were all historical figures who battled very real enemies. In 1958 the American poet Archibald MacLeish updated the story of Job as a verse drama entitled *J. B.* Premiered at Yale, where MacLeish was a professor, the play tells the allegorical tale of a successful businessman, J. B., whose family possessions are destroyed as a test of his faith. While J. B. wrestles with his soul, the audience is reminded that he is no different from them, and that tomorrow could bring them such trials. J. B. is a modern-day Everyman whose antagonist is God.

MacLeish set his play in a circus tent. Two out-of-work actors, getting by as circus concessionnaires, decide to cast themselves as God and Satan. Their play-acting becomes real, and the three rings of the circus become the worlds of God, Satan, and, in the center ring, J. B. The Broadway production starred Christopher Plummer and Raymond Massey, as Satan and God, and Pat Hingle as J. B., and was staged and designed by Elia Kazan and Boris Aronson. The play won the 1959 Tony as Outstanding Play.

Not all plays feature great struggles against kings and gods. Broadway has played host to many inspirational tales of men and women battling a lesser, but equally frightening, foe: themselves.

Illness has often been seen as a metaphor for life. Illness reminds one of the inevitability of death or the possibility of a lifetime of physical and mental hardship. Many people, confronted with such possibilities, faint or fail. Some few find new courage; it is through the stories of these that we derive inspiration.

Broadway has welcomed, and the Tony Awards have honored, many such plays. In 1958 Dore Schary's *Sunrise at Campobello* recounted Franklin Roosevelt's triumphant victory over polio. Two years later *The Miracle Worker,* by William Gibson, overwhelmed audiences with the dogged battles between the deaf, dumb, and blind Helen Keller, and her teacher, Anne Sullivan. The moment when Helen finally recognizes the correspondence between a rush of water and the word *water* is a stunning dramatic event almost unparalleled in the modern theater.

Nineteen eighty brought Broadway Mark Medoff's *Children of a Lesser God,* which depicts the struggles between a deaf woman and her hearing husband. This play is not the story of a disabled person adapting to the world of the "able-bodied." The hearing James sets himself up as the standard of normality; but the deaf Sarah does not accept this, protesting that "all my life I have been a creation of other people." *Children* so captivated audiences and critics that the show became one of the longest-running nonmusicals in Broadway history. Phyllis Frelich, the original Sarah, became the first deaf actress to win a Tony Award.

One of the finest of Broadway's inspirational stories was that of John Merrick, known to history as the "Elephant Man." Born horribly deformed, a victim of neurofibromatosis (a disease in which the skin grows into large, bony masses resembling brown cauliflower), Merrick was cast out by society and forced into the life of a freak in a traveling sideshow. Rescued by Dr. Frederick Treves, Merrick lived the remaining six years of his life in London Hospital. He became famous, and all Europe's renowned clamored to visit and befriend him. For them it was a good deed; for him it was the human contact he had so long been denied.

Anne Bancroft and Patty Duke in The Miracle Worker *(1960)*

Philip Anglim and Carole Shelley in
The Elephant Man *(1979)*

Bernard Pomerance's *The Elephant Man* subtly sketches Merrick, his relationship with Dr. Treves and with the actress Madge Kendal. While the actor portraying Merrick used no make-up—conveying his deformity only through a slight change in carriage and voice—the horrible irony of a beautiful spirit encased in an ugly body was profoundly communicated. The childlike innocence of Merrick ("Sometimes I think my head is so big because it is so full of dreams") won over audiences as easily in the 1980s as it had in the 1880s.

EMANUEL AZENBERG & JOSEPH PAPP

Emanuel Azenberg and Joseph Papp have won nearly fifty Tony Awards between them for their Broadway productions. They are today's finest theatrical producers, the heirs of David Belasco and John Golden, Kermit Bloomgarden and the Shubert brothers. Azenberg and Papp have conquered Broadway from opposite directions: Azenberg the consummate insider, Papp the renegade outsider.

Emanuel Azenberg spent three and a half years as a company manager for producer David Merrick. He studied firsthand Merrick's ability to combine quantity with quality, producing good shows one after another. With fellow Merrick protégé Eugene Wolsk, Azenberg began producing on Broadway. *The Lion in Winter* (1966) and Hal Holbrook's *Mark Twain Tonight!* (1966) were two early hits.

When Azenberg went solo he continued to produce plays and musicals of comparable literary worth. Such Tony Award-winning hits as *Ain't Misbehavin'*, *Sunday in the Park with George*, *Whose Life Is It Anyway?*, *Children of a Lesser God*, and *'Master Harold' . . . and the boys* were successful with both critics and audiences. Azenberg's concern for the written word may have come from his grandfather, Charles, whose advice to relatives about to move from their native Poland to join

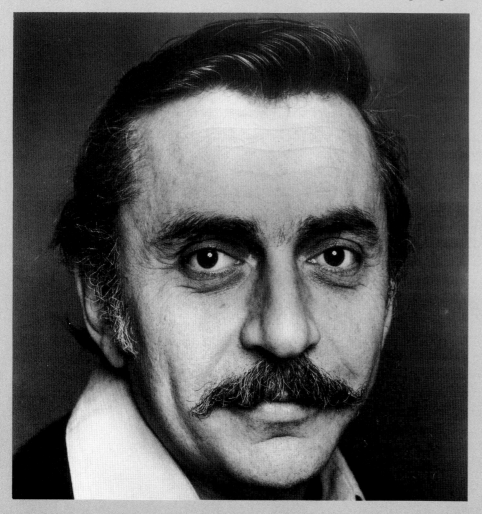

Emanuel Azenberg

him in his new home in London was, "You must read all of Dickens and all of Thackeray."

In 1972 Azenberg began producing the plays of Neil Simon. From *The Sunshine Boys* to *Broadway Bound*, Azenberg and Simon visited Broadway almost every year. Azenberg's ability to produce such weighty or ephemeral plays as *'Master Harold' . . . and the boys* and *Whoopi Goldberg* rested on the financial foundation of Simon's comedies. Laughter paid for tears.

The comedies and tragedies of Shakespeare served as English primers for the young Yiddish-speaking Joseph Papp.

born. In 1967 Papp opened the Public Theatre in the former Astor Library, and his theater had a year-round home.

Papp has produced more than three hundred plays and musicals, directing more than forty of them himself. The New York Shakespeare Festival has a staff of more than a hundred and a multimillion dollar budget. The head of all this is Joseph Papp. As playwright Thomas Babe has said, "The institution is Joe, and Joe is the institution."

Dozens of Public Theatre offerings have moved to Broadway to win Tony Awards, *The Pirates of Penzance, That Championship Season,* and *The Mystery of Edwin*

Joseph Papp

After a stint in the Navy, Papp returned to New York to found a Shakespearean workshop in a church basement. A year later, in 1954, he presented his first show, *An Evening with Shakespeare and Marlowe.* Two years after that, Papp and his New York Shakespeare Festival began producing free plays in Central Park, and a staple of New York's theater life was

Drood among them. In 1976 Papp moved *A Chorus Line* to Broadway and helped rewrite the history of the American musical. Much as Emanuel Azenberg has dealt with the largesse created by Neil Simon, Papp has been able to transform the revenues from *A Chorus Line* into financial backing for many worthy but commercially marginal plays.

In 1952 Samuel Beckett's *Waiting for Godot* changed the theater forever. This play about two vagrants and their endless waiting for a character who never appears redefined everyone's idea of the limits of drama. Suddenly theater seemed precisely to address the predicament of the modern man, mirroring his despair in the postwar nuclear age. Instant mass death had called into question the continued existence of man. Samuel Beckett met the horror of this situation with absurdity and translated his perceptions onto the stage in a drama without overt action.

In 1958 John Osborne's *Look Back in Anger* revealed the possibilities of the theater in yet another way. Jimmy Porter, the protagonist of the play—who came to exemplify the "Angry Young Man"—captured the frustrated malaise of postwar youth. Porter served both as observer and symbol. Savaging England's icons, he at first reflected the day's social disillusionment and then rekindled social protest.

Look Back in Anger served to liberate playwrights of Osborne's generation. The proverbial good taste and understatement of the English were supplanted by a willingness to show fury. As Osborne observed: "We English are more violent than we allow ourselves to know. That is why we have the greatest body of dramatic literature in the world."

Osborne added further to that literature with *The Entertainer* (1958), an allegory of the British Empire set in a crumbling music hall and starring Laurence Olivier in his finest nonclassical performance; then came the Tony Award–winning *Luther* (1963), a Brechtian story of the great Protestant leader, and *Inadmissable Evidence* (1965).

Harold Pinter's first plays were full of seemingly inconsequential speeches, arbitrary actions, and sinister characters. They were met with scorn by confused audiences and derisive critics. Pinter's style has since become more familiar, and audiences and critics have come to value its poignancy and embrace its humor.

Pinter, the only child of a tailor, attended the Royal Academy of Dramatic Art during the late forties. He refused to fulfill his National Service and was twice tried as a conscientious objector. Each time, prepared to be sent to prison, Pinter brought his toothbrush to court, only to be released.

In 1950 he had two poems published and got his first acting job. Over the next seven years he toured, played in rep (under the stage name of David Barron), and worked various odd jobs. In 1957 he wrote a short play, *The Room,* for a teacher friend who needed a play for his students to perform in a competition. The judge of the contest, *Sunday Times* critic Henry Hobson, wrote appreciatively of *The Room,* and the play was optioned by a commercial producer.

In the same year Pinter wrote *The Dumb Waiter* and *The Birthday Party*.

Following years brought *The Caretaker* (1961), *The Collection* (1962), *The Homecoming* (1967), *Old Times* (1971), *No Man's Land* (1976), and *Betrayal* (1980). Pinter has since become a sought-after screenwriter and director, making a specialty of directing the plays of Simon Gray *(Butley, Otherwise Engaged, Quartermaine's Terms)*.

Pinter's dramatic style is distinctive and readily recognizable. His dialogue is full of the circular irrationality of "real" speech; characters have no history, existing only onstage; themes concern the fear of dispossession and the womb-like safety of one's own room. Pinter's conviction that there is only the slimmest of lines separating the real from the unreal, the true from the false, drives him to create mystery after unsolvable mystery. His best plays have the inevitability of great thrillers.

Who's Afraid of Virginia Woolf? thrust Edward Albee to the forefront of the American theater. The passion and power of his characters as they struggle toward understanding display the great flight through illusions we all must make

George Grizzard, Uta Hagen, and Arthur Hill in Who's Afraid of Virginia Woolf? *(1963)*

and endure. The play's Broadway director, Alan Schneider, called it "a dark legend of truth and illusion, musical in its structure and style." Albee saw it as a study of "the success or failure of American revolutionary principles."

In 1963, when *Virginia Woolf* was produced, the theater was looking for the Great American Playwright. Eugene O'Neill was dead; Arthur Miller and Tennessee Williams were in decline. Albee became the choice of the day—and yet he never fulfilled his promise.

Audiences wanted another *Virginia Woolf* and instead got mysteries like *Tiny Alice* (1969) and *Seascape* (1975), adaptations like *The Ballad of the Sad Café* (1963) and *Malcolm* (1966), and such incomprehensible sideshows as *The Lady from Dubuque* (1980) and *The Man Who Had Three Arms* (1983). Time after time it seemed as though the playwright were merely speaking for himself and to himself. Only *A Delicate Balance* (1966), which explored the limits of personal responsibility, had substantial theatrical viability and success.

★ ▓▓▓▓

David Rabe and Lanford Wilson are two American playwrights who have grown in stature and accomplishment throughout their careers. Between them they have seven Tony Award nominations for Outstanding Play.

Rabe's career began with his explorations of the effects of the Vietnam War on its combatants and their families. *The Basic Training of Pavlo Hummel* (1971) followed a misfit in his attempts to achieve the manly ideal touted in Army recruitment posters. *Streamers* (1976) showed blacks and homosexuals trying to gain the respect of the white, heterosexual Army. *Sticks and Bones* (1972), a Tony Award–winning play, was a searing combination of satire and sitcom, showing a typical middle-class American family—Ricky, Ozzie, and Harriet—who deflect the reality of the war as represented by the blinded son David.

Rabe's *Hurlyburly* (1984), set in Hollywood, depicts the refuge failed men find in alcohol, cocaine, and sex. The play was inspired by the years Rabe had spent as a screenwriter. This sprawling drama of Hollywood was cast with some of film's brightest new performers—William Hurt, Christopher Walken, and Sigourney Weaver.

The plays of Lanford Wilson are no less passionate, but their expression is gentler. Most often Wilson's plays are defined by "lyric realism," presenting recognizable characters and stories seen through poetic eyes.

Wilson had gone to college in San Diego as an art major and had worked at an ad agency in Chicago before moving to New York. He began writing plays during the early years of Off-Off-Broadway at the famed Caffe Cino. There, through the production of dozens of short plays, Wilson and so many other playwrights learned their craft. His *Balm in Gilead* became the first full-length original play to be produced Off-Off-Broadway.

In 1969 Wilson made his Broadway debut with *The Gingham Dog,* a flop. Not until 1980 did he return. The years in between were spent at the Off-Broadway

THE SHUBERT ORGANIZATION
ELIZABETH I. McCANN   NELLE NUGENT
ROGER S. BERLIND
present

IAN McKELLEN
TIM CURRY JANE SEYMOUR

in

AMADEUS

by

PETER SHAFFER

with

GORDON GOULD   PAUL HARDING   PATRICK HINES
NICHOLAS KEPROS   LOUIS TURENNE   EDWARD ZANG

Production Designed by
JOHN BURY

Associate Scenic Designer   Associate Costume Designer   Associate Lighting Designer
URSULA BELDEN   **JOHN DAVID RIDGE**   **BEVERLY EMMONS**

Music Directed and Arranged by
HARRISON BIRTWISTLE

Directed by
PETER HALL

THE WORLD PREMIERE OF AMADEUS WAS GIVEN IN LONDON
BY THE NATIONAL THEATRE OF GREAT BRITAIN.

♿ BROADHURST THEATRE
235 West 44th Street

VAN NUTT

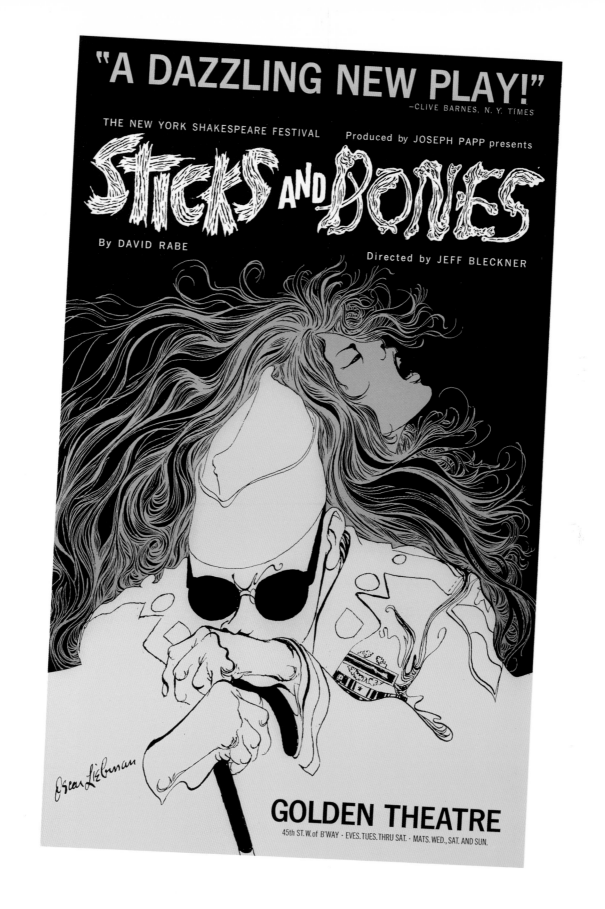

Circle Repertory Theatre, a company of actors, directors, designers, and playwrights cofounded by Wilson, his longtime director, Marshall W. Mason, actress Tanya Berezin, and producer Rob Thrielkeld. All of Wilson's plays were premiered and developed there, including *The Rimers of Eldritch* (1967), *Hot l Baltimore* (1973), *The Mound Builders* (1986), and *Angels Fall* (which was transferred to Broadway in 1983).

In 1980 *Talley's Folly* was moved to Broadway from Circle Rep. This Pulitzer Prize–winning ''valentine'' about an accountant and a shy Missouri spinster captivated audiences. The following year brought *Fifth of July,* a play set thirty-three years after *Talley's Folly.* It was the second of a proposed five-play cycle concerned with the Talley family of Lebanon, Missouri, and featured Kenneth Talley, a homosexual schoolteacher who had lost his legs in the Vietnam War. The action hinged on the threatened disbanding of the family home— itself a major character in this Talley cycle.

Peter Shaffer and his twin brother Anthony have won three Tony Awards for Outstanding Play in just four nominations. Anthony won for *Sleuth* (1970). Peter, the more prolific playwright of the two, was nominated for *Black Comedy,* and won for *Equus* and *Amadeus.*

Amadeus *(1980)*

Peter Shaffer's childhood in Liverpool was interrupted when he was conscripted in 1944 to work in the coal mines. After university and a stint at a music publishing house, Shaffer began to write plays. His success was early and considerable: *Five Finger Exercise* (1959), *The Private Ear/The Public Eye* (1963), and *The Royal Hunt of the Sun* (1965), about Pizzaro's conquest of Peru. Unlike John Osborne, Shaffer was not an angry young man but simply a man of the theater.

His first Broadway hit (in 1967), *Black Comedy* (a long one-act play preceded by the shorter sketch *White Lies*), was based on a simple theatrical trick. The play begins in the dark, and at the moment in the play when the electricity fails, the stage lights come on. The audience can see; the characters cannot.

Equus (1974) and *Amadeus* (1980) typify Shaffer's mature style. Well-crafted, they center around effective "star" roles and constantly evoke the conflict between the rational, mortal man (Dysart and Salieri) and the instinctual, sainted man (Alan and Mozart). Neither play is completely realistic; both synthesize various theatrical styles and conventions. Shaffer's philosophy is this: "The more naturalistic the style, the more you lose touch with the audience's own imagination."

Athol Fugard is a playwright whose work serves to instruct the conscience of his native land, South Africa. He tells the stories of blacks and whites living under apartheid, the South African system of racial separation. Fugard's Broadway debut was in 1975 with *Sizwe Banzi Is Dead* and *The Island,* two one-acts devised by Fugard and the play's actors, John Kani and Winston Ntshona. The plays had been developed earlier at the Serpent Players, a South African theatrical company, of which the three men were leaders.

A Lesson from Aloes (1980) and *'Master Harold' . . . and the boys* (1982) showed the crushing pressures that marriage and friendship are subject to under the reign of apartheid. *'Master Harold'* was the first and only of Fugard's plays to be premiered outside South Africa. It explores Fugard's own youth, his relationship with his alcoholic father, and the eternal embarrassment he causes himself by humiliating his family's friend and servant, Sam.

In 1986 Fugard was nominated for a Tony Award for *The Blood Knot.* Fugard's first major work, the play had been written and premiered twenty-five years before it reached Broadway. On Broadway Zakes Mokae and Fugard himself played the two roles: half-brothers, one black, and one light-skinned enough to "pass."

Fugard's plays always deal with simple human stories set against a complex political world. They are not meant solely for entertainment but as programs for positive action. He fervently believes that "an evil system isn't a natural disaster. There's nothing you can do to stop a drought, but bad laws and social injustices are man-made and can be unmade by men."

Debbie Allen in the Broadway revival of West Side Story *(1980)*

CLASSIC REVIVALS

By the mid seventies, revivals were playing a bigger and bigger part on Broadway. It is believed that reviving a popular show reduces the financial risk for the producer: if a play was a success ten or twenty years ago, it might work again. In reality, revivals fail with the same regularity as new shows.

In 1977 the Tony Awards began to honor revivals by choosing the finest or most innovative re-productions. Some revivals were re-creations of theater history—*West Side Story* (1980), *My Fair Lady* (1982), and *The Caine Mutiny Court Martial* (1983). Others completely revamped the original production, as in *Timbuktu!* (1978), which brought *Kismet* from Arabia to Africa, and *The Pirates of Penzance* (1981), which delighted audiences by blasting the hidebound traditions of Gilbert and Sullivan productions with a new unabashed irreverence.

The first Tony Award for ''Most Innovative Production of a Revival'' was given to the Houston Grand Opera production of George Gershwin's *Porgy and Bess*. For the first time Broadway saw Gershwin's original operatic conception, not something performed in a style similar to his more typical musicals. True, *Porgy and Bess* is by its nature a hybrid of opera and musical, but never had the show's music been treated with the full measure of its due respect.

The revivals of *Dracula* (1927;1977), *Morning's at Seven* (1939;1980), and *On Your Toes* (1936;1983) did not have the inherent strength of the script and score of *Porgy and Bess* (1935;1976). These three Tony-winning revivals were reignited through brilliant performances—Frank Langella's sensual Count Dracula; the four lovable sisters played by Maureen O'Sullivan, Elizabeth Wilson, Nancy Marchand, and Teresa Wright; and American Ballet Theatre star Natalia Makarova in her Broadway debut as Vera Barnova, the Russian prima ballerina.

Othello, Death of a Salesman, and *Joe Egg* can stand up to lesser productions; given brilliant treatment, they soar. The *Othello* revival in 1980 starring James Earl Jones, Christopher Plummer, and Dianne Wiest was favorably compared to the landmark 1943 production featuring Paul Robeson, José Ferrer, and Uta Hagen. Dustin Hoffman's Willy Loman in 1984 was not only considered on a par with Lee J. Cobb's (1949), but many critics and theatergoers who had seen both actually preferred Hoffman's bantamweight fighter to Cobb's hulking victim. The 1985 revival of Peter Nichols's *Joe Egg* was more successful, both artistically and commercially, than the original production produced on Broadway in 1968 as *A Day in the Death of Joe Egg.*

5 MUSICALS

THE R & H FACTOR

When Cole Porter was asked to name the most profound change in musical comedy, he replied simply: "Rodgers and Hammerstein."

More than a quarter-century after the premiere of their last show together, the work of Richard Rodgers and Oscar Hammerstein II remains the benchmark against which audiences and professionals alike judge the worth of new musicals. Rodgers and Hammerstein wrote with eloquence and beauty about the essentials of humanity—love, death, suffering, prejudice, fear—all that is timeless. Their work together was a perfect match of verbal invention and musical expression.

Rodgers and Hammerstein served as midwives to the musical theater we know today. The contemporary integration of words, music, story, and dance, each sustaining and intensifying the others, first came to fruition in *Oklahoma!* Gradual changes in the musical form were taking place before then: Richard Rodgers's earlier musicals *On Your Toes* (1936) and *Pal Joey* (1940), both written with Lorenz Hart, had used dance to a greater extent than other musicals, and Oscar Hammerstein's work with Jerome Kern on *Show Boat* (1927) had expanded the musical form by exploring serious, mature themes through a score more closely related to character and dramatic situation than usual for that day. But *Oklahoma!* marked the emergence of revolution from this evolution.

The work of Cole Porter, Irving Berlin, George and Ira Gershwin, and Richard Rodgers and Lorenz Hart defined the musicals of the thirties, elegant song-and-dance entertainments that were bright, chic, and joyously frivolous. These musicals were marked by plenty of dancing girls, a strong, almost relentless emphasis on comedy, and a collection of songs that often demonstrated more of the writer's wit than the characters'. Songwriters were expected to provide hits —not necessarily germane to situation or character—that could be readily moved into another musical if not immediately successful.

Rodgers and Hammerstein's *Oklahoma!*, a musicalized version of Lynn Riggs's play *Green Grow the Lilacs,* changed everything. When the curtain rose on March 31, 1943, no gaudily gowned chorus line burst into full voice. The stage, but for an old woman churning butter, was empty. Quietly, *offstage,* a man's voice was heard: "Oh, what a beautiful mornin' . . ."

And *Oklahoma!* was begun.

Hammerstein's sunlit lyrics exhibited a seemingly effortless natural quality that belied what was actually painstaking artistry. He spent an entire week debating whether "Oh" should or should not begin the first two lines of the chorus of that opening song. Rodgers, whose work with Lorenz Hart had been the height of sophistication, had found in Hammerstein an even closer soul mate. It took the composer only ten minutes to set Hammerstein's words to music.

There was nothing extraneous in *Oklahoma!* One admirer remarked that the orchestrations sounded the way the costumes looked. Thirteen songs were sung, reprised, and quoted as background scoring, knitting the text and music into a seamless whole. Six of these songs were restated to create the dream ballet "Laurey Makes Up Her Mind." Choreographed by modern-dance pioneer Agnes de Mille, the ballet was founded on the characters' subtextual yearnings, adding to the further integration of music, story, and dance. The musical comedy had become the musical drama.

Rodgers and Hammerstein followed *Oklahoma!* two years later with *Carousel,* a work that pushed the boundaries of the musical even further, and solidified Rodgers and Hammerstein's position as the dominant figures in musical theater. In *Carousel,* Rodgers and Hammerstein gave us an unheroic hero who is killed midway through the action. This tragedy, giving the work an almost operatic stature, brought new worlds to the musical theater.

Joshua Logan rehearsing South Pacific *(1950)*

Carousel almost equaled *Oklahoma!* as a bursting of traditions. As Richard Rodgers put it, "You can do anything in the theatre—just so long as you do it right." With *Carousel,* Rodgers and Hammerstein knew no rivals.

South Pacific (1949) was the first of Rodgers and Hammerstein's musicals to be produced after the advent of the Tony Awards. It won, and it remains for many the perfect musical, the ultimate musical drama. The wartime romance of a naive girl from Little Rock, Arkansas, and an expatriate Frenchman became so popular that the following joke quickly made the rounds. When asked about an empty seat in an otherwise sold-out theater, a woman whispered that her husband had died. "Tsk, tsk," solicited the inquirer, "couldn't you get a friend to come with you?" "No," the lady whispered back, "they're all at the funeral."

Basing the musical on two stories, "Fo' Dolla" and "Our Heroine," in James Michener's Pulitzer Prize–winning *Tales of the South Pacific,* Rodgers and Hammerstein, joined by director and colibrettist Joshua Logan, devoted almost four months to conferences before a single word or note of music was put down. With consummate craft, they created an almost seamless connection between music and action that perfectly balances comedy, drama, dialogue, and song.

Ezio Pinza, Barbara Luna, Michael DeLeon, and Mary Martin in South Pacific *(1949)*

Each song in *South Pacific* is right for that character in that dramatic situation. As Richard Rodgers explained, "[Nellie Forbush's] musical and cultural background would have been confined to radio, a certain number of movies, and perhaps one trip to Chicago where she saw a touring musical comedy."

In "A Wonderful Guy" Rodgers and Hammerstein showed what happens to an unsophisticated, uncomplicated girl bowled over by love for the first time. The melody blossoms into a romantic yet simple waltz—what more appropriate music for a country girl singing of love?

South Pacific marked a deepening of the craft with which Rodgers and Hammerstein approached their material. In other hands *South Pacific* could easily have been a simple musical comedy love story played out against a background of exotic "natives." Rodgers and Hammerstein offered a dual love story in the form of a musical drama that explores the relationship between Nellie from Little Rock and the older European sophisticate Emile de Becque. The story also develops a secondary romance, between an American soldier and a Polynesian girl. Both stories are touched by the theme of racial prejudice—the Frenchman having had two children by a native woman.

Even more astonishing than an *Oklahoma!* followed by a *Carousel* was *The King and I* coming on the heels of *South Pacific*. Imagine what Rodgers and Hammerstein faced in adapting Margaret Landon's novel *Anna and the King of Siam:* the absence of a love story; leading characters consisting of a middle-aged widow and the King of Siam; and a story ending with his death. And the whole thing had already been a successful nonmusical film only six years earlier.

That there was no conventional love story was perhaps the greatest challenge. Musicals had always been about two characters falling in love. Yet, in the "real" musicals of Rodgers and Hammerstein, a Welsh governess and the King of Siam could hardly fall in love. Oscar Hammerstein put it this way: "The intangibility of their [Anna and the King's] strange union was a challenge to us as librettist and composer. In dealing with them musically, we could not write songs which said 'I love you' or even 'I love him' or 'I love her.' We were dealing with two characters who could indulge themselves only in oblique expressions of feeling for each other, since they themselves do not realize exactly what these feelings mean."

The King and Anna, their thoughts and feelings, don't really come together until the penultimate musical number of the show, and, even then, their feelings for each other are not rendered by open declaration but through Anna's singing the words of a man she *imagines* speaking to her—"Shall we dance?"

Rodgers and Hammerstein followed *The King and I* with three musicals that made but few dents in Tony history. *Me and Juliet* (1953), a backstage romance, *Pipe Dream* (1955), based on John Steinbeck's short story "Sweet Thursday," about a madam with a heart of gold, and *Flower Drum Song* (1958)—as Hammerstein put it, "an Oriental *Life with Father.*"

In the late fifties Rodgers and Hammerstein were asked to provide a single song for a new musical about the life of the Trapp family singers. The remainder of the score was to have been authentic folk and religious songs the family had sung in their own shows. (Indeed, the song "Edelweiss" added to the show during out-of-town tryouts, was actually mistaken for an authentic Austrian folk song.) Rodgers and Hammerstein did not agree to this request, but they were willing to write a complete score. *The Sound of Music* was not a ground-breaking musical, but it was perhaps the epitome of what a Rodgers and Hammerstein musical had come to be: a strong story filled with fully realized characters, a score of beauty and scope, lyrics full of humanity and optimism.

The songs in *The Sound of Music* were not as fully integrated into the show as those in other Rodgers and Hammerstein musicals. The show opens without overture, revealing a young postulant on a mountainside, listening to the "sound of music" drifting up the hills. It comes to a musical and emotional climax with "Climb Ev'ry Mountain," a stirring hymn that sums up the religious and personal strength of the Trapp family as they leave their homeland to escape the growing Nazi menace.

Yul Brynner and Gertrude Lawrence in The King and I *(1951). Lawrence died of cancer just three weeks after leaving the show. At her request, she was buried in her "Shall We Dance" ball gown.*

Mary Martin and Theodore Bikel in
The Sound of Music *(1959)*

The Sound of Music contained the final lyrics of Oscar Hammerstein, who died nine months after the show opened. Following the death of Oscar Hammerstein, Richard Rodgers continued writing musicals, though none reached the heights of his previous work. *No Strings* (1962), the only musical for which Rodgers supplied his own lyrics, examined an interracial love affair. In addition, the orchestration reflected the title in its omission of stringed instruments, save a harp and one string bass.

Rodgers's other work, *Do I Hear a Waltz?* (1965) with Stephen Sondheim, *Rex* (1976) with Sheldon Harnick, and *Two by Two* (1970) and *I Remember Mama* (1979), both with Martin Charnin, were graced only by flashes of the master's former brilliance. Yet, through the years, the musicals of Rodgers and Hammerstein have been produced more often than those of any other composer-lyricist team. Yearly productions of *Oklahoma!* top six hundred, and *The Sound of Music, South Pacific, The King and I,* and *Carousel* are all given between three and four hundred professional and amateur productions each year.

*Patricia Morison and Alfred Drake in
Kiss Me Kate (1948)*

Songs like "I Get a Kick Out of You," "You're the Top," "It's De-Lovely," "My Heart Belongs to Daddy," and "Night and Day" had assured Cole Porter's fame in the thirties and forties. *Kiss Me, Kate* (1948), the first musical to win a Tony, brought Porter's art to an even more exalted level and revealed the influence of earlier Rodgers and Hammerstein musicals on the older Porter, who knew what the so-called R & H Factor had meant to his usual run of fluffy shows: "The librettos are much better, and the scores are much closer to

the librettos than they used to be. Those two [Rodgers and Hammerstein] made it much harder for everybody else."

The idea for *Kiss Me, Kate* came when producer Saint-Subber, then a back-stage worker for the Theatre Guild's production of *The Taming of the Shrew*, realized that its stars, Alfred Lunt and Lynn Fontanne, argued almost as much off-stage as husband and wife as they did onstage as feuding lovers.

The play-within-a-play story gave Porter the idea of using Shakespearean-influenced songs for the onstage characters (who, in the story, are performing a production of Shakespeare's *The Taming of the Shrew*) and reserving his own inimitable style for the off-stage, "contemporary" characters.

The score, blending Shakespeare and sex, urbane melody and jazz, is Porter's acknowledged masterpiece. Using Shakespeare as a point of departure, Cole Porter created "I've Come to Wive it Wealthily in Padua," "Were Thine That Special Face," "Why Can't You Behave?," "Too Darn Hot," and "Brush Up Your Shakespeare"—a delightful duet that shows how two singing gangsters could prove critic George Jean Nathan's early belief that, "when it comes to lyrics, this Cole Porter is so far ahead of the other boys in New York that there just is no race at all."

★ ▓▓▓

From third prize in a harmonica-playing contest when he was a teenager to writing five Broadway musicals—including one, *Guys and Dolls,* recognized as among the greatest—Frank Loesser's career was marked by a succession of glories. He started out as a lyricist; his first lyric, "In Love with a Memory of You," was set by no less than William Schuman, later a Pulitzer Prize–winning "serious" composer. Then Jerome Kern offered the budding lyricist a piece of advice: "Your lyrics make the writing of a melody a cinch. You're a sucker to let others do it." Loesser learned. The first song for which he wrote both music and lyrics was the 1942 success "Praise the Lord and Pass the Ammunition."

Loesser's first show, *Where's Charley?* (1948), was an old-fashioned musical comedy. His second was *Guys and Dolls* (1950), depicting the unlikely pursuit of a Salvation Army lady by a brash Broadway gambler. It was "the model of what an ideal musical comedy should be," according to one critic.

After Loesser had rejected eleven librettos, Abe Burrows, who had no theatrical experience, wrote an entirely new book, which he fitted to Loesser's already completed score. Based on Damon Runyon characters and stories, the new book, perhaps the funniest in Broadway history, was subtitled "A Musical Fable of Broadway" and retained all the swagger of the Runyon originals.

Loesser's score had nary a weak spot, from the big romantic melodies of "I'll Know" and "I've Never Been in Love Before," to the brassy punch of "Sit Down, You're Rockin' the Boat" and "Take Back Your Mink," a wacky striptease. "Adelaide's Lament," a brilliant comic song about unrequited love and psychosomatic flu, was a perfect example of Loesser's desire to "examine characters, not events."

Loesser's next show, *The Most Happy Fella* (1956), took four years to write. Loesser wrote not only the music and the lyrics, but also the book, which he based on Sidney Howard's *They Knew What They Wanted,* a tale of an aging California vintner and his mail-order bride. There were more than forty musical numbers, and, as with operatic productions, the theater program did not list them individually. However, Loesser refused to call it an opera, insisting that it was merely "a musical—with lots of music."

Robert Morse in How to Succeed in Business Without Really Trying *(1961)*

Loesser had won a Tony Award for *Guys and Dolls* and would win another for *How to Succeed in Business Without Really Trying* (1961), based on the satirical how-to manual of the same title. Again set to a book by Abe Burrows, the show won a Pulitzer Prize.

Loesser wrote just five Broadway shows in thirteen years—"I don't write slowly. It's just that I throw out fast"—but he was always available with aid and advice for fellow composers. He also had quite a knack for recognizing talent in others and encouraged Meredith Willson to write down his tales of boyhood life in small-town Iowa. This became the 1957 Tony Award–winning *Music Man*.

★▨▨

When Frank Loesser suggested the writing team of Richard Adler and Jerry Ross to director George Abbott for a musical version of Richard Bissell's *7 ½ Cents,* he couldn't really have known that Adler and Ross would come up with such hit songs as "Hey There," "Hernando's Hideaway," and "Steam Heat." The product of a naive collaboration of neophytes, *The Pajama Game* (1954) was the first time around for Adler and Ross, choreographer Bob Fosse, and producers Frederick Brisson, Robert Griffith, and Harold Prince. The success of their "happy cartoon" about a wage strike at the Sleep-Tite Pajama Factory in Cedar Rapids, Iowa, was immediate.

Adler and Ross each wrote music and lyrics; their first hit song, in 1953, was "Rags to Riches." Theirs was a complete collaboration. They were anything but old pros, having begun on Broadway the year before by writing several

How to Succeed in Business Without
Really Trying *(1961)*

*Janis Paige, John Raitt, and Buzz
Miller in* Pajama Game *(1954)*

songs for the revue *John Murray Anderson's Almanac,* and felt that they were "writing the way our generation demands we write." Adler and Ross were not trying for major statements or exciting innovations but were "writing for the man on the street," trying "to write universal truths in colloquial terms."

Just one year after *Pajama Game* came *Damn Yankees* (1955), using the same producers, choreographer, musical director (Harold Hastings), orchestrator (Don Walker), and director as the first Adler and Ross hit. *Damn Yankees,* like *The Pajama Game,* was not particularly innovative (it *was* the first musical about baseball), yet it had a vibrancy and youthful verve that captivated audiences.

Shortly after the success of *Damn Yankees,* Jerry Ross died of a lung ailment he had contracted early in life. His death also marked the end of his partner's Broadway success.

★▓▓▓▓

"You are Alan Jay Lerner? You write good lyrics. I am Frederick Loewe. I have something to say to you." With that exchange at the Lambs Club in 1942 a musical team was born.

Lerner, the Harvard-educated writer, and Loewe, alumnus of the Viennese operetta tradition, inherited the Rodgers and Hammerstein traditional-book musical and refined it in such work as *Brigadoon* (1947) and *Paint Your Wagon* (1951).

The project of musicalizing Bernard Shaw's *Pygmalion* had been offered first to Rodgers and Hammerstein, who turned it down—as did Noel Coward, Cole Porter, E. Y. "Yip" Harburg, and the team of Arthur Schwartz and Howard Dietz. The problem was trying to make a standard book musical out of *Pygmalion.* It just didn't work. There was no subplot, a traditional element in a musical. There was no one to serve as the chorus. The nonlove story called for nonlove songs, and who would go see that? Lerner and Loewe tried, failed, and gave it up. "For years Fritz and I floundered around, trying to find our natural way of writing. *My Fair Lady* revealed it to us. . . . We are the means by which [the characters] express themselves, not vice versa. When we felt we really knew them, then we began to work on the score."

So sympathetically were the characters captured that when Eliza at last succeeded in her pronunciation lesson, a palpable sense of relief coursed through the audience. Her tango of celebration, "The Rain in Spain," in which Higgins and Pickering join, is a high point of musical comedy.

The overwhelming success of *My Fair Lady* led many to believe Lerner and Loewe had replaced Rodgers and Hammerstein as the premier writers of musicals. Lerner: "Neither Fritz nor I believe we're *that* good. It's just that the time was ripe for something gay and theatrical, something that was not two lonely people finding each other in a dark alley. *My Fair Lady* fit the bill." It was all a matter of contrasts: Loewe's graceful Viennese melodies were quite the opposite of the broader, more majestic tunes of Rodgers, and Lerner's lyrics were more consciously sophisticated than Hammerstein's.

Their next and last stage collaboration was *Camelot* in 1960, after which Loewe retired. *Gigi* (1973), which won a Tony Award for its score, was merely a stage adaptation of their film, with the addition of four more songs. For all their individual joys, Lerner's later efforts—*On a Clear Day You Can See Forever* (1965), *Coco* (1969), *1600 Pennsylvania Avenue* (1976), *Carmelina* (1979), and *Dance a Little Closer* (1983)—were not commercially successful.

Katharine Hepburn in Coco *(1969). This was Hepburn's only Broadway musical.*

THEME AND VARIATIONS

The shadow cast by Rodgers and Hammerstein loomed even larger after they stopped writing musicals. Though audiences continued to flock to old-fashioned musical comedies, many had come to recognize the form Rodgers and Hammerstein had created—melody, seriousness of purpose and content, integration of medium and message—as *the* way to write a musical. Broadway producers recognized this also, and the recognition led to variation after variation on the R&H theme.

Zero Mostel and cast recording A Funny Thing Happened on the Way to the Forum

For all the millions who come to New York to see the original stars in hit Broadway musicals, there are untold millions more who experience those performances through recordings. The first Broadway musical to be recorded in full by its original cast was Rodgers and Hammerstein's *Oklahoma!*. The advertisements back then bragged, "Now you can hear the Broadway show in your own living room." The original cast recording of *My Fair Lady* sold an all-time record six million copies. Besides spreading a score near and far, an original cast recording also preserves performances for the ages. Without recordings of *Gypsy* and *South Pacific* would future generations understand the Merman-Martin idolatry? And without the recording of such an unsuccessful show as *Anyone Can Whistle*, would we appreciate the early genius of Stephen Sondheim?

Thomas Z. Shepard, producer of the original cast recordings of *Company*, *Sweeney Todd*, and *La Cage Aux Folles*, among many others, explains: "The job is to absorb the intention of the show—what the director has put on the stage—and convey it in nonvisual language. There are no sets, no lights, no costumes on a rec-ord. You have to recreate the experience without any of those things." The good producers—Shepard and his mentor, Goddard Lieberson—realize this essential difference.

These aural photographs are generally taken on the Monday following opening night, usually a day with no theater performance. In one sixteen- to eighteen-hour day the entire show is put on tape. It is recorded with the orchestra and singers in one room. If a mistake is made by a single person, the take must be redone. Often there are changes in the orchestration, pieces of dialogue removed or added, new beginnings or endings of songs produced, but only for this one performance, only to create an experience for the listener as profound and immediate as an actual viewing of the show.

The chances to see such ever-popular shows as *Hello, Dolly!*, *The Music Man*, and *Annie*, are many. And seeing every musical in full production would obviously be ideal. Yet the opportunity to savor on disc the delights of such beautiful but seldom-produced scores as *Bells Are Ringing*, *She Loves Me*, and *Follies* is for most of us a blessed compromise.

Early in his career Jule Styne received a bit of advice from Richard Rodgers: "Don't be a minor Cole Porter. Be yourself and the critics will gradually have respect for you." Gradually they did. Critic Kenneth Tynan referred to Styne as "the most persistently underrated of popular composers," even though he was popularly appreciated—indeed, the most prolific and one of the most successful composers of the postwar years. Year after year a new Jule Styne musical came to Broadway: *Bells Are Ringing, Do Re Mi, Two on the Aisle, Hazel Flagg, Peter Pan, Say, Darling, Subways Are For Sleeping, Fade Out–Fade In, Look to the Lilies, Sugar*—twenty-three in all, between 1944 and 1976.

Jule Styne is perhaps the finest creator of vehicles for female stars in Tony history. Judy Holliday, Ethel Merman, and Barbra Streisand had their biggest Broadway successes in Styne musicals. He was a master at writing songs that not only suited character and dramatic situation, but also the performer. Styne recognized the overwhelming importance of the singer: "Without the rendition there is no song."

And what songs they were—"Everything's Coming Up Roses," "People," "The Party's Over," and "Make Someone Happy." The songs flowed from his fertile imagination. Styne once let out the secret of such productivity: "You know what songwriters do when they're tired? They doodle. Know what they doodle? Songs." He and his lyricists "doodled" over two thousand of them.

Styne won Tony nominations for *Bells Are Ringing* (1956), *Gypsy* (1959), *Do Re Mi* (1960), *Funny Girl* (1964), and *Hallelujah, Baby!* (1967), winning the Outstanding Musical award only for the last. That award notwithstanding, the greatest of these was *Gypsy*.

Originally, the young Stephen Sondheim was to have provided the music and lyrics for the musicalization of the life story of stripper Gypsy Rose Lee. Ethel Merman, who was to star, insisted on a composer more experienced than Sondheim, and eventually Styne was brought on board by producer David Merrick. Sondheim remained as lyricist. Mama Rose was the last stage role Merman created, and it became the greatest musical role of the musical's greatest star.

The exceptionally strong book by Arthur Laurents and the Styne-Sondheim score moved the audience, introducing them to Mama Rose and her children in the world of vaudeville and then into the coarser world of burlesque. Simultaneously, the audience was shown Mama Rose's singleminded devotion not to her children as such, but to their careers. As Laurents put it, "What we've got here is a mother who has to learn that if you try to live your children's lives, you'll end up destroying yourself."

As Jule Styne put it, "The answer to the entire play is in that song."

At times called *A Very Special Person, My Man,* or *The Luckiest People,* and alternately announced as starring Mary Martin, Anne Bancroft, or Carol Burnett, the musical biography of Fanny Brice finally made it to Broadway as

Ethel Merman in Gypsy *(1959)*

Barbra Streisand and Danny Meehan in Funny Girl *(1964). Both performers were nominated; neither won.*

Funny Girl (1964). It starred Barbra Streisand. Styne wrote the show with Bob Merrill, composer-lyricist of *New Girl in Town* and *Carnival,* and after going through four directors, five postponements of opening night, and dozens of rewrites of the final scene, what remained most memorable were such new Styne delights as ''People,'' a popular hit that quickly became a Streisand signature song. *Funny Girl* made Streisand a star on Broadway. Four years later she became a star in Hollywood when the film version was released.

★▓

Musical effortlessness has been a hallmark of each Cy Coleman song or score. While he does feel that ''the score is the sub-text of the entire piece,'' Coleman's work has always been more that of a songwriter than a composer.

Jim Dale and Glenn Close in Barnum *(1980)*

His musicals almost always contain at least one song that has a popular success, including "I've Got Your Number," "Hey There, Good Times," "It's Not Where You Start (It's Where You Finish)." Coleman believes that "somehow people feel cheated if they don't hear a few songs they can latch on to."

Marvelous songs like "If My Friends Could See Me Now," "Big Spender," and "I'm a Brass Band" highlight his most popular show, *Sweet Charity* (1966). Running 608 performances during its first Tony-nominated Broadway engagement, the show won a Tony for Best Re-production in 1986, and enjoyed another healthy run.

Coleman's work on *Little Me, Seesaw, I Love My Wife, On the Twentieth Century,* and *Barnum* also received Tony nominations.

Good producers raise money. Great producers develop productions, create audiences, provide artistic guidance, and, of course, raise money—lots of it. David Merrick is one of the greatest producers.

David Merrick began as a lawyer, worked as a press agent and stage manager, and became Broadway's most prodigious and most highly rewarded producer. Merrick's ninety-plus Broadway produc-

tions have received more than one hundred Tony nominations. Merrick himself has received two special Tony Awards for his service to the Broadway theater. Not a week goes by without a performance of one of the plays or musicals he originally produced appearing before an audience somewhere in the world. Within one week in 1960, Merrick opened *Irma La*

Douce, A Taste of Honey, and *Becket.* And those were just three of eleven shows he had running that season.

Not only did Merrick get shows on the boards, he also kept them there through a genius for promotion. He was the first to advertise in taxicabs. As *Flower Drum Song* became more popular than one of his own shows, Merrick had the Rodgers and Hammerstein show picketed by signs reading, "The only authentic Oriental show on Broadway is *The World of Suzie Wong.*" When the newspaper reviews for his production of *Subways Are for Sleeping* weren't to his liking, he found ordinary citizens with the same names as the newspaper critics—"Walter Kerr," "Douglas Watt," "Clive Barnes"—and advertised *their* high praise.

Merrick knows that while hit musicals might not always be great art—"to be successful, a musical must be simple-minded" —they are what audiences want. He has produced some of the most popular: *Gypsy, Carnival, Oliver,* and *I Do! I Do!.* It was Merrick who thought of changing the film *The Apartment* into the musical *Promises, Promises,* and of turning Thornton Wilder's *The Matchmaker* (which Merrick had previously produced as a play on Broadway) into *Hello, Dolly!.* He extended the run of *Hello, Dolly!* by using an all-black cast headed by Pearl Bailey. Merrick's productions of dramas have mainly been London imports: *Look Back in Anger, The Entertainer,* and *Travesties.*

Merrick has become rich from his productions. At its highpoint, *42nd Street,* which Merrick completely owned, poured $500,000 a week into his pockets. Luckily for the theater, Merrick returns much of that money to Broadway by producing more shows. "I have only two interests: Broadway and women." Merrick has been married five times.

Preparing a musical version of Thornton Wilder's *The Matchmaker*, producer David Merrick auditioned several composers and lyricists before finally giving the nod to Jerry Herman. Once Herman got the assignment he quickly went to work writing a star vehicle for Ethel Merman. *Ethel Merman?* Though *Hello, Dolly!* was written for her, she turned the project down without hearing the score. Only later, after Carol Channing, Ginger Rogers, Martha Raye, Betty Grable, Bibi Osterwald, Pearl Bailey, and Phyllis Diller, did Merman play Dolly Levi on Broadway. At that time Herman reinstated two songs that had originally been written for Merman, but were dropped as uncomfortable for Channing.

Hello, Dolly! became the first of Herman's Tony-winning musicals. He also won for *La Cage Aux Folles*. All of Herman's work (including his other musicals, *Milk and Honey, Mack and Mabel, The Grand Tour, Dear World*) are firmly in the realm of the big, splashy Broadway musical.

Herman is not an innovator, nor is he influenced by contemporary musical sound. He believes that theater music should be melodic and memorable, and to insure this, the melodies are simple and the audience's memory is helped by reprise after reprise. Herman himself admits: "If I had had the choice of being the most brilliant and sophisticated writer that ever came down the pike or of being the simple melodic songwriter that I am, I still would have chosen the latter." And, "If they can't hum it when they leave the theatre, it doesn't work."

His characters, usually well into their middle years, are often larger-than-life, independent-minded women. His songs tend either to be glorifications of the show's star—"Hello, Dolly!," "Mame," "When Mabel Walks in the Room"—or sentimental ballads—"If He Walked into My Life," "Time Heals Everything," "Song on the Sand."

La Cage Aux Folles in 1984 was Herman's tenth score and first hit since *Mame* in 1966. Based on the drama of the same name, about a St. Tropez transvestite nightclub, the show was another Broadway musical spectacle—the form that Herman has so thoroughly mastered.

Herman understands the niche he fills in the American musical, and he has learned never to stray far from it. "Some writers write for themselves alone. I have to please myself first—but I also am here to entertain. That is my credo. That is what I'm all about. That's why I write simple melodic music. I want to please the audience and I want to make them happy and entertained. If they're not, I'm doing something wrong."

Charles Strouse writes American musicals. Nothing set in Siam or Russia. He even wrote a show called *All American* (1962). Strouse has won three Tony Awards for Best Musical, American subjects all: *Bye, Bye Birdie* (1960), the earliest musical about the rock 'n' roll phenomenon; *Applause* (1970), a Hollywood tale of the rise and fall of stars; and *Annie* (1977), the quintessential Amer-

ican comic strip brought to musical life. Strouse has written music to the lyrics of Alan Jay Lerner, Martin Charnin, and, most often, Lee Adams.

The composer's musical background is a combination of classical studies with Aaron Copland and Nadia Boulanger, plus long stints as a Broadway rehearsal pianist. Strouse puts his talents to work daily; he is probably the most prolific Broadway composer writing today. ''One of the supreme pleasures in putting down all of these notes is that there will be somebody in an evening somewhere in the future, who will sit down with one of my works. It's nice to have an audience at one with you.''

Bock and Harnick. They brought to new heights the Rodgers and Hammerstein ideal of songs so completely in tune with the world of the show's characters as to be inseparable from it. Theirs were carefully crafted, carefully integrated shows, not mere successions of scene, song, and dance.

Jerry Bock and Sheldon Harnick's first Tony-winning musical, *Fiorello!* (1959), was also awarded a Pulitzer Prize. The show was unique in that the leading character, New York's legendary Depression-era mayor, Fiorello LaGuardia, didn't dance and didn't sing much either. The team's second Tony Award–winning musical, *Fiddler on the Roof* (1964), was the first show that Bock and Harnick initiated (they had been hired for their earlier work only *after* the shows were in development). Based on the fiction of the turn-of-the-century Yiddish short-story writer Sholom Aleichem, *Fiddler* defied the standard logic of the commercial theater by daring to treat religious persecution, poverty, and the loss of old-world traditions in the face of a rapidly approaching modern world. These universal themes, unfolded in simple but elegant songs and a touchingly humorous book, were masterfully handled by director-choreographer Jerome Robbins and by Zero Mostel, whose lovable antics as Tevye captivated audiences.

Fiddler on the Roof broke the performance record of *My Fair Lady,* setting a new mark of 3,242 performances. This mark has since been broken only by *Grease, Oh! Calcutta,* and *A Chorus Line*.

''When we're doing our best we sound like one person.'' In fact, most people don't know which of the Kander and Ebb team is the composer and which is the lyricist. John Kander (music) and Fred Ebb (words) found early and lasting fame writing *Cabaret* (1966), based on *Goodbye to Berlin* by Christopher Isherwood.

Featuring a story and characters that few composers of the forties or fifties would touch, yet songs even they would applaud, for many *Cabaret* is *the* Kander and Ebb musical. The majority of the songs were not integrated into the musical's book in the R & H fashion, but were set in the show's nightclub, which, in turn, was the hub of the entire production. The songs echoed the music of Kurt Weill and counterbalanced with a decadent joy the bleak book, which depicted Berlin amid the burgeoning Nazi threat.

MUSICAL DIRECTORS AND CONDUCTORS

From 1948 until 1964 a Tony Award was given to the outstanding musical director-conductor of each season. Though the jobs of musical director and conductor are usually taken by a single person, they are two different jobs. The musical director teaches the music to the principal and chorus singers and often helps the composer and orchestrator arrange the music for those voices. A production's conductor actually leads the singers and orchestra night after night.

The conductor is responsible for pacing the show—fighting the indifference that can plague any long run—and leading each performance, which may include sections of ballet, pure orchestral interlude, spoken

Richard Rodgers rehearsing the orchestra for South Pacific *(1950)*

dialogue underscored by music, and, of course, a dozen or more songs. Also, the timing of lights, curtains, and actors' entrances is often set to the conductor's cues.

Franz Allers, musical director and conductor for *My Fair Lady,* had to find special nonmusical cues to use with Rex Harrison, a nonmusical actor. Harrison wasn't able to begin his songs on musical cues from the orchestra, so, in reverse of the usual method, Harrison would "cue" Allers and the orchestra with a glance, an emphasized word, or the emphatic pointing of a pencil. Allers, who won Tony Awards for his work on *My Fair Lady* and *Camelot,* was a Vienna-trained musician who had served as conductor of the Ballet

Russe de Monte Carlo and had led the premiere of Agnes de Mille's choreography to Aaron Copland's *Rodeo.*

Allers and Maurice Abravanel, Tony Award winner in 1950 as musical director and conductor for Marc Blitzstein's *Regina,* worked to raise the musical standards of performers and orchestral musicians. They were joined by the most-rewarded musical director-conductor in Tony history, Lehman Engel.

Engel was born in Jackson, Mississippi, and was captivated at an early age by the orchestra that played at the local silent movie theater. He studied composition with Roger Sessions at the Juilliard School, served as the chief composer during World War II for the Navy's film division, and conducted the first American production of Kurt Weill's *Threepenny Opera.*

Engel worked as musical director-conductor on almost two hundred shows, including the Broadway productions of *Li'l Abner, Fanny, Do Re Mi,* and *Destry Rides Again.* He received Tonys for his work on Gian Carlo Menotti's *The Consul* and Bernstein's *Wonderful Town,* and additional nominations for *Goldilocks, What Makes Sammy Run?,* and *Take Me Along.*

Engel's most enduring legacy is his numerous books on the musical and the musical-theater workshops he founded, which are today run by the music-licensing organization BMI. These workshops bring together experienced Broadway composers and lyricists with younger aspirants; together they hone new songs and shows. Among the musicals that have come out of these Lehman Engel workshops are *The Best Little Whorehouse in Texas, Nine, Raisin, You're a Good Man, Charlie Brown, Little Shop of Horrors,* and *A Chorus Line.*

Kander and Ebb's other shows, *Chicago, Zorba, The Act, Woman of the Year,* and *The Rink* are filled with many musical delights, and, as performer vehicles, are of the highest Broadway standard. At times their songs can be weak as individualized statements of character, but more often their work stands as a tribute to the Broadway songwriter's craft.

The entertainment world has never been able to put Leonard Bernstein into a neat, comfortable category—composer? pianist? conductor? educator? writer? His work for the Broadway stage has been similarly hard to classify. *Wonderful Town* (1953) (a production boasting the same team—Bernstein, Comden, Green, Robbins, and Abbott—as the earlier *On the Town*) is a fairly standard book musical. *Candide* (1956), surviving its checkered production history, is a delightful pastiche of operettalike music. *West Side Story,* one of the finest of all American musicals, comes as close to opera as possible without actually going over the line.

Bert Convy, Joel Grey, and Jill Haworth in Cabaret *(1966)*

Rosalind Russell in Wonderful Town
(1953)

Eight years before *Wonderful Town*, Bernstein and Jerome Robbins had expanded their ballet *Fancy Free* into a stage musical, *On the Town* (1944). Contractual agreements concerning *Wonderful Town* gave Bernstein, Comden, and Green only five weeks to complete the score, or the star, Rosalind Russell, would be lost to the production. The songs—''A Little Bit in Love,'' ''Christopher Street,'' and ''Ohio''—poured out, and the show was a hit, winning a Tony as Best Musical.

It has taken years for *Candide* to be recognized as a major work. The show was a flop, due in part to the leaden book by Lillian Hellman and the ungainly staging of Tyrone Guthrie (who confessed, ''My direction shipped along with the effortless grace of a freight train heavy-laden on a steep gradient''). Eighteen years after its initial Broadway run, *Candide* was successful, revamped with a new book by Hugh Wheeler, additional lyrics by Stephen Sondheim, and a new staging concept by Harold Prince. Crowning this new success was the introduction of the show into the repertory of the New York City Opera with a further revised and augmented score.

Scheduling conflicts among Jerome Robbins, Leonard Bernstein, and Arthur Laurents kept *East Side Story,* a musical about the love between a Jewish girl and an Italian Catholic boy, from getting under way. After several years, in 1957, this modern-day version of Shakespeare's *Romeo and Juliet,* now featuring a Puerto Rican girl and an ''American'' boy, came to Broadway as *West Side Story*.

Writing the book—the dialogue scenes—for a musical is a thankless task. The writer's best, his most dramatic, emotional, or comic scenes, are taken by the lyricist and turned into songs. The writer is then asked to construct dialogue to lead into and out of his musicalized scene.

When the musical is in trouble, either out of town or in Broadway previews, the book is the first thing blamed. If the show is a failure, the standard cry is "Great score, but what an awful book." Moreover, it is much easier to rewrite the book and have the actors memorize a few new scenes than to write a new lyric and melody, have it orchestrated and rehearsed, memorized, and performed. A new scene can go in tomorrow night, a new song might take a week; and with millions of dollars riding on the success of this new musical, a week is often too long to wait.

Many writers have produced books for musicals, and some—Joseph Stein, Michael Stewart, Arthur Laurents, Hugh Wheeler—have produced a number of exceedingly fine musical books. Book writers don't become stars, yet when one speaks of them two names always come up, Comden and Green. They are linked so inextricably that few know their first names (Betty and Adolph), and many believe they are married to each other (nope).

Betty Comden and Adolph Green have been writing books and lyrics for musical shows since the early forties, and neither has written a lyric, libretto, or screenplay without the other. The success of their nightclub act, The Revuers, and the ever-increasing demand for new, royalty-free material, was the start of their writing career.

The duo's Broadway career began in 1944 when they furnished book, lyrics, and their own onstage performances for Leonard Bernstein and Jerome Robbins's *On the Town*. Comden and Green went on to deliver the book and/or lyrics for such shows as *Wonderful Town, Bells Are Ringing* (starring former co-Revuer Judy Holliday), *Do Re Mi, Hallelujah, Baby!, Applause,* and *On the Twentieth Century*. On Broadway (twice) and throughout the country, Comden, Green, and their regularly revived revue, *A Party with Betty Comden and Adolph Green,* have charmed audiences, who are thrilled to hear again the highlights of years of lyric writing.

"Why haven't we broken up? Because we cling together out of fear." With Green pacing, thinking aloud, and Comden typing, the team has produced work that has received nine Tony Award nominations, winning five: the books and lyrics for *On the Twentieth Century* and *Hallelujah, Baby!* (one of eight shows with Jule Styne) and the book for *Applause*. The pacing and typing and forty-plus years together demonstrate the remarkable match of the satirical Comden with the madcap Green. They are compatible but not interchangeable. As composer Styne puts it, "Betty is realistic, and Adolph is dream-istic."

Amazingly, after all these years, and all this success, Comden and Green, pessimistic native New Yorkers to the core, "still feel we're on the brink of some terrific career."

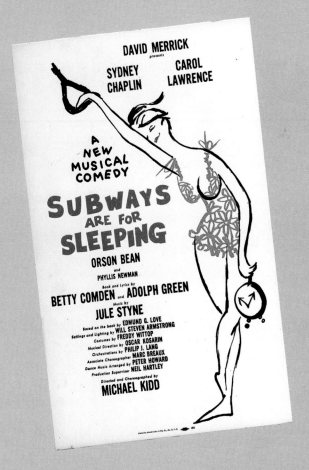

The production team, joined by lyricist Stephen Sondheim, knew they wanted to create something more than just another Broadway musical comedy. Arthur Laurents, who wrote the book, revealed their underlying notion: "We all knew what we did not want—neither formal poetry nor flat reportage; neither opera nor split-level musical comedy; neither zippered-in ballets nor character-less dance routines. We didn't want newsreel acting, blue-jean costumes, or garbage-can scenery any more than we wanted soap-box pounding for our theme of young love destroyed by a violent world. What we did was to aim at a lyrically and theatrically sharpened illusion of reality." Leonard Bernstein recorded in his diary the problems inherent in writing *West Side Story*. "Chief problem: to tread the fine line between opera and Broadway, between realism and poetry, ballet and 'just dancing,' abstract and representational."

Their brilliant success at treading these lines thrilled audiences. Robbins's choreography made the music a vibrant physical presence. Laurents's book captured the feeling of youthful slang without sacrificing the universal themes of Shakespeare's original. But most of all, it was Bernstein's music, full of soaring melodies and syncopated urban rhythms, that set *West Side Story* in the pantheon of immortal American musicals.

THE SONDHEIM ERA

In 1971, 1972, and 1973 Stephen Sondheim won Tony Awards for his scores to *Company, Follies,* and *A Little Night Music*. No other composer has done this. Nor can any match Sondheim's record of five Tony Awards in twelve nominations. As Rodgers and Hammerstein revolutionized the musical in the forties, so Sondheim altered the course of the musical theater in the seventies and eighties.

The musical theater form that Rodgers and Hammerstein developed, the "integrated" musical, became formulaic in the fifties and sixties. What worked for Rodgers and Hammerstein worked because it was fresh; other writers who tried to write a "Rodgers and Hammerstein" show became, in effect, their own predecessors. Rodgers and Hammerstein broke with the traditional musical of their day by letting their choice of subject matter determine structure. "We just took a story and worked it out to what we thought was its logical conclusion, and the hell with the old type of show with its sequence of scene, song, and dance."

Sondheim, often working with director Harold Prince, experimented with having a production's style of presentation take precedence over the story itself; no longer was there a single, standard "Broadway musical" production style. Both the matter and the manner of the musical were balanced, neither predominated. Sondheim chose not to reject the work of Rodgers and Hammerstein but rather developed it to ends its creators had not imagined. There was no turning back to an earlier day.

Stephen Joshua Sondheim was born on March 22, 1930. He studied music with the distinguished American "serious" composer Milton Babbitt, and he

SIDE BY SIDE BY SONDHEIM

A Musical Entertainment

HAROLD PRINCE
in association with RUTH MITCHELL
presents
by arrangement with
THE INCOMES COMPANY LTD.

SIDE BY SIDE BY SONDHEIM

A Musical Entertainment

with

**MILLICENT MARTIN
JULIE N. McKENZIE
DAVID KERNAN
and NED SHERRIN**

MUSIC & LYRICS BY

STEPHEN SONDHEIM

and music by

LEONARD BERNSTEIN   MARY RODGERS
RICHARD RODGERS   JULE STYNE

Directed by NED SHERRIN
Musical Director RAY COOK

Pianists·DANIEL TROOB and ALBIN KONOPKA
Musical Staging by BOB HOWE
Scenery by PETER DOCHERTY
Costumes by FLORENCE KLOTZ
Lighting by KEN BILLINGTON
Scenery Supervision JAY MOORE
Musical Supervision PAUL GEMIGNANI

Original Cast Album & Tapes **RCA** Records

MUSIC BOX THEATRE
239 W. 45th St. · 246-4636

studied the musical with Oscar Hammerstein. "What I . . . learn[ed] from Milton was basic grammar—sophisticated grammar, but grammar. It was a language, whereas what I learned from Oscar was what to do with language."

Sondheim's classmate at the George School in Pennsylvania was Hammerstein's son, Jimmy, and their friendship led to the protégé-mentor relationship of Sondheim with Hammerstein. In 1946, for the George School, Sondheim wrote a student musical, *By George,* with three classmates. Sondheim took it to Oscar Hammerstein and asked for his comments, pressing for a professional critique. Hammerstein went though *By George* line-by-line, meticulously passing on the fundamentals of musical theater. Sondheim later admitted that he learned more during that one afternoon than many students of the musical learn in a lifetime.

Hammerstein laid out a course of study that would make Sondheim into a writer of musicals. "Professor" Hammerstein's program was, first, to take a good play and turn it into a musical. Sondheim chose *Beggar on Horseback.* Second, to take a not-so-good play and turn that into a musical. Sondheim chose *High Tor.* Third, to take a nontheatrical work and musicalize it. Sondheim chose *Mary Poppins.* Fourth and last, to write an original musical. Sondheim wrote one called *Climb High.*

After these years of study Sondheim was prepared. He began writing a new musical, *Saturday Night,* which, due to the death of producer Lemuel Ayers, was never produced. During the same time, Arthur Laurents, Jerome Robbins, and Leonard Bernstein were working on the musicalized version of Shakespeare's *Romeo and Juliet.* Laurents heard *Saturday Night* at a backers' audition and suggested Sondheim to the others as lyricist for what would become known as *West Side Story.*

Though Sondheim has always considered himself more a composer than a lyricist, it was his lyrics that first got him work. While he is unsurpassed as a writer of tricky, sophisticated lyrics, his straightforward ballads, such as "Somewhere" in *West Side Story,* are masterpieces of simplicity.

After *West Side Story* Sondheim was offered the assignment of writing a musical version of Gypsy Rose Lee's memoirs. When Ethel Merman was hired to play the leading role of Rose, Gypsy's mother, she insisted on a more experienced composer than Sondheim to produce the music. The project was offered to Irving Berlin and Cole Porter, and several other composers were auditioned, until finally Jule Styne was chosen. Sondheim had wanted desperately to write both music and lyrics, and stayed with the project, as lyricist, only at the urging of Oscar Hammerstein.

Following *Gypsy* (1959) Sondheim was finally able to finish his first musical for which he wrote both music and lyrics. The book by Burt Shevelove and Larry Gelbart used the comedies of the Roman playwright Plautus as inspiration for a story of a slave, Pseudolus, willing to do anything to gain his freedom. *A*

Funny Thing Happened on the Way to the Forum was the antithesis of an integrated musical. The songs could have been removed from the show with no effect on the action; they were not plot-advancers, but plot-stoppers. As Sondheim put it, "The score interrupts the action instead of carrying it on, because there are no songs that develop the characters and the story. They simply pinpoint moments of joy or desire or fear, and they give the performers a chance to perform."

A Funny Thing Happened on the Way to the Forum was given a Tony Award as the outstanding musical of 1963. *Forum* also brought Tonys for the acting of Zero Mostel and David Burns, for Burt Shevelove and Larry Gelbart's book, and for George Abbott's direction. Stephen Sondheim's score was not even nominated.

After two failures in 1964 and 1965, *Anyone Can Whistle* and *Do I Hear a Waltz?* (lyrics to Richard Rodgers's music), Sondheim's *Company* not only won as Outstanding Musical of the theatrical season, but Sondheim received two Tony Awards for his score—1971 was the first and only year that separate Tonys were given for the music and the lyrics of a score.

Company was the first of six Stephen Sondheim musicals directed and produced by Harold Prince. It and the other Sondheim-Prince musicals that followed marked a change in the way musicals were written. In the new "concept" musicals, the style of telling the story was as important as what was being told; the musicals were organized around a theme rather than a narrative. The songs in *Company* are sung as commentary on or counterpoint to the action rather than, as in a Rodgers and Hammerstein musical, the bursting forth of emotion that advances the plot.

Company presents five separate stories of different married couples, the stories held together only by the couples' shared friendship with a character named Bobby. It is not a linear musical of cause and effect, but rather an almost plotless collection of vignettes. There is no chorus, no dancers, no singing ensemble.

Follies (1971) has former show girls and their guys gathered to bid adieu to the theater that was home to their careers and is about to be torn down and turned into a parking lot. Sondheim's score uses sentimental pastiche songs in the period flashbacks, saving the more modern idiom for the present segments. The human follies of those assembled are presented through stingingly intense irony that says one thing in the lyrics while the music says something quite different, thereby conveying the cruel contrast between the public and private emotions of the characters.

Written exclusively in three-quarter time, or multiples thereof, the score of *A Little Night Music* (1973) is a tribute to Sondheim's compositional talents. More than half of the score was unfinished when the production went into rehearsals, and the pressure of an impending opening night brought great inspi-

ration to Sondheim. Out of this came his first great popular hit, "Send in the Clowns," which has been recorded by singers as diverse as Barbra Streisand, Judy Collins, and Frank Sinatra.

Few Broadway musicals have ever dared so much in so many ways as *Pacific Overtures* (1976). The tale, a narrative of the opening of Japan by the nineteenth-century American Commodore Oliver Hazard Perry, is told from the Japanese point of view in a form approximating Kabuki. The music was more faithful to the sounds of the Orient than anything heard before on Broadway—yet it was not Japanese, but unmistakably Sondheim. His lyrical mastery can be heard in the narrative of "Someone in a Tree" and in the intricate construction of "Chrysanthemum Tea." Perhaps most audacious was Sondheim's writing of a song consisting of stanzas in haiku.

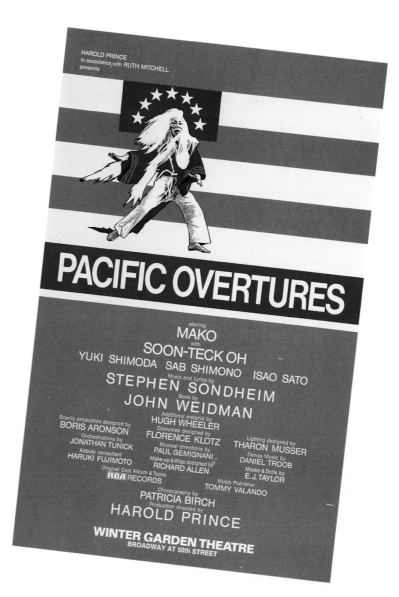

Sweeney Todd (1979) is the logical successor to *Porgy and Bess*, *The Most Happy Fella*, and *West Side Story* as the closest thing we've heard to a Broadway opera. The almost continuous underscoring and the constant interweaving of musical themes, combined with a vast emotional scale, made this a natural choice of the New York City Opera as a 1984 addition to their repertory.

Based on Christopher Bond's play of the same name, *Sweeney Todd* is Broadway's most grisly musical ever, the story of a demonic barber whose victims end up as meat-pie filling. Not a single emotion, from lust and revenge to love and affection, is missed as fate moves the characters to their blood-soaked destinies. Again, the score is wedded to its dramatic foundation, so Sondheim's songs for *Sweeney Todd* have seldom been taken up by popular singers; they remain the property of the character.

Merrily We Roll Along (1981) is Sondheim's most "Broadway" score. Consciously setting out to write a score that was more "hummable" than previous ones, Sondheim was nevertheless not content with anything ordinary. Based on a play by George S. Kaufman and Moss Hart, the show is a show-biz tale of lost innocence. But it is told in reverse—in fact, if one could hear the score played from finale to opening, a progression of recurring themes and built-upon motifs would be discerned.

Sondheim won the Pulitzer Prize for *Sunday in the Park with George* (1984). Inspired by Georges Seurat's painting, *A Sunday Afternoon on the Island of La Grande Jatte,* Sondheim's musical has a unifying theme rather than a story. It is founded on character, not action. It is about art and creation, artistic sacrifice and artistic influence, and it is perhaps the most autobiographical of Sondheim's work.

At each step in his career, Stephen Sondheim has been reproached for his choice of subjects and for the dominance of rigorous intellect over emotional warmth: Commodore Perry's opening of Japan to the West; a murderous barber

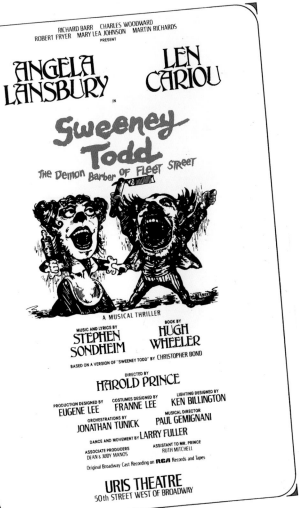

whose female friend cooks the customers into pies; the creation of a pointillist painting. None of his subjects lends itself to the traditional plot comforts of boy-meets-girl. Sondheim's music tends to be precise, restrained, and sophisticated rather than "accessible," the chief characteristic of the Broadway melodies of his predecessors.

At the end of *Sunday in the Park*, George, an artist, is given advice that enables him to bypass the never-ending criticism:

> *Stop worrying where you're going—*
> *Move on.*
> *If you can know where you're going,*
> *You've gone.*
> *Just keep moving on.*
>
> *Stop worrying if your vision*
> *Is new.*
> *Let others make that decision—*
> *They usually do.*
> *You keep moving on.*
>
> *Look at what you've done,*
> *Then at what you want,*
> *Not at where you are,*
> *What you'll be.*

Sondheim once said, "I have nothing large to say, just a lot of small things. I think I have a style but I don't think I have a tone. The tone varies from piece to piece." From the urban chatter of *Company* and the world-weary heartache of *Follies,* to the intricate word play of *A Little Night Music* and *Sunday in the Park with George,* Sondheim has shown that he is not only the heir to a great musical-theater tradition but is the creator of yet another.

TRENDS AND TRANSITIONS

Except for Stephen Sondheim and the British composer Andrew Lloyd Webber, the Broadway musical of the seventies and eighties has been characterized less by particular composers than by various trends, the most prevalent of which have been genre musicals, such as black musicals, dance musicals, rock musicals, and revues. These have had successes and failures on Broadway, but, by definition, a genre musical works within a set form, and thus isn't as influential or as innovative as the individual expression of one musician. A revue maintains its and-then-he-wrote structure no matter who "he" is. A dance musical purports to tell its story more through dance than words or even music.

Mabel King in The Wiz *(1975)*

Carolyn Mignini, Trey Wilson, Jerry Zaks, Mary Catherine Wright, and Lynne Thigpen in Tintypes *(1980). Zaks won a 1986 Tony Award for his direction of a revival of* The House of Blue Leaves.

Beginning in 1898 with *A Trip to Coontown*, black musicals have had a long, marvelous history on Broadway. The work in the twenties of Eubie Blake and Noble Sissle was succeeded by that of Melvin Van Peebles (*Ain't Supposed to Die a Natural Death*), Micki Grant (*Don't Bother Me, I Can't Cope*), and Charlie Smalls (*The Wiz*) in the sixties and seventies.

Revues about black composers Thomas ''Fats'' Waller (*Ain't Misbehavin'*), Duke Ellington (*Sophisticated Ladies*), and, the father of them all, Eubie Blake (*Eubie!*) were joined on Broadway by revues incorporating turn-of-the-century immigrants (*Tintypes*), young rock 'n' rollers (*Leader of the Pack*), and South American dancers (*Tango Argentino*). Revues differ from true musicals in that instead of a plot there is usually just a musical survey of a subject or a period of time.

Andrew Lloyd Webber, whose musical idol is Richard Rodgers, has reversed the tide of American musicals being exported to London by first producing his shows in Britain and then bringing them to Broadway. Lloyd Webber has shattered the myth that the quintessentially American form of theater, the musical, can be mastered only by Americans.

Writing with lyricist Tim Rice, Lloyd Webber began his Broadway career in 1971 with *Jesus Christ Superstar*. Begun as an album (when no backers for a stage production could be found), then as a series of concert performances, the

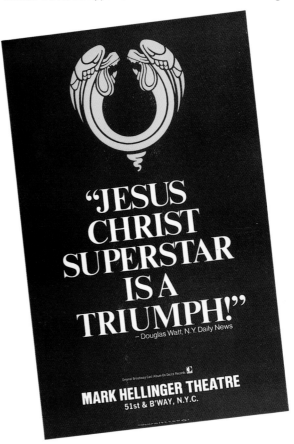

show was finally transformed into a "rock opera" and brought to the stage. Lloyd Webber and Rice later imported two other rock-flavored shows: *Evita*, about the rise and fall of Argentina's Eva Perón, and *Joseph and the Amazing Technicolor Dreamcoat*, the biblical tale of Joseph and the coat of many colors told through diverse musical styles. Both shows were nominated for Tony Awards; *Evita* won.

Rock musicals had a brief Broadway reign. The strong, rigid beat and the short, repetitive phrases of rock music did not suit the theater's need for drama nor the audience's need for melody.

Jeff Fenholt (Jesus) and Paul Ainsley (Pontius Pilate) in Jesus Christ Superstar *(1971)*

Striking out on his own, Webber musicalized T. S. Eliot's *Old Possum's Book of Practical Cats*. Previously, Lloyd Webber had always written the music first and Rice filled in the words later. With *Cats,* Lloyd Webber had his first experience in composing to set lyrics: ''I suddenly realized that there were very musical rhythms in them, an extraordinary rhythm that really is the rhythm of lyrics. The words themselves dictate that certain musical phrases have to be there. I mean the conjuring cat, who has a chorus each time which goes, 'Oh! Well, I never! Was there ever a cat so clever as the magical Mister Mistoffo-lees!' Well, you say that to yourself a few times and the tune begins to appear.'' *Cats,* which opened in 1982, winning a Tony Award as Outstanding Musical, continues to be one of Broadway's all-time hits.

Andrew Lloyd Webber, who comes from a musical family, writes shows full of spectacle and memorable anthems, ''I Don't Know How to Love Him,'' ''Don't Cry for Me Argentina,'' and ''Memory.'' Yet, as he has not developed his own musical voice, relying instead on his formidable gifts as a parodist of a wide range of musical genres, Lloyd Webber's influence has been slight.

Aside from Sondheim and Lloyd Webber, few composers of recent years have had more than one Broadway success. Single Tony Awards have been won by Maury Yeston in 1982 for his show *Nine,* a musical version of Federico Fellini's film, *8 ½*; by singer-songwriter Roger Miller in 1985 for *Big River,* based on Mark Twain's *Adventures of Huckleberry Finn*; and by Marvin Hamlisch and lyricist Ed Kleban in 1976 for *A Chorus Line,* Broadway's longest-running musical. At this writing, the show is approaching five thousand performances.

From its propulsive rock opening to its brazen Broadway finale, *A Chorus Line* has captivated audiences throughout the world. The story of a group of dancers auditioning for a new musical—and about anyone who has ever put himself on the "line"—the show boasts roots in dance, rock, and concept musicals of the past. *A Chorus Line* combines the best of the musical's past with a new, more vital belief in the form itself, and has sent the American musical into a bright future.

The musical grew in America from the English ballad-opera, Viennese operetta, and black-face minstrel shows. From *Kiss Me, Kate,* the first Tony Award–winning musical, to *The Mystery of Edwin Drood,* the latest, the musical theater has continued to grow, embracing thousands of influences foreign and domestic. Yet the musical remains quintessentially American—brash, high-spirited, and big-hearted.

Betty Buckley in Cats *(1982)*

6 MOVERS AND SHAKERS

The work of directors and choreographers is the most ephemeral of all theater art. A play can be read, a musical score can be heard or played, designs can be photographed, even performances are now preserved on film and videotape. When we watch a taped performance we see the influence of the director on the actor, much as we "see" the wind in the blowing of leaves. A director produces only his influence on others, the roads he pointed down but did not himself travel.

A choreographer's work can be judged more easily; after all, the dancers didn't make up those steps. Yet even the most sophisticated choreographic recording systems have not fully preserved the choreographer's work. It comes down to us either through filmed records or through the memories of the dancers themselves.

Directors and choreographers stand between us and the production onstage. We see, feel, and think *through* them.

DIRECTORS

No one has yet learned to teach the art that enables a great director to extract a playwright's thoughts and emotions from a text, interpret them, and then inspire actors and designers to turn those feelings into a flesh-and-blood reality.

Harold Clurman, himself a director, once defined his profession as being the "author of the stage performance." In other words, the director is responsible for everything the audience sees and hears. The director chooses the actors, the scenic, costume, and lighting designs, and determines the style of performance. Throughout months of preparation, collaborating with the playwright and the designers, and additional months of rehearsals with the actors, the director must develop a consistent approach to the play that will reveal the playwright's work sensitively and insightfully.

After all this preparation and work, the director's contribution to the production is subordinated and ultimately supplanted by the physical reality of the actors living a playwright's dream before an audience.

During the 1940s and 1950s Arthur Miller and Tennessee Williams were America's finest active playwrights. They were nearly polar opposites: Miller was the intellectual master of well-made social dramas; Williams, the instinctual creator of tragic poems. For all their differences, both Miller and Williams found their greatest interpreter in director Elia Kazan.

Kazan's ability to embody the disparate dreams of Miller and Williams is echoed in one of his own statements: "I tried to think and feel like the author so that the play would be in the scale and in the mood, in the tempo and feeling of each writer. I tried to be the author. I was many men, but none of them was myself."

For years Kazan was every playwright's first choice as director. He served not only the play but the playwright through his cogent analysis of structure and style, stimulating new ideas and concepts. Most notably, Kazan encouraged Williams to rewrite the third act of *Cat on a Hot Tin Roof,* bringing back the indelible character of Big Daddy for a climactic confrontation with his son, Brick.

A Greek born in Istanbul, Kazan came by his directorial skills through academic instruction and practical trial-and-error. He studied at Yale under the renowned George Pierce Baker (playwriting teacher of George Abbott, Philip Barry, and Eugene O'Neill, among others), worked as an actor for the Group Theater, and helped found, with Lee Strasberg, the Actors Studio—the group responsible for introducing "method acting" to America.

Determined to "get poetry out of the common things in life," Kazan, often joined by Actors Studio alumni, was well suited to the work of Miller and Williams. Joining forces with master designer Jo Mielziner, Kazan made Miller's "common man" tragedy, *Death of a Salesman,* a wrenching emotional reality against a backdrop of fantasy. Kazan tempered the languid qualities of Williams's *Cat on a Hot Tin Roof* by staging the action as a series of deadly duels before an audience nominated as both judge and jury.

Well rewarded for his work, Kazan won Tony Awards for his direction of Miller's *All My Sons* and *Death of a Salesman,* and for Archibald MacLeish's *J. B.,* a modern verse retelling of the biblical story of Job. Kazan's other Tony nominations were for Williams's *Cat on a Hot Tin Roof* and *Sweet Bird of Youth* and William Inge's *The Dark at the Top of the Stairs.* Ironically, Kazan's finest work, on Williams's *A Streetcar Named Desire,* did not win a Tony, although Kazan did go on to direct the film version, starring Marlon Brando and Vivien Leigh.

After Kazan "named names" to the Communist-hunting House Un-American Activities Committee in the McCarthy 1950s, many theater colleagues refused to work with him. A second blow came a decade later, when he was codirector of the theater company at Lincoln Center. Vicious reviews of his direction of the Jacobean tragedy *The Changeling* edged Kazan into retirement from the theater altogether.

All My Sons *(1947)*

Paul Newman and Geraldine Page in
Sweet Bird of Youth *(1959)*

American playwrights found another tireless champion in Marshall W. Mason. Cofounder of the Circle Repertory Company in lower Manhattan, Mason has directed the premieres of over one hundred new American plays. Almost a quarter of those have been by fellow Circle Rep cofounder Lanford Wilson, one of America's most successful realistic playwrights.

Although Circle Rep is an Off-Broadway theater company, many shows begun there have been moved—intact—to Broadway. Circle Rep's renowned standard of excellence is based on its being a *company*—a company of playwrights, directors, actors, and designers. Playwrights like Wilson, Jules Feiffer, Corinne Jacker, and Milan Stitt are inspired to write specific roles for specific actors, strengthening the bond between the actor and the character and allowing the actor and playwright to grow and develop together. Circle Rep boasts an acting company with such well-known performers as William Hurt, Jeff Daniels, Judd Hirsch, Richard Thomas, Trish Hawkins, and Lindsay Crouse. Circle Rep's artists are bound by a belief in creating "real plays about real people."

Noted for his detailed and highly textured productions, Mason has been nominated for Tony Awards for his direction of Lanford Wilson's *Talley's Folly, Fifth of July,* and *Angels Fall,* Jules Feiffer's comedy *Knock, Knock,* and William Hoffman's drama about AIDS, *As Is.*

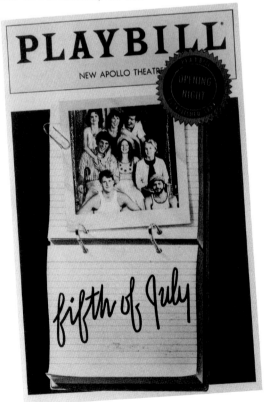

Alan Schneider, foremost American director of the avant-garde, was born during the Russian Revolution. The day-old baby and his mother caught the last train out of the city of Kharkov. Reunited with husband and father, they made their way through Europe and, six years later, to America. Arriving in New York Harbor on the Fourth of July, the frightened Schneiders thought the fireworks heralded yet another revolution.

After a period of directing commercial Broadway fare, Schneider became a theater revolutionary and introduced to America the plays of Samuel Beckett and Harold Pinter. He also directed most of the plays of Beckett's protégé, Edward Albee (indeed, four of Schneider's five Tony Award nominations were for Albee plays).

Endgame, Happy Days, Krapp's Last Tape, The Dumb Waiter, The Birthday Party, The Ballad of the Sad Café, A Delicate Balance: while these plays are now revered and regularly taught in college literature courses, when Schneider tackled them they were often considered playwrights' pranks. Schneider realized that "my best work is often done on shows that are commercial failures," what he called "unexplored territory." Schneider excelled in small-cast shows that, squeezed into near-claustrophobic settings, generate intense theatrical power. The searing drama of Albee's *Who's Afraid of Virginia Woolf?* (1962) not only created but also cauterized the emotional wounds of the characters. Schneider's production was relentless in its temper and passion. As choreographed by Schneider, the characters alternated as bull and matador in a vicious contest to the death.

While crossing a London street in 1984, Schneider was struck by a motorcyle and killed. He had just finished directing a series of new one-act plays by Samuel Beckett and was about to begin rehearsals for a play by a novice American playwright. The theater was robbed of a director of vision and devotion. Perhaps the best summation of his career came in Schneider's posthumously published autobiography, *Entrances*:

> *I have always favored the poetic over the prosaic, siding with instinct over reason, swayed by the power of symbols, images, metaphors, all of the substances lurking behind the closed eyelids of the mind. To me, these are more faithful signs of essential truths than all those glossy photographs that seek to mirror our external world. I've always preferred Chekhov to Ibsen, Tennessee Williams to Arthur Miller, and Dostoyevsky to Tolstoy; but Beckett's metaphors reach deepest into my subconscious self.*

Unlike Schneider, Peter Brook is not associated with the plays of a major living writer. His finest work has generally been with classics or with new plays created by his company of actors at the International Center for Theater Research.

Born into a nontheatrical family in Texarkana, Texas, Joshua Logan became an award-winning director and writer. Three times Logan's career was interrupted by nervous breakdowns. Each time, after electroshock or drug therapy, he returned to Broadway to further success.

After attending Princeton University (mainly to join in the famed Triangle Club's dramatic activities), Logan traveled

each won Tony Awards for Outstanding Play, and Logan won another as Outstanding Director.

Two years later he won yet another Tony Award, this time for cowriting the book for *South Pacific*. While Logan shared the authorship credit with Oscar Hammerstein II, he did not share in the royalties. Rodgers and Hammerstein decided that they would rather not do the

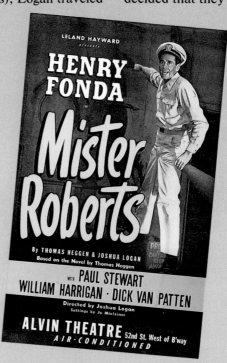

to Moscow to study with Constantin Stanislavski, the celebrated director and acting teacher. Back in New York, he shared an apartment with Henry Fonda and Jimmy Stewart, friends from summer stock, while acting small parts and working as an assistant stage manager for various productions.

In 1948 Logan cowrote and directed a dramatic version of Thomas Heggen's novel, *Mister Roberts*. Heggen and Logan became fast friends—"I was a corpulent manic depressive and Heggen was a thin manic depressive." The coauthors, who wrote their second act in just one night,

show if it meant sharing the show's copyright. Nor at first did his name appear on the Pulitzer Prize certificate—though this was later amended.

Logan was strongest in his ability to analyze a script and repair the deficiencies, either through judicious criticism or by application of his own pen. His many directorial successes include *Annie Get Your Gun, Knickerbocker Holiday, Fanny, Charley's Aunt, The World of Suzie Wong,* and *Picnic*. Logan directed the film versions of *Camelot, Paint Your Wagon,* and, with Marilyn Monroe, *Bus Stop*.

A boy wonder, in 1946 Brook directed *Love's Labours Lost* at Stratford-upon-Avon when he was just twenty-one. Three years later he was made head of production at the Royal Opera at Covent Garden. Brook became known as a supreme interpreter of plays, a director capable of forging a synthesis between a centuries-old text and a contemporary audience. He made the familiar new. He made a living theater.

In 1971 Brook brought to Broadway his interpretation of Shakespeare's *A Midsummer Night's Dream*. All too often the play is set in a leafy "Peter Pan" realm of child-fairies. Brook defied these traditional expectations. Brook and his acrobatically trained Royal Shakespeare Company brought with them a world of white walls punctuated with doors and ladders and dotted with trapezes. Oberon's magic flower was a dish set spinning atop a juggler's stick. Bottom was bedded not in Titania's usual bower but atop a gently swaying red-feather cloud. Bottom's ass's head was nothing more than a clown's red nose. Such was the power of Brook's imagination that his nontraditional production became in itself a new tradition, influencing countless subsequent productions.

A number of years earlier, Brook and the RSC had prepared a season based on the theories of Antonin Artaud. The so-called Theater of Cruelty did not mean violence but an immediacy and intensity of physical rather than verbal expression. (Brook: "I do not believe in the word much today, because it has outlived its purpose.") Peter Weiss's historically based script, *The Persecution and Assassination of Jean-Paul Marat as Performed by the Inmates of the Asylum of Charenton Under the Direction of the Marquis de Sade* (this, the longest title in Broadway history, is usually abbreviated *Marat/Sade*), told the story of a

Marat/Sade, *1966*

liberal asylum superintendent who used theatrical entertainment as a form of therapy. The inmate-director was Sade, and it was fashionable in Parisian society to attend not only for the entertainment, but also for the opportunity to watch the caged lunatics *au naturel.*

Brook's acting company spent months studying the behavior of the insane and, in a great technical *tour de force,* brilliantly recreated that behavior onstage. Fashionable New York audiences flocked to see the spectacle. Brook's finest touch came when, as the play ended, the actors fought, smashing through toward the audience. Suddenly all noise and movement stopped, and the audience, sensing the natural ending, applauded. Slowly, insanely, the actors applauded back. "If we had conventional curtain calls, the audience would emerge relieved, and that's the last thing we want." Theater as shock therapy.

Brook received Tony Awards for directing *Midsummer* and *Marat/Sade.* He received nominations for his work on Friedrich Dürrenmatt's *The Visit* (which served as the farewell to Broadway of the acting team of Alfred Lunt and Lynn Fontanne) and for the musical *Irma La Douce.* For most of the seventies and eighties Brook has devoted his time to the International Center for Theater Research, every so often bringing work to New York.

* ▨

More instinctual and less intellectually oriented than Brook is his friend and colleague Peter Hall. The only son of a railroad stationmaster, Hall made his professional directing debut at age twenty-three, missing Brook's mark by two years.

In addition to directing England's first production of *Waiting for Godot,* Hall has closely associated himself with the works of Harold Pinter and Peter Shaffer. On Broadway he has directed, among others, Pinter's *The Homecoming* (which provided Hall his first Tony), *No Man's Land, Betrayal,* and Shaffer's *Royal Hunt of the Sun, Equus,* and *Amadeus* (which got Hall a second Tony Award).

Hall's special abilities as a director of new plays are grounded in his belief that the author is the final authority on a play. Hall will argue, suggest, cajole, but in the final measure, it is the author's wishes that he honors. He sees his task as *transmitting* the author's play to the audience rather than interpreting it for them. "Very few people should be allowed to use their imaginations. Mostly what is wanted is the obvious, *but very well done.*"

Peter Shaffer's *Amadeus,* produced on Broadway in 1980, is an example of Hall's finest work. He not only made clear the play's complex passages backward and forward through time, but emotionally underlined Shaffer's principal theme: the war between genius and mediocrity.

* ▨

Just as Elia Kazan was Broadway's director of choice in the forties and fifties, Mike Nichols has become everyone's first choice as director since the seventies. He is this generation's super director. Nichols has won five Tonys and has been nominated for five others. And he is also one of Hollywood's finest directors, having directed such films as *The Graduate, Catch-22,* and *Silkwood.*

Four of Nichols's five Tony Awards have come for directing the plays of Neil Simon—*Barefoot in the Park, The Odd Couple, Plaza Suite,* and *The Prisoner of Second Avenue.* Nichols comes by his mastery of comedy firsthand. In the fifties he and Elaine May, both alumni of the Chicago improvisatory theater group Second City, kept Broadway and America laughing with their improvised sketches. They relied not on funny lines but on the effect of humanity skewered by irony. Through improvisation, Nichols learned that comedy is more dependent on situation than punch lines alone. "What is happening is always very complicated and often interesting, while what is being said is not."

Bolstered by classes with Method master Lee Strasberg, Nichols and his career have moved from the rapid-fire comedy of Neil Simon to more challenging and abrasive plays, including *The Real Thing, Comedians, Streamers,* and Chekhov's *Uncle Vanya.* He has moved beyond merely delivering funny lines to conveying life itself through language and behavior.

★▧

While in high school in Hackensack, New Jersey, Gene Saks wanted to be a professional basketball player. When he got out of the Navy, he wanted to be a nightclub comedian. After studying acting on the GI Bill, Saks became an actor and was featured in *South Pacific, The Tenth Man,* and, as Chuckles the Chipmunk in *A Thousand Clowns.* Scenes Saks directed at the Actors Studio brought him the opportunity to direct on Broadway in 1963. His debut was *Enter Laughing.* It was a hit, and acting—not to mention basketball and nightclubs—was summarily relegated to the background.

The next four plays Saks directed were all hits as well. In 1977 he had three plays running simultaneously on Broadway. In 1985 he repeated this feat and topped himself by making them all Neil Simon shows. Saks's work with the Actors Studio and his experience as an actor have enabled him to encourage actors to invest Simon's comedies with a reality that makes the laughter human. Saks has won two of his three Tonys for the direction of Simon shows, *Brighton Beach Memoirs* and *Biloxi Blues.*

If always speaking in punch lines is not "real," neither are singing and dancing onstage. Yet Saks can direct actors to make sentimental ballads as real and believable as he makes comic lines. In addition to his work on comedies by Simon and others, he has had great success in directing musicals, winning a Tony for *I Love My Wife,* and having been nominated for *Half a Sixpence* and *Mame* (which featured Bea Arthur, his wife at the time).

★▧

The difference between directing plays and directing musicals is more than just coping with the addition of music. The director of a contemporary musical

Patti Lupone, Bob Gunton, and Mandy Patinkin in Evita *(1979)*

must blend the work of composer, lyricist, book writer, choreographer, designers, and actors into a seamless whole. More often than not the "director" of a musical is in reality a director-choreographer. With fewer composers of genius working in the musical theater, the balance of power and the responsibility for a show's style have shifted to the hybrid director-choreographer. As Stephen Sondheim is the only contemporary composer with the prestige and influence to match that of the reigning director-choreographers, Harold Prince is the only nonchoreographing director who can match the success of the finest director-choreographers.

Prince, winner of six Tony Awards for the direction of musicals, joined forces with Sondheim to revolutionize the genre. Beginning with *Company* in 1970 and continuing through six musicals culminating in *Merrily We Roll Along* (1981), Prince and Sondheim have not only entertained in the finest traditions of the musical, but have also stimulated the intellect.

Beginning as a "go-fer" for the renowned director George Abbott, Prince graduated to an Abbott stage manager and, at the age of twenty-six, coproduced a new musical by Richard Adler and Jerry Ross, *The Pajama Game* (1954). Prince and his coproducers Frederick Brisson and Robert Griffith tracked down 161 backers to raise the money for the show (to cut costs Prince and Griffith doubled as the production's stage managers). Prince hired Abbott and Jerome Robbins to codirect and newcomer Bob Fosse to choreograph. This first producing effort ran 1,063 performances and won Prince his first Tony Award.

His second Tony came the following year when he put *Damn Yankees* on Broadway, again with Brisson, Griffith, Adler, Ross, Abbott, and Fosse. This show ran 1,019 performances.

Despite these early successes, Prince's real goal in theater was to direct. In 1963 he served as producer and director of Bock and Harnick's *She Loves Me*. "I hired myself, which is more than anyone else would do."

Prince supplies his productions with exciting stage pictures; he is as visual a director as any choreographer-director. The ten-stage "environmental" production of Bernstein's *Candide,* the Industrial Revolution scenery of *Sweeney Todd,* and the decadence of prewar Berlin in *Cabaret* are all testimony as much to the original talent of Prince as to that of the set designers.

CHOREOGRAPHERS

A composer works at a piano. The lyricist works on paper. The choreographer works with human bodies. No matter how powerful his imagination, the choreographer cannot know if a dance number will actually work until it is set and seen in action. Steps become combinations; combinations become dances; dances become choreography.

Early musicals used dances as isolated bits of entertainment. Just as the musical grew and changed from a collection of songs to a cohesive score, dances moved toward true choreography. The catalyst was Agnes De Mille. Though De Mille's father wanted her to become a championship tennis player—and had

"The Dream Ballet" from Oklahoma! *(1943)*

given her her own tennis court—at the age of eight young Agnes saw the famed Anna Pavlova dance. From that moment on, the life of Agnes De Mille and the history of the American musical were changed. She used choreographic form, pattern, and style not only to entertain, but also to tell the musical's story, create atmosphere, and reveal character. Other choreographers have followed her lead.

The integration of dance into the regular fabric of music and dialogue made Rodgers and Hammerstein's *Oklahoma!* revolutionary. The "Dream Ballet," during which young Laurey's fears are dramatized through dance, was among the first uses of dance to further a musical's plot. The twenty-seven minutes of

Brigadoon *(1947)*

dance in *Oklahoma!* were second in importance only to the score itself in telling the story. De Mille's treatment of dancers as individual characters enabled the chorus dancers to become actors in a play.

De Mille's gift for narrative dance came directly out of her work in the world of modern dance. Such works as "Rodeo" and "Fall River Legend" not only told stories, but each step and gesture came out of an individualized conception of each character's motivation. Realizing that both dance and theater were fundamentally means of communication, De Mille's dances told folk tales in *Oklahoma!,* Scottish tales of marriage and death in *Brigadoon,* and the simple, daily incidents of New England village life in *Carousel*. Each De Mille show was graced by her mastery of lyrical, purposeful movement—the physical technique of modern dance put to the service of the theater.

★ ▧▧▧

The crossover of choreographers from ballet and modern dance to the theater has been active since George Balanchine choreographed the ballet "Slaughter on Tenth Avenue" for the 1936 Rodgers and Hart musical *On Your Toes*.

The most successful choreographer (and sometime director) of the fifties and sixties was Michael Kidd. Winner of five Tony Awards for choreography—*Finian's Rainbow, Guys and Dolls, Can-Can, Li'l Abner,* and *Destry Rides*

Destry Rides Again (1959)

Again—Kidd was a former soloist with the Ballet Theater (later called the American Ballet Theatre) who had come to the attention of Broadway with his ballet "On Stage."

Kidd's work on Broadway was marked by exuberant acrobatics that choreographically explored each dance situation. He used bullwhips and lassos in *Destry Rides Again,* developed a show-stopping ballet out of a crap game in *Guys and Dolls,* and captured the comic-strip antics of a helter-skelter Sadie Hawkins Day chase in *Li'l Abner,* all with a quality of limitless invention.

If Agnes De Mille integrated dance into the musical in *Oklahoma!,* Jerome Robbins integrated the musical into dance in *West Side Story*. *Oklahoma!* was revolutionary in 1943; fourteen years later, *West Side Story* was the peak of an

West Side Story *(1957)*

intervening evolution. The first musical to be conceived, choreographed, and directed by one man, *West Side Story* has one of the shortest musical books. The show is plotted by dance rather than by dialogue: the ''Prologue'' initiates the action of the gang rivalry; the ''Dance at the Gym,'' where Tony and Maria (*West Side Story's* Romeo and Juliet) first meet and fall in love, advances the action; and the ''Rumble'' completes the arc of the play. The score, ranging from lyrical ballads to jazz, was mirrored by Robbins's choreography.

Though the dances are separately named, there is perpetual dance movement, the characters always moving in dance form. At the beginning of *West Side Story,* the Jets are seen loitering on a street. The mere shift in body position, in time to the music, shows the audience character, attitude, and environ-

"The Wedding Dance" from Fiddler on the Roof *(1964)*

ment without any singing or speaking. At other times, Robbins moves the story along by creating the theatrical equivalent of a cinematic dissolve. Maria, at work preparing for her first American party, twirls with happiness in her new dress. Other girls, also twirling in party dresses, move in behind Maria, and we are transported to the "Dance at the Gym." What in the traditional musical would have been a blackout becomes a dissolve.

Jerome Robbins, the greatest American-born choreographer, came to Broadway from ballet. A dancer with the Ballet Theater, Robbins choreographed Leonard Bernstein's "Fancy Free," the tale of three sailors on leave in New York City. This ballet then became a full-fledged musical, *On the Town* (1944). From that show on, Broadway was his, and Robbins became a pioneer in combining the positions of director and choreographer, later winning Tony Awards in both categories.

Robbins's work on such shows as *The King and I, High Button Shoes, Peter Pan,* and *Gypsy* cemented his reputation as an innovative perfectionist. *Fiddler on the Roof* moved him into the world of myth. He captured an entire ethnic culture through the vocabulary of theater dance, creating a magical world. Robbins then reentered ballet, joining the New York City Ballet and George Balanchine. Except for overseeing the revival of several of his earlier successes, he has not returned to Broadway.

While Jerome Robbins disappears into the world of each musical he choreographs, Bob Fosse boldly stamps his unique personality on each of his projects. "As a dancer, I was no choreographer's dream. I just *couldn't* pick up anyone else's style. I was very limited as a dancer. I had to adjust everyone's work to fit my own body." He has transformed his own limitations into a razzle-dazzle trademark.

Bob Fosse choreographing Pleasures and Palaces *(1965). This Frank Loesser musical never made it to Broadway, closing in Detroit.*

Buzz Miller, Carol Haney, and Peter Gennaro in Pajama Game *(1954)*

The son of a Chicago vaudeville trouper, Fosse came to choreography from burlesque, not ballet. The stage-struck youth became a chorus dancer and developed into the most highly rewarded of Broadway's choreographers. In 1973 he scored a unique triple-play by becoming, for his work on *Cabaret, Pippin,* and *Liza with a Z,* the only director to win the Oscar, Tony, and Emmy in a single year. In addition to his two Tony Awards (direction and choreography) for *Pippin,* Fosse has won seven others for *The Pajama Game, Damn Yankees, Redhead, Little Me, Sweet Charity, Dancin',* and *Big Deal.* He is the most consistently successful of all Broadway's director-choreographers.

His choreographic signature, best remembered from his film of *Cabaret* (Ron Field choreographed the show on Broadway) and the "Steam Heat" number from *Pajama Game,* is to treat the dancer's body as a collection of isolated parts. The convulsively hyperactive loins suddenly freeze, then release in neatly syncopated motion. Fosse's subtle use of rhythm and counterpoint brings the sexuality implicit in all dance into sharp, contemporary focus.

A solid pro rather than an innovator, Gower Champion was as much a showman as Fosse. A creator of rousing, old-fashioned Broadway dances, Champion came to public attention as half of a popular dance team with his then-wife, Marge. He began his Broadway career by staging a revue, *Lend an Ear* (1948), winning a Tony Award for choreography, while Marge was recovering from a severely sprained ankle.

Champion was capable of switching gracefully from the rock 'n' roll dances of *Bye, Bye Birdie* to the sad and lyrical movements in *Carnival* a season later. Champion's ability to capture with energy and spirit the dances of earlier eras was best seen in the famous waiters' dance to the title song in *Hello, Dolly!* and the propulsive tap opener of *42nd Street*. On the opening night of this last show —a paean to the "naughty, bawdy, gaudy, sporty" street on which he'd spent most of his career—Gower Champion died of a rare blood disease.

Gower Champion's heir as Broadway's foremost showman is Tommy Tune. A protégé of Michael Bennett, Tune danced in the choruses of numerous shows: *A Joyful Noise, Irma La Douce,* and the ill-fated *Baker Street.* Tune came to the full attention of Broadway audiences dancing in Bennett's *Seesaw.* The image of a six-foot-six dancer perched atop four-inch clogs, prancing up and down a staircase and through a sea of hundreds of balloons while singing "It's Not Where You Start (It's Where You Finish)" was an unforgettable delight. It won Tune a

Tommy Tune in Seesaw *(1973)*

A Day in Hollywood/A Night in the Ukraine *(1980)*

Tony as Featured Actor in a Musical. He is the only Tony-winning choreographer also to have won as a performer.

There aren't many jobs for dancers who are, as Tune puts it, "five foot eighteen," and after *Seesaw,* he couldn't get work. Tune moved into directing. His work on such Off-Broadway shows as *The Club* (1976) and *Cloud 9* (1981) brought him acclaim. His work on Broadway in *The Best Little Whorehouse in Texas* (1978), *A Day in Hollywood/A Night in the Ukraine* (1980), and *Nine* (1982), brought him Tony Awards and further accolades.

Tune's inventiveness, coupled with an aura of sheer innocence, was seen to advantage in *Whorehouse,* where he staged a cheerleaders' dance using a chorus line of live dancers partnered by life-size dolls, and in *Hollywood/Ukraine,* in which he choreographed a legs-only tribute to the ''Famous Feet'' of Fred Astaire and Ginger Rogers, Mickey and Minnie Mouse, and Charlie Chaplin.

Tune's finest work was on Maury Yeston's *Nine.* He developed the show through workshop productions, finally creating a beautifully stylized presentation that featured twenty-one women and just one man, the Casanova-like Italian film director suggested by Federico Fellini's film *8½.*

A Chorus Line *(1975)*

Deborah Burrell, Sheryl Lee Ralph, and Loretta Devine in Dreamgirls *(1981)*

As if to cement the dominance of the director-choreographer, Michael Bennett's *A Chorus Line* (1975) has been an unprecedented success. It could never have been done by a director and choreographer working separately. The show was conceived by Bennett, and it was Bennett who nursed and developed it through four different workshop productions, finally winning Tonys for both his direction and his choreography.

This, the most original musical since *West Side Story,* was the first major musical developed through workshops rather than out-of-town working previews. Since *A Chorus Line* more productions have been coming to Broadway through the workshop approach than from the traditional out-of-town tryouts. *Nine, Sunday in the Park with George,* and *The Mystery of Edwin Drood* owe their success in part to the path blazed by Bennett.

In a workshop, the show is slowly developed through a free-flowing collaboration of writers, actors, designers, and the director-choreographer. It is tried out and built upon the talents of those specific contributors rather than those of writers working in an isolated studio. Bennett realized that what had worked for Shakespeare and Molière would work for him: "To write for a performer is much more successful than writing a whole show and then looking for a person to match what you've seen in your head." By making shows less expensive to produce, workshops have become increasingly necessary during harder financial times on Broadway.

Michael Bennett dropped out of high school to join the chorus of dancers in Jule Styne's *Subways Are For Sleeping* (1961). Bennett danced in more and more chorus lines until he was finally given the opportunity to choreograph. His work in *A Joyful Noise* (1966), *Promises, Promises* (1968), and *Coco* (1969) brought him into collaboration with Harold Prince, for whom Bennett choreographed *Company* (1970) and *Follies* (1971). With *Follies,* which he codirected, Bennett began his directing apprenticeship. He furthered his education by directing such nonmusicals as Neil Simon's *God's Favorite* (1974), and *Twigs* (1971), for which he received a Tony nomination. Bennett applied his directing experience to choreography. "My approach to everything in dancing is not in the step kick, step kick, back, change, step kick. That's not my bag. What I want to do is to make the movement give a psychological insight into a character, to advance the story, and make a point quickly, as in a cartoon."

From *A Chorus Line,* Bennett directed and choreographed *Ballroom* (1978) with twirling, swirling ballroom dances, and *Dreamgirls* (1981), an ever-changing theatrical spectacle in which even the set was choreographed. Bennett won Tony Awards for his choreography in both of these shows. His work—especially on these last three shows—has influenced not only other choreographers, but also composers, designers, and directors. His ability to combine show-stopping theatricality with sheer physical beauty has set new standards for the production of musicals.

7 DESIGNS AND DESIGNERS

Designers spend months preparing, revising, and refining their designs. They hold countless meetings so that each member of the production team understands clearly the essence of the play and the ways in which it will be presented visually to the audience. Then, after all these months of dedicated work, designers can look forward at most to one-line mentions in newspaper reviews. The day after the show closes, the designer's work is torn down, trucked to New Jersey, and either burned or sold off at bargain-basement prices.

A stage set is not a picture, not a mere background, but an atmosphere, an environment. Costumes are not fashion, but clothes for characters. Lighting is not just for visibility, but for the illumination of the text. Producing a play or musical is a process of making a physical reality of what is often insubstantial suggestion. The playwright imagines characters and a story and puts them down in ink. The director and actors take these words and create characters and behavior. It is the designer who gives these creations a home.

Applause that comes upon the raising of the curtain is meaningless to a designer; great designs are imbued with their full meaning only through the progress of the play. Theater designers deal not only in the standard three dimensions, but also in the fourth: time. Unlike a painted picture, a theater design must grow and develop as it is displayed before the audience. Designers aren't hired to provide pretty pictures but to create a rich environment in which the characters can live and grow.

Perhaps the hardest aspect of designing is that all design questions have to be answered before rehearsals begin. Generally four weeks before the start of rehearsals, the scenic and costume designs go into workshops to be constructed. While the actors are exploring possibilities in their characters, and the director and playwright are finding new possibilities in the script daily, the physical boundaries of the production are set. This offers little or no time for the set designer to explore the vast array of his choices. He is forced to keep his eye on what *will* be rather than what *might* be.

Theater design consists of three traditional areas: scenery, costumes, and lighting; a fourth design specialty, sound, is not yet recognized by a Tony Award. While people often speak of "a great set design" or "terrific costumes," all three design elements—sets, costumes, and lighting—are actually completely interdependent. A "great" set design will not look good if the lighting doesn't work. Costumes that do not complement the scenery often are invisible or else woefully conspicuous. It has been proved that if the stage is so dark that the audience can't see the actors' lips, their lines are simply not heard.

Great theater design embodies the playwright's themes, the director's concept, and the actor's goals in a single physical reality. Anna's Victorian gowns in *The King and I,* completely surrounded by Siamese characters dressed in native *panungs,* constantly remind us of the great gap that separates these two cultures. The gauzy scrim between the set and the audience in *A Streetcar Named Desire* engages us in the battle between Stanley's brutal reality and Blanche's ethereal self-delusions. The confrontational spotlights turned on the audience at the end of *Marat/Sade* force us to decide just whose insanity—the characters' or our own—is to be believed.

Such design coups, created in a flash of insight or after months of painful trial and error, are the essence of the designer's art, the concrete creation of a fictive world, the tangible admixture of the poet's fantasy with the craftsman's accuracy.

SCENIC DESIGNERS

For generations Broadway scenic design consisted mainly of variations on perspective scenery. Backdrops painted in perspective served to give depth and a sense of grand space to stages that were sometimes barely thirty feet from the audience to the building's back wall. The designer's aim was always to fool the audience into believing the "reality" created by the scene-painter's craft. Producers, notably David Belasco, went so far as to fill the stage with real props— *real* cattle carcasses in a butcher's shop setting, the frying of *real* flapjacks in a restaurant setting—all the better to convince the audience of the reality of what was presented on stage. Yet for all the scene painter's efforts, the audience was presented not with actors *in* a set, but in *front* of a set.

Between the world wars, Edward Gordon Craig and Adolphe Appia, an Englishman and a Swiss, began to replace this notion of realism with a more poetic expression. These two and their followers urged a simplified realism that would capture and interpret the spirit of the text, not merely form a backdrop for the script. Their ideas became known as "the new stagecraft."

But Craig and Appia were visionaries who seldom actually built any of the designs they drew. It fell to Robert Edmond Jones (1887–1954), the first great American stage designer, to take their philosophy and transmit it to the stage. Design now moved from preparing a painted background to sculpting a theater space to surround, to house a play. Designers stopped being painters and became builders of buildings inside of buildings.

Scenic design is not merely a matter of creating a ground plan that meets the play's set requirements for action, or tastefully decorating around these boundaries, or providing comfortable furniture and costumes for the actors. Today's theater audiences are increasingly more visually sophisticated. For them, the set must capture, complement, and heighten the moods and ideas of the text. A designer must read between the lines of the text, almost as a director or actor does. Jo Mielziner said that "literalism has no place in the theater." This is true. The design, like the acting, directing, and the play itself, must not be a *copy* of life (at this film excels), but a revealing, usually heightened *simulation* of life. Jo Mielziner, one of the greatest scenic designers in American theater history, once offered a recipe for the ideal scenic designer: he should be equal parts painter, draftsman, architect, sculptor, couturier, electrical engineer, and dramatist—a balance of the technician with the artist. Naturally, all designers have weighed these ingredients differently. Designers of the forties relied heavily on painted scenery. Designers of the fifties used modern advances in lighting and photographic projection to their advantage. The seventies and eighties have seen a preoccupation with mechanics in a perhaps futile attempt to mimic the fluidity of film. Contemporary designers have sometimes forgotten that significant essentials are more powerful than a glut of detail. As Voltaire once said, "The secret of being a bore is to tell everything."

All modern scenic designers can be summed up by saying that there are only two kinds, those who combine architecture and painting, and those who combine architecture and lighting. It is convenient, though coincidental, that America's two greatest scenic designers of the Tony years fall into each of these categories: Boris Aronson, the master architect/scene painter, and Jo Mielziner, the master architect/lighting designer.

Born in Kiev, the son of a rabbi, Boris Aronson was one of ten children. One day at school, at the age of eight, Boris drew a fly on his school book. His teacher, passing by, tried to flick the fly away. Discovering that the "fly" was a pencil sketch, the teacher informed Aronson's parents. Aronson remarked, "I learned two things. First, that it's easy to fool people in art, and second, if you can make a fly look like a fly, you're in."

Aronson was encouraged to study art and did so in Kiev, Moscow, and later, Paris. While in Moscow, he came under the influence of Alexandra Exter, the leader of Russia's radical stage designers and a devotee of the school of constructivism. Exter encouraged Aronson to go into theater design. It was the beginning of a career that would last more than fifty years.

Arriving in New York in 1923, Aronson first found work in the flourishing Yiddish theater and with Eva Le Gallienne's Civic Repertory Theatre. In 1932

Set design for The Rose Tattoo *(1951)*

he made his Broadway debut designing the sets for *Walk a Little Faster*, a musical by S. J. Perelman, Vernon Duke, and E. Y. "Yip" Harburg, starring Beatrice Lillie.

Designing for the Group Theater in the 1930s and 1940s, Aronson created sets for such plays as *Awake and Sing, Cabin in the Sky, Paradise Lost,* and *Three Men on a Horse,* but he was quick to differentiate between work that was "documentary—totally based on research" and work that was "imaginative." Examples of his imaginative designs from the same period are *The Merchant of Yonkers, The Time of Your Life,* and *R.U.R.,* the science fiction play by Karel Capek that gave us the word *robot*. Besides theater design, Aronson worked in the opera and ballet and created interior art for synagogues and paintings for several galleries.

One of the founders of the Group Theater, Harold Clurman, judged Aronson to be the only designer after Robert Edmond Jones who earned the right to be called a "master visual artist of the stage." Perhaps the strongest support for this assessment is that in all of Aronson's one hundred–plus Broadway productions there exist no Aronson "trademarks." The designer was reborn with each assignment.

Critic Brooks Atkinson praised Aronson this way: "His greatest quality is his understanding of the theatre and theatre scripts and the excitement with which he is able to identify with them. Every design is fresh and original. Like all first-rank artists, Boris never repeats himself." From the theatrical realism of *The Diary of Anne Frank* (1955) and *The Crucible* (1953) to the highly interpreta-

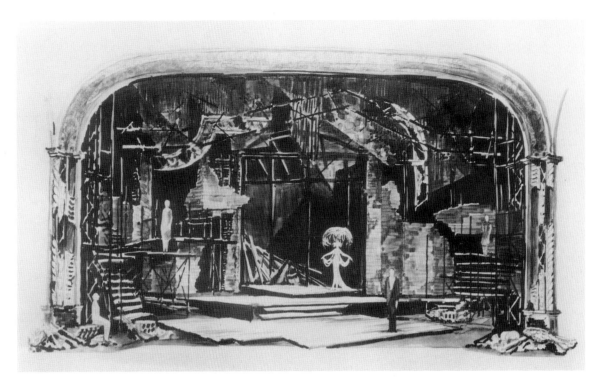

Set design for Follies *(1971)*

tive designs for *J. B.* (1958) and *The Rose Tattoo* (1951), Aronson never did repeat himself—regardless of the demands of the "organized calamity" of commercial theater.

The final period of Aronson's life and career was spent in partnership with producer Harold Prince. Aronson designed *Fiddler on the Roof* (1964), *Cabaret* (1966), *Zorba* (1968), *Company* (1970), *Follies* (1971), *A Little Night Music* (1973), and, his final work for Broadway, *Pacific Overtures* (1976). The last four productions were, of course, Stephen Sondheim musicals. Aronson won three of his six Tony Awards for *Company, Follies,* and *Pacific Overtures.* His other Tonys came for *Zorba, Cabaret,* and the season during which he designed *The Rose Tattoo, The Country Girl,* and *The Season in the Sun.* Six other times during his career he received Tony Award nominations.

Aronson's breadth of imagination was staggering: by using painted plastic in *A Little Night Music* he captured both old-world Sweden and the "new" musical world of Sondheim; *Company's* set of steel and plastic reflected the cold, isolated urban environment of New York City; the mirror overhanging the stage in *Cabaret* became the mirror of society—reflecting the audience back toward itself and inviting self-examination.

Probably the best way to sum up the uncompromising design philosophy of Boris Aronson would be to quote his answer to a reporter's question as to what he considered his "greatest achievement." The answer: "Some of the smash hits I turned down." Aronson died in 1980.

When Jo Mielziner died in 1976, four days short of his seventy-fifth birthday, he was completing the designs for his 302nd Broadway production, *The Baker's Wife,* which, as if jinxed, never opened. Mielziner was the most prolific designer in Broadway history and was for over half a century the designer producers sought first. Such was the respect for Mielziner's taste that one playwright regularly sent him manuscript copies of his plays, knowing that if Mielziner agreed to design the production, getting a producer to pay for it would be easy.

Mielziner was born of American parents in Paris. His father was a famous portraitist and trained his son in what Mielziner senior called "essentialization"—the ability to look at a subject for a short while, turn away to the canvas, and capture its essential nature. Deciding on a career as a theater designer, Mielziner studied the work of Craig and Appia (going so far as to track down the aging Swiss artist to spend a mere three hours in his presence). In addition, on the advice of his brother, actor Kenneth MacKenna, he joined a stock company in Detroit as an actor and general "go-fer" in order to augment his limited theater experience.

Mielziner next apprenticed himself to Robert Edmond Jones, Joseph Urban, and Lee Simonson, the principal designers for the Theatre Guild. After serving as assistant to stage managers as well as designers, he was given the assignment of designing scenery for the Alfred Lunt–Lynn Fontanne production of *The Guardsman* in 1924. After its smashing success there was no turning back.

Mielziner later designed for the opera and the ballet, produced Broadway shows (including *Happy Hunting* with Ethel Merman), during World War II devised camouflage for the OSS (forerunner of today's CIA), and served as codesigner, with Eero Saarinen, of the theater at Lincoln Center in New York.

In 1949, Mielziner's twenty-fifth season on Broadway, he designed *Death of a Salesman, South Pacific, Summer and Smoke, Anne of the Thousand Days,* and *Sleepy Hollow.* Still running from previous seasons were such hits as *Mister Roberts* and *A Streetcar Named Desire.* Yet, at the time, Mielziner was less than halfway through his career and still had such productions as *The King and I, Cat on a Hot Tin Roof,* and *Gypsy* ahead of him.

His design for Arthur Miller's *Death of a Salesman* has often been called the finest in Broadway history. The *Salesman* set is so inherently dramatic that it is truly a part of the play itself. Every designer today who approaches *Salesman* must do battle with the genius of Mielziner's design.

The original typescript of the play gave no description of the physical situation. Miller did include a brief paragraph that indicated a general direction and then said: "The designer of this play must use a great deal of imagination and work out an extremely simple solution to this obviously difficult scenic problem." Mielziner's solution was indeed simple: the delicate tracery of the set

Jo Mielziner

Set design for Death of a Salesman
(1949)

outlined Willy Loman's own fragile mental state. Willy's struggle against reality was mirrored in the half-naturalistic, half-impressionistic set. By using lighting as the medium to suggest Willy's mental leaps in time from past to present, Mielziner gave a weightless impact to the transitions. The scenic projections, which created various environments, were impressionistic, not naturalistic, and became not mere background, but active products of Willy's imagination.

With his designs for *Death of a Salesman,* Mielziner set a high-water mark for American theater design. In this set one sees not only the essentials of good design but the essentials of Mielziner's art: truth, balance, and self-effacement.

Death of a Salesman *(1949)*

Set designs for Camelot *(1960)*

Until the deaths of Boris Aronson and Jo Mielziner, all scenic designers labored in their shadows and in their debt. Probably the finest, most visually gifted designer who created his own niche during the Aronson–Mielziner years was Oliver Smith. Besides being a prolific stage designer (in 1957, seven of twenty-four shows running at season's end had his designs), Smith served as production designer for the film versions of *Oklahoma!, Guys and Dolls,* and *Porgy and Bess,* produced the stage versions of *On the Town* and *Gentlemen Prefer Blondes,* and was the codirector of the American Ballet Theatre for thirty-five years. Slightly outside his theatrical bailiwick were Smith's designs for restaurants and his work coordinating the interior renovation of several Broadway theaters and the Grand Ballroom of the Waldorf-Astoria, site of many Tony Award ceremonies.

Born in Wisconsin, Smith was accepted into the play-writing program of the Yale School of Drama. He never went. Instead, he moved to New York, apprenticed himself to Lee Simonson, and quickly made his mark on Broadway. His first Tony nomination—and his first win—was for *My Fair Lady* in 1957. Other Smith designs included in that first nomination were *Auntie Mame, Candide, A Clearing in the Woods, Eugenia,* and *A Visit to a Small Planet.*

Smith's next four Tony-nominated productions—*West Side Story, The Sound of Music, Becket,* and *Camelot*—all won the Scenic Design award. Smith won additional Tony Awards for his designs for *Hello, Dolly!* and *Baker Street.* Indeed, his seven awards for Scenic Design is a Tony record.

Costume sketches for Camelot *(1960)*

Set designs for My Fair Lady *(1957)*

Smith was probably Broadway's finest designer of musicals. The American musical makes more, and more complicated, demands on the scenic designer than any other type of theatrical production. The designs must accommodate large scenes of chorus spectacle without overwhelming the smaller book scenes that propel the plot. In addition, the designs have to be engineered to move quickly and silently, allowing the show to go on while the set is changed from, say, a small convent to a clearing in the Austrian Alps.

Smith designed musicals with an easy command of technique, while achieving the musicals' special design goals with grace and beauty. The silhouetted fire escapes of *West Side Story*, Dolly's staircase in *Hello, Dolly!*, and the cozy comforts of Professor Higgins's *My Fair Lady* library have been etched into theater history.

Five young designers have ruled Broadway and the Tony Award in the most recent past. What David Mitchell, Robin Wagner, Santo Loquasto, Tony Walton, and John Napier hold in common is a chameleon-like ability to move from the fantastical demands of the large Broadway musical to intimate, naturalistic drama. These men are not architect/scene painters, like Boris Aronson, or even architect/lighting designers, like Jo Mielziner, but Scenic Designers—the truest exemplars of Mielziner's ideal.

Beginning as an assistant to master designer Ming Cho Lee—the starting point for many of today's designers—David Mitchell has made his biggest splash designing musicals. Winning his two Tonys for *Annie* and *Barnum,* Mitchell has also been nominated for his designs of a rural Appalachian home in *Foxfire* and the Vietnam War setting of *The Boys of Winter.*

His musical designs, including his work on *La Cage Aux Folles* (1983), are marked by sure technical achievement and the ability to mimic the fluidity of cinematic movement. The opening scene of *La Cage* features the theatrical equivalent of a cinematic tracking shot. We are first presented with a free-standing building on the French Riviera. Then the building opens up, forming a street of buildings. The main building comes downstage and curtains fly in to create a nightclub interior. The opening number of Zaza's nightclub act—and the show—has begun.

Barnum (1980), perhaps Mitchell's wittiest design, gave us flash to equal the master circus showman himself. Mitchell used the St. James Theatre from top to bottom. In fact, he even designed a balloon that was to carry Barnum and Jenny Lind at the end of the first act from the stage, up and over the audience, to the balcony. The idea was finally dropped, ostensibly for insurance reasons, though Mitchell has since declared that the real problem was that no one could figure out how to come up with a second-act finale that would "top" the balloon.

Designer of the most successful musical in Broadway history, Robin Wagner came to *A Chorus Line* with no formal training. The single white line set against a mirrored back wall has been called one of the best designs in contemporary theater. Wagner stripped away all formal scenery and left the barest of essentials, those few elements that, in themselves, tell the musical's story.

Winning a Tony Award for *On the Twentieth Century,* Wagner brought a dynamic set to Broadway, an Art Deco railroad train that, with a mind of its own, roared across (and up and down) the stage.

Designer of more than one hundred productions, Wagner is a master of working hand-in-hand with a production's other designers. Known on Broadway as "The Group," Wagner and his frequent partners, costume designer Theoni V. Aldredge and lighting designer Tharon Musser, have had many successes. The cohesive designs for *A Chorus Line, Ballroom,* and *Dreamgirls* are the result of perfect collaboration. As Wagner has said: "Theatre is a collaborative art form. It's the process of merging visions into some kind of oneness. It's like fibre optic strands that eventually throw a great beam of light—but only because they are made up of a series of minute little channels of energy focused in the same direction.''

While at the Ross Common Playhouse in Pennsylvania, Santo Loquasto designed his first productions, *Gigi* and *Picnic*. He was sixteen. Though Loquasto spent time in acting school, he later enrolled in the Yale School of Drama as a graduate student in design.

While Loquasto works generally in the "sculptural" tradition of theater design, he is also a master of a naturalism that is anything but literal. His first and still most famous Broadway design, for *That Championship Season,* showed the audience only one room, but Loquasto worked out the ground plan and architecture for the entire house. Though the house was that of an unmarried high school basketball coach, the furniture and other decor conveyed the impression that his house had until recently been coinhabited by the coach's mother and was still more hers than his.

Like most of today's designers, Loquasto feels that his first assignment is to serve the play and the director rather than the designer's ego: "The success of establishing a total concept for a production, regardless of period, centers on a total understanding of the play by both the director and the designer, and I feel strongly that the designer is to serve the production and not to overwhelm it or insist on doing his thing to the point where he's in one place and the production is in another.''

★ ▓▓▓

The invasion of new plays and musicals from London to Broadway has, of course, carried along the original British designers. Usually the London designs are either transferred with the show or recreated by the same designers in New York. Less often have new designs or new designers been used. Naturally, if a production worked well enough in London to be exported to Broadway, it doesn't pay to tamper with success. British designers Tony Walton and John Napier have had great success on Broadway. Both work here often; Walton now lives in New York.

Born at Walton-on-Thames and formerly married to actress Julie Andrews, Tony Walton has designed costumes and sets for theater, opera, ballet, and film. Nine times he has worked with director Mike Nichols; seven times with film director Sidney Lumet. Among Walton's film designs are those for *Mary Poppins, All That Jazz, Murder on the Orient Express,* and *The Wiz.* His Tony-winning designs for *Pippin* and the Broadway revival of *The House of Blue Leaves* share a vibrant sense of theater. The strange little house in *Blue Leaves,* surrounded by the skyscrapers of Manhattan, gently reminds the audience what it means to live in Queens when you really want to be living in Manhattan—the central dream of Artie, the leading character.

Cats *(1982)*

John Napier is a sculptor rather than a painter. He does no formal drawings while preparing his designs, but instead creates model after *working* model. Napier has called his approach "instinctive" and "irrational," far removed from the strictures of schoolbook design technique. He has no diplomas, no degrees; he was not schooled in design. Like many other self-created artists, Napier is little stimulated by routine assignments. His artistic sense is excited by new challenges: "I'm not interested in any script that is hugely naturalistic or that lays down strict requirements. I'm not interested in one that says we must have two doors, a sofa, a french window, a brick fireplace. I like to work on something that needs investigation, followed by manufacture out of unusual elements. I enjoy the process of discovery and invention."

The Life and Adventures of Nicholas
Nickleby (1981)

Napier's designs for *The Life and Adventures of Nicholas Nickleby* and for *Cats* demonstrate his great talent. *Nicholas Nickleby* was a marvel of props and scenery constantly being adapted to yet another locale or setting. The eight-hour production was never constrained or circumscribed by the scenery. The stroke of genius behind *Cats* was to remake the entire theater, both stage and audience, in cat scale. Disorienting the audience, it also created the marvelous spectacle that continues to please.

Bill Nolte making up for a national (touring) company presentation of Cats (1982). Although make-up can be instrumental in the success of a production, no Tony Awards are given for make-up design.

COSTUME DESIGNERS

Over and over again costume designers tell you that they don't design costumes. They design *clothes*.

It was not always so. In the early years of Tony costume-design history, the designers of costumes were really not much more than dress designers who created gowns with barely a glancing reference to character. The stars of the period were clotheshorses for whom looking good was more important than looking and feeling in character. The development of the integrated musical and the corresponding rise in serious American drama led to the conviction that all elements of a production should contribute to a unified conception. No longer were costumes thought of as individual creations, but as design elements to be seen in the context of the entire production. Costumes were an aspect of characterization, almost as much as the walk or tone of voice the actor chose for his character.

Naturally there were producers who fought these new ideas about costumes. A costume designer's demand for more intricate and telling detail would be met with the reply that "No one will notice but another designer." Producers would balk at having costumes individually created and tailored when store-bought outfits could pass. Not many producers understood when the costumer explained that clothes off the rack just do not have the right dimensions and proportions necessary to "carry" the message to the audience.

Costumes don't just materialize; they must be designed, and, like many producers, audiences don't always realize the amount of work and effort that goes into them. While it is costumes for musicals that garner the most attention, costumes for plays are actually much more difficult to design. A simple white linen suit for a leading actor doesn't seem quite as complicated as a beaded and spangled gown for a leading lady. It is true that the gown is more complicated to build, but the suit is probably more "complicated" to create, since the fewer the options available to the designer, the more difficult it is to meet the goals of the design vision.

When one does a period show, costume designing is not merely a matter of recreating period fashions, but rather of creating the effect of the period while proportionately maintaining the costumes' contribution to the concept of the production. In doing costumes for choruses, the designer must fit his work into an overall pattern so that the chorus remains identifiably the chorus, separate from the leading players, yet also recognizable as individuals.

Whereas the history of Tony scenic design is almost completely dominated by men, Tony costume history is more balanced between the genders. But above all costume designers hovers one name: Irene Sharaff.

For years she was to the theater what Edith Head was to film—the "only" costume designer. It was Sharaff who shaved Yul Brynner's head and began the importation to America of Thai silk for *The King and I*: "The stage precedes fashion cycles." It was Sharaff who, asked if she was awed by dressing Broad-

198 ⋆

Irene Sharaff

way's and Hollywood's biggest stars, answered: "In underwear, they all look alike."

Yet even with popular recognition and ever-more-numerous job offers from producers, Sharaff realized the fleeting nature of renown: "You can roll up a big reputation designing one show a year, if it is a hit. But you can't live on one show a year, and you can't eat a reputation."

From designing costumes and scenery for Eva Le Gallienne's famed production of *Alice in Wonderland* in 1932, to *re*designing her classic costumes for the revivals of *The King and I* and *West Side Story* in the seventies ("Everything exists to be improved upon!"), Sharaff built a professional career.

And professionalism is highly valued in the theater. It means not only doing a job well but bringing it in on time and on budget, all the while remaining calm under the most adverse conditions. To add artistic insight to this professionalism, as Sharaff did, is something of a bonus.

Sharaff believed that the design process was "like working out a mathematical problem," finding the right combination of elements to work out the shared vision of the production team. After the solution was found, the actual execution, the building, of the costumes was the "hardest part of the job." Though Sharaff sometimes made light of the difficulties of designing, she realized all too well that in any good design there is a melding of practicality and vision, of craft and art: "Clothes are not just the whim and fancy of the designer who sits down and conjures them forth from his brain, but fashion really is the manifestation and reflection of the political, economic and social development of its day."

★ ▓▓▓

If Irene Sharaff was the First Lady of Broadway costume, then the First Gentleman was Cecil Beaton. Born in London in 1904, Beaton got his interest in theater from his father. The younger Beaton often carried his father's fieldglasses to the theater, the better to study the actresses' make-up and dress. Later, while a member of the Marlowe Dramatic Society at Cambridge, the self-taught Beaton began designing sets and costumes. Some of his work attracted the attention of the London critics. Beaton's theatrical design career was leavened by stints as playwright, actor, journalist, and, throughout his life, as a photographer, both to royalty and to the common rich.

While Beaton did contribute some uncharacteristically realistic designs to the theater, it was in romantic and slightly fantastical musicals that he was at his best: "Whenever I am embarking on the designs for a new production, early impressions of the theatre come back to mind, and many of my most successful effects have been dividends that have been paid to me from the past. Some of the most successful dresses have been inspired by memories of early playgoing days."

Nostalgia played a dominant role in Beaton's artistic consciousness. He was fated to design for *My Fair Lady*. The combination of the period in which the show was set with the Pygmalion-Galatea plot of an ugly duckling turned into a ravishing princess was tailor-made for him. The justly famous black-and-white designs for the Ascot Races scene made the entire stage resemble nothing so much as a Cecil Beaton photograph of beautiful people. Interestingly, the dress he designed for the character of Mrs. Higgins was, in reality, a copy of a dress Beaton's own mother had worn.

Cecil Beaton. *The women are wearing Beaton's costumes for* Saratoga *(1959).*

Beaton's *My Fair Lady* costumes helped define the spectacle of musical theater in the 1950s, a tradition that has been carried forward to the present day. Perfect evocations of Edwardiana, the *Fair Lady* costumes bore out Beaton's definition of theater, ''which at its finest should be an opulent cornucopia showering the spectator with golden illusions not to be found at home.''

201 ⋆

Born in Holland, and internationally known as Federico Rey, the Spanish dancer Freddy Wittop (*né* Koning) gave Broadway its single most famous costume: Carol Channing's red dress for the title-song scene in *Hello, Dolly!* (1964). This dress and the Tony Award it brought to him are even more remarkable in light of the following confession: "I don't even know how to cut a costume. I do the sketches and others have to carry on from there. I'm glad I don't know all the difficulties included in actually making the costumes because if I did, I probably wouldn't create such striking things."

Later, as his designs for such shows as *The Roar of the Greasepaint/The Smell of the Crowd, The Happy Time,* and *I Do! I Do!* became more assured, so did he. "I don't think of costumes as being pretty masonry. I study the walk, the sit, the movement of each character to determine the flow of material."

Costume sketch for Hello, Dolly! *(1964)*

■ ★ ■

Another of the old-guard costume designers, Lucinda Ballard, began her work at the age of seventeen with the Walter Hampden–Ethel Barrymore Shakespearean Repertory Company. Ballard moved on in later years to design costumes for *The Sound of Music, J.B., Cat on a Hot Tin Roof, Annie Get Your Gun, A Streetcar Named Desire, The Glass Menagerie,* and *I Remember Mama.*

"I tried to think out a character for each individual who appears on stage. I tried to show how the people look to each other; to dress each character in his own taste." It was Ballard's ability to put herself into the minds of her characters that led her to dress Marlon Brando's Stanley Kowalski in wetted, and thus form-fitted, blue jeans. This singular design stroke created a powerful male image that has persisted for decades.

★ ■

The three costume designers who have reigned over recent Tony history are Theoni V. Aldredge, Florence Klotz, and Patricia Zipprodt. Their work is marked by wit, humanity, and, when required, opulence. Among them, they have ten Tony Awards in twenty-five nominations.

Coming to the United States at the age of seventeen, Theoni V(achlioti) Aldredge, a "tall, weird foreigner who loved dimestores," has received twelve Tony nominations, more than any other costume designer. From dramatic classics such as *The Devil's Advocate* and *Much Ado About Nothing,* to musical fantasies like *42nd Street* and *Dreamgirls,* there is no style or period of which Aldredge is not master. Her greatest accomplishment is in creating costumes that seem truly inevitable and alive, yet are comfortable for the performers. For *La Cage Aux Folles,* Aldredge created women's clothing for the male chorus that in no way inhibited vigorous dancing, yet these Tony Award–winning dresses were pretty and elegant.

A Chorus Line is one of over eighty productions Aldredge has designed for producer Joseph Papp, and one of her almost two hundred Broadway productions. The assignment of designing the spare, simple designs for *Chorus Line* was at the opposite end of the spectrum from her extravagant costumes for *La Cage:*

> *It is much more difficult to do a rehearsal garment than it is to do a beaded dress. To find a character in each dancer took us six months. I was in rehearsal every day with my Polaroid, and I watched the kids because they brought their own personalities. And I just borrowed from what they brought. That was a very difficult show, and nobody understood that. I took it as a compliment if people thought "Well, they're just wearing their own clothes." That is what it should look like.*

"Flossie" Klotz began in the Broadway design world as an assistant to Irene Sharaff, working on the costumes for *The King and I.* Klotz's four Tony Awards (out of four nominations) came for her contributions to *Follies, A Little Night*

Irene Ryan in Pippin *(1972). Ryan died during the run of the show.*

Costume sketches for Pippin *(1972)*

Music, Pacific Overtures, and *Grind*—four Harold Prince musicals. Obviously, she has a good eye: "You're only as good as your material. If you've got a good script and a director with a point of view, someone who knows what he's looking for visually, your work will be that much better."

Her *Follies* costumes—especially those for the Loveland sequences, which smack of Las Vegas as painted by Watteau—were so heavily beaded that they had to be folded each night; hangers could not hold them. In *Pacific Overtures,* in which all of the women's roles are played by men, Klotz confronted and surmounted the extra problems without a hitch.

Patricia Zipprodt also apprenticed herself to Irene Sharaff. Zipprodt's Tony-winning designs for *Fiddler on the Roof, Cabaret,* and the Broadway revival of *Sweet Charity* share an innate sense of the humanity of the character, combined with a rare ability for telling us a "secret" about the character through the design.

Her designs (in collaboration with Ann Hould-Ward) for *Sunday in the Park with George* beautifully captured the world of Seurat's painting. Zipprodt used no black, as Seurat didn't consider that a color, but employed a series of nets

204 ★

Sunday in the Park with George *(1984)*

Georges Seurat, A Sunday Afternoon on the Island of La Grande Jatte, *1884–86. Oil on canvas, 81 x 120⅜"*
Helen Birch Bartlett Memorial
Collection, Art Institute of Chicago

and overhangs to give the illusion of the painter's pointillistic technique without actually using dotted fabrics. The costumes were a triumph of creativity over the production style's inherent restrictions.

Zipprodt sees herself as more than a costumer: "In this business you have to know a lot of things in addition to being able to draw. You have to know all about textiles, how color dyes will look under lighting. You must coordinate closely with the scenic designer. You have to be a psychologist and a cost accountant, too."

LIGHTING DESIGNERS

The art of theatrical lighting has had a much shorter history than its sister arts of scenic and costume design. Lighting design was first recognized by the Tony Awards in 1970, though for years—from the work of Jo Mielziner to that of Jean Rosenthal—it had ceased to be mere illumination of the actors on stage. Continual technological breakthroughs have increased the demand for lighting experts. Scenic designers, burdened by the demands of their own art, were scarcely able to stay abreast of these technical advances and thus weren't able to exploit them fully. As the techniques of lighting became more than a means of providing visibility, designers came to understand that lighting had moved from craft to art, that the technician had to be replaced by the artist. Lighting designers paint the stage with light, creating mood, locale, time of day, season, and geographical location.

Lighting design is still so little understood that it is often only the most obvious effects that impress the givers of prizes. But lighting, if it is really good, should go unnoticed. The moment the audience wonders how some effect was achieved, they have been taken away from the play. As lighting designer Jules Fisher once said, "Anyone can put a lightbulb on stage, but lighting design is *selecting* what the audience will see at each moment."

Edward Gordon Craig, a vigorous proponent of the dramatic use of lighting —a "plastic" medium, he called it—observed that "the relation of light to the scene is akin to that of the sun on the leaves, the moon on a river or sea, to that of the bow to the violin or of the pen to the paper. For the light travels over the scene—it does not stay in one fixed place . . . traveling, it produces the music."

While such scenic designers as Robert Edmond Jones, Lee Simonson, and Jo Mielziner were true musicians when working with lighting, the history of lighting design has been dominated by two women, Jean Rosenthal and Tharon Musser.

Most of Rosenthal's career preceded by years the Tony Award for Lighting Design. Beginning by designing the lighting for Leslie Howard's *Hamlet* in 1937, Rosenthal went on to design for such productions as *West Side Story, Fiddler on the Roof,* and *Cabaret.*

Many lighting designers have won one or two Tony nominations or Awards —Jo Mielziner (*Child's Play*), John Bury (*Amadeus*), Jennifer Tipton (*Cherry Orchard*), David Hersey (*Evita, Cats*). Three have figured most prominently in Tony history: Tharon Musser, Jules Fisher, and Ken Billington.

From a Broadway debut designing the lighting for *Long Day's Journey into Night,* to bringing the first computerized lightboard to Broadway, Tharon Musser has carried the craft of lighting design to the higher realm of art. Lighting design is, as Musser has put it, "as real as sugar in coffee, and as abstract as Jackson Pollack." Musser fights the temptation to which many directors yield, to see the lighting designer not as an artist but as a mere technician, "Talk to me like you talk to an actor," Musser says, "and I'll take care of the technical end."

Musser brings memories of her rural Virginia childhood to the theater. "I was raised in the country and it was a long time before my family could afford electricity. I think candlelight and oil lamplight are still most beautiful. . . . [Now] I just use colored light to re-create real light on stage."

In her more than two hundred productions Musser learned to maintain her sanity and joy in lighting design by tempering the "formula" world of Broadway with more satisfying fare. "You do musicals to survive economically and Shakespeare to survive spiritually."

Receiving Tony nominations for *42nd Street, Applause, A Little Night Music, Pacific Overtures, The Good Doctor, The Act,* and *Ballroom,* Musser has won for her work on *Follies, Dreamgirls,* and *A Chorus Line.* Musser's Tony tally could have been much higher: in 1968, just two years before Tony Awards were given for lighting design, she had seven productions running on Broadway.

Jules Fisher is a producer, director, theater consultant, and lighting designer, with more than one hundred productions to his credit. Relatively young (he graduated from Carnegie Institute of Technology in 1959), Fisher has won three Tony Awards—for *Pippin, Ulysses in Nighttown,* and *Dancin'*—in eight nominations. Because of the demands of his now multifaceted career, he is generally able to design only one production a year.

Jules Fisher is a practical man:
You don't have to know anything technical. It's only common sense and good taste. Does the furniture look good? Does the skin look good? Is there a focus? Does the lighting tell me where to look? Does it communicate an idea, express a mood? Tragedy isn't bright. Farce isn't dark. It's all obvious.

Jules Fisher knows his place in history:
Stage lighting is relatively new in the theatre. When you realize that it only came into its own with the advent of electricity and was introduced into an art form that goes back as far as recorded history, we realize how much we have yet to learn.

Jules Fisher is an artist:
[Stage lighting is] the discipline of knowing the optical, electrical, physical, and psychological sciences and their interrelationship—the proximity to creation in trying to use the arts of painting, sculpture, dance, architecture and music to express an idea, a feeling, an emotion.

Ken Billington skipped college, went straight to New York, and apprenticed himself to Tharon Musser. From there he has gone on to design lighting for dozens of Broadway shows, opera, nightclub performers, and even architectural lighting. "What I do is cue, color, and focus." Even given the evidence of Billington's five Tony nominations, lighting design is much more difficult than what is contained in that sentence: "For [a dress rehearsal of] *Sweeney Todd,* I had a full orchestra playing while I was trying to light. Six hundred invited people and I had not lit one cue in the first act. . . . And Hal Prince said, 'Turn on the lights, Ken.' "

8 THE FORGOTTEN AND THE REMEMBERED

Richard Burton in Camelot *(1960).
Burton received a Special Tony Award
in 1976, for his performance in* Equus.
*The award is noteworthy in that
Burton was not the originator of the
role; major stars seldom came to
Broadway as replacements.*

*Maurice Chevalier received a Special
Tony Award in 1968 for his long,
distinguished career.*

From the beginning of the Tony Awards in 1947 there have been performers
and productions that simply did not fit into existing award categories. At first
new categories were added: "Outstanding Performance by Newcomers," "Outstanding Foreign Company," and "Contribution to Theatre Through a Publication." Finally, in 1950, the Tony Award committee chose to consolidate all
extraordinary presentations under the category of Special Awards.

While often given to acknowledge a particular piece of work that lies outside the realm of the regular annual categories, Special Tony Awards are also
given in recognition of an artist's lifelong contribution to American theater. An
artist whose career may have been unintentionally forgotten will be remembered
in the twilight of his or her life.

Recipients of Special Tony Awards, like the other Tony Award winners, are
given the famous medallion bearing the faces of Comedy and Tragedy. The special awards are voted on only by the select Tony Award committee and not by
the Tony voters at large.

Artists from every area of theatrical expertise have been honored with Special Tony Awards. Performers, authors, composers, directors, designers, and
producers have been regular recipients. Yet the special awards have also been
given to publications (*Playbill,* 1971), libraries (The Theatre Collection of the
New York Public Library, 1956, and The Theatre Collection/Museum of the City
of New York, 1983), and entire productions (*The Threepenny Opera,* 1956, and
La Tragedie de Carmen, 1984). Almost each year a Special Tony Award is
bestowed upon a regional theater company in symbolic recognition of Broadway's dependence upon the creative productions that begin beyond its boundaries. Theater companies such as the Negro Ensemble Company, the National
Theatre for the Deaf, the Guthrie Theatre of Minneapolis, and the Steppenwolf
Theatre Company of Chicago have received special awards.

Alfred Lunt and Lynn Fontanne
received Special Tony Awards in 1970
for their lifetime achievement in the
American theater.

Betty Comden, Rosalind Russell,
Adolph Green, George Abbott,
Lehman Engel, and Leonard
Bernstein rehearsing Wonderful Town
(1954). Bernstein received a Special
Tony Award in 1969 for having worked
so successfully as a composer for the
stage, films, and concert halls. Abbott
received a Special Tony Award in 1987
on the occasion of his 100th birthday.

Bette Midler in Fiddler on the Roof
(1964). She received a Special Tony
Award in 1974 for her one-woman
show, Bette at the Palace.

Brooks Atkinson, former drama critic of the New York Times, *received a Special Tony Award in 1962 for "being the ideal of what a critic should be."*

Eva Le Gallienne, celebrating her fiftieth year as an actress, received a Special Tony Award in 1964 for her work with the National Repertory Theatre.

Gower Champion, Jerry Herman, Carol Channing, David Merrick, and Freddy Wittop after winning Tony Awards for Hello, Dolly! *(1964)*

Special Tony Awards offer the greatest opportunity for the American Theatre Wing and the League of American Theatres and Producers to honor individual lifetime achievement. Critics Brooks Atkinson and Elliot Norton were given medallions. Al Hirschfeld received his Special Tony for capturing the essence of Broadway through his caricatures. Liza Minnelli, Diana Ross, and Lena Horne brought new audiences to Broadway through their singing and were rewarded with medallions. Noel Coward, Alfred Lunt, and Lynn Fontanne—three careers without which Broadway would have been dimmer—are notable special-award winners.

It is more in keeping with the memory of Antoinette Perry to honor great accomplishment rather than the performance of a particular feat. Therefore, the annual Tony Awards are given not for "the best" of the season, but for "distinguished achievement." Nevertheless, these men and women of the American theater, all winners of Special Tony Awards, are indeed "the best."

NOTE ON SOURCES

The text of *The Tony Award Book* is based on the scripts, scores, designs, and critical reviews of the plays and musicals discussed, the extensive holdings (periodical clippings files, scrapbooks, ephemera, etc.) of the Billy Rose Collection at the Lincoln Center branch of the New York Public Library, such standard reference books as *Current Biography, Theatre World, Who's Who in the Theatre,* and *Who Was Who in the Theatre,* and the following list of studies, autobiographies, and biographies of and by various theater personalities. Where there were conflicting dates or versions of stories, the author followed those cited by the most authoritative or contemporaneous source.

Abbott, George. *Mister Abbott*. New York: Random House, 1963.

Atkinson, Brooks. *Broadway*. New York: Limelight Editions, 1985.

Ciment, Michel. *Kazan on Kazan*. New York: Viking, 1974.

de Mille, Agnes. *Dance to the Piper*. Boston: Little, Brown & Co., 1951.

————. *And Promenade Home*. Boston: Little, Brown & Co., 1956.

Ewen, David. *Richard Rodgers*. New York: Henry Holt & Co., 1957.

Fordin, Hugh. *Getting to Know Him: A Biography of Oscar Hammerstein II*. New York: Random House, 1977.

Gelb, Arthur and Barbara. *O'Neill*. New York: Harper & Brothers, 1962.

Green, Stanley. *Broadway Musicals Show by Show*. Milwaukee: Hal Leonard Books, 1985.

Harrison, Rex. *Rex: An Autobiography*. London: Macmillan, 1974.

Hayman, Ronald. *Harold Pinter*. London: Heinemann, 1980.

Lerner, Alan Jay. *The Street Where I Live*. New York: W. W. Norton, 1978.

Logan, Joshua. *Josh: My Up and Down, In and Out Life*. New York: Delacorte Press, 1976.

Martin, Mary. *My Heart Belongs*. New York: William Morrow & Co., 1976.

McGovern, Edythe M. *Not-So-Simple Neil Simon: A Critical Study*. Van Nuys, California: Perivale Press, 1978.

Merman, Ethel, with George Eells. *Merman*. New York: Simon & Schuster, 1978.

Prince, Hal. *Contradictions: Notes on Twenty-Six Years in the Theatre*. New York: Dodd, Mead & Co., 1974.

Rodgers, Richard. *Musical Stages*. New York: Random House, 1975.

Schneider, Alan. *Entrances: An American Director's Journey*. New York: Viking, 1986.

Teichmann, Howard. *Fonda: My Life*. New York: New American Library, 1981.

Trewin, J. C. *Peter Brook: A Biography*. London: MacDonald, 1971.

Wellard, Dennis. *Miller: A Study of His Plays*. London: Eyre Methuen, 1979.

Zadan, Craig. *Sondheim & Co*. London: Macmillan, 1974.

The categories and their citations changed periodically during the forty years of Tony Award history, and, over the years, a number of nominees changed their names; for instance, George Scott became George C. Scott, Harold S. Prince became Harold Prince, Ron Field became Ronald Field. All categories, citations, and nominees are listed as printed in each year's award ceremony program. When available, the texts of citations for Special Tony Awards are given verbatim as worded in each year's award ceremony program, telecast videotape, or press release.

The names of all nominees were not made public until the Tenth Annual Tony Awards in 1956; prior to this, only the winners were announced. In this listing, from the 1956 awards on, nominees are printed in regular type and winners indicated by boldface type.

1st ANNUAL TONY AWARDS
PRESENTED APRIL 6, 1947
WALDORF-ASTORIA

OUTSTANDING PERFORMANCE
Ingrid Bergman, *Joan of Lorraine*
Helen Hayes, *Happy Birthday*
José Ferrer, *Cyrano de Bergerac*
Fredric March, *Years Ago*

OUTSTANDING DEBUT PERFORMANCE
Patricia Neal, *Another Part of the Forest*

OUTSTANDING MUSICAL PERFORMANCE
David Wayne, *Finian's Rainbow*

OUTSTANDING SCORE
Kurt Weill, *Street Scene*

OUTSTANDING PLAYWRIGHT
Arthur Miller, *All My Sons*

OUTSTANDING DIRECTOR
Elia Kazan, *All My Sons*

OUTSTANDING DANCE DIRECTION
Agnes De Mille, *Brigadoon*
Michael Kidd, *Finian's Rainbow*

OUTSTANDING SCENIC DESIGN
David Ffolkes, *Henry VIII*

Jessica Tandy in A Streetcar Named Desire *(1947)*

OUTSTANDING COSTUME DESIGN
Lucinda Ballard, *Happy Birthday, Another Part of the Forest, Street Scene, John Loves Mary,* and *The Chocolate Soldier*

SPECIAL AWARDS
Ira and Rita Katzenberg, for enthusiasm as inveterate first-nighters.
Vincent Sardi, Sr., for providing a transient home and comfort station for theatre folk at Sardi's for twenty years.
Dora Chamberlain, for unfailing courtesy as treasurer of the Martin Beck Theatre.
Burns Mantle, for the annual publication of *The Ten Best Plays*.
Jules J. Leventhal, for the season's most prolific backer and producer.
P. A. McDonald, for intricate construction for the production of *If a Shoe Fits*.

Award for women: initialed sterling silver compact cases

Award for men: engraved gold bill clips

2nd ANNUAL TONY AWARDS
PRESENTED MARCH 28, 1948
WALDORF-ASTORIA

DISTINGUISHED PERFORMANCE BY AN ACTRESS
Judith Anderson, *Medea*
Katherine Cornell, *Antony and Cleopatra*
Jessica Tandy, *A Streetcar Named Desire*

DISTINGUISHED PERFORMANCE BY AN ACTOR
Henry Fonda, *Mister Roberts*
Paul Kelly, *Command Decision*
Basil Rathbone, *The Heiress*

DISTINGUISHED MUSICAL STAGE PERFORMANCE
Grace Hartman, *Angel in the Wings*
Paul Hartman, *Angel in the Wings*

OUTSTANDING PERFORMANCE BY NEWCOMERS
June Lockhart, *For Love or Money*
James Whitmore, *Command Decision*

OUTSTANDING PLAY
Mister Roberts, by Thomas Heggen and Joshua Logan

OUTSTANDING DIRECTOR
Josh Logan, *Mister Roberts*

OUTSTANDING DANCE DIRECTION
Jerome Robbins, *High Button Shoes*

OUTSTANDING SCENIC DESIGN
Horace Armistead, *The Medium*

OUTSTANDING COSTUME DESIGN
Mary Percy Schenck, *The Heiress*

OUTSTANDING ORCHESTRA CONDUCTING
Max Meth, *Finian's Rainbow*

OUTSTANDING BACKSTAGE TECHNICIAN
George Gebhart

OUTSTANDING FOREIGN COMPANY
The Importance of Being Earnest, directed by John Gielgud

SPREADING THEATRE TO THE COUNTRY WHILE THE ORIGINALS PERFORM IN NEW YORK
Mary Martin, *Annie Get Your Gun*
Joe E. Brown, *Harvey*

EXPERIMENT IN THEATRE
Experimental Theatre, Inc., John Garfield, accepting

PROGRESSIVE THEATRE OPERATORS
Robert W. Dowling, president of City Investing Company, owner of several theatres in New York
Paul Beisman, operator of the American Theatre, St. Louis

CONTRIBUTION TO THEATRE THROUGH A PUBLICATION
Rosamond Gilder, editor, *Theatre Arts*

CONTRIBUTION TO DEVELOPMENT OF REGIONAL THEATRE
Robert Porterfield, Virginia Barter Theatre

DISTINGUISHED WING VOLUNTEER WORKER THROUGH THE WAR AND AFTER
Vera Allen

SPECIAL AWARD
George Pierce, for twenty-five years of courteous and efficient service as a backstage doorman (Empire Theatre).

Award for women: gold bracelets, each with a disk inscribed with the actress's initials and the name of the prize

Award for men: gold bill clips, inscribed with the actor's initials and the name of the prize

3rd ANNUAL TONY AWARDS
PRESENTED APRIL 24, 1949
WALDORF-ASTORIA

OUTSTANDING LEADING PERFORMANCE IN A PLAY
Martita Hunt, *The Madwoman of Chaillot*

Rex Harrison in Anne of the Thousand Days *(1948)*

Rex Harrison, *Anne of the Thousand Days*

OUTSTANDING SUPPORTING PERFORMANCE
Shirley Booth, *Goodbye, My Fancy*
Arthur Kennedy, *Death of a Salesman*

OUTSTANDING MUSICAL PERFORMANCE
Nanette Fabray, *Love Life*
Ray Bolger, *Where's Charley?*

OUTSTANDING MUSICAL
Kiss Me Kate. Music and lyrics by Cole Porter; book by Bella and Sam Spewack. Produced by Saint-Subber and Samuel Ayers.

OUTSTANDING PLAY
Death of a Salesman, by Arthur Miller. Produced by Kermit Bloomgarden and Walter Fried.

OUTSTANDING DIRECTOR
Elia Kazan, *Death of a Salesman*

OUTSTANDING CONDUCTOR AND MUSICAL DIRECTOR
Max Meth, *As the Girls Go*

OUTSTANDING DANCE DIRECTOR
Gower Champion, *Lend an Ear*

OUTSTANDING SCENIC DESIGN
Jo Mielziner, for his work throughout the season [which included *South Pacific*]

OUTSTANDING COSTUME DESIGN
Lemuel Ayers, for various contributions throughout the season

First awarding of the Tony medallion designed by Herman Rosse. The face of the medallion carries an adaption of the traditional comic and tragic masks and the reverse side, carrying a relief profile of Antoinette Perry, is engraved with the award citation and the name of the winner.

The producers of Outstanding Musical and Outstanding Play received scrolls, not medallions.

4th ANNUAL TONY AWARDS
PRESENTED APRIL 9, 1950
WALDORF-ASTORIA

OUTSTANDING DRAMATIC ACTRESS
Shirley Booth, *Come Back, Little Sheba*

OUTSTANDING DRAMATIC ACTOR
Sidney Blackmer, *Come Back, Little Sheba*

OUTSTANDING MUSICAL ACTRESS
Mary Martin, *South Pacific*

OUTSTANDING MUSICAL ACTOR
Ezio Pinza, *South Pacific*

OUTSTANDING SUPPORTING ACTRESS
Juanita Hall, *South Pacific*

OUTSTANDING SUPPORTING ACTOR
Myron McCormick, *South Pacific*

OUTSTANDING MUSICAL
South Pacific. Music by Richard Rodgers; lyrics by Oscar Hammerstein II; book by Oscar Hammerstein II and Joshua Logan. Produced by Leland Hayward, Oscar Hammerstein II, Joshua Logan, and Richard Rodgers.

OUTSTANDING SCORE
Richard Rodgers, *South Pacific*

OUTSTANDING LIBRETTO
Joshua Logan and Oscar Hammerstein II, *South Pacific*

OUTSTANDING PLAY
The Cocktail Party, by T. S. Eliot. Produced by Gilbert Miller.

OUTSTANDING DIRECTION
Joshua Logan, *South Pacific*

OUTSTANDING SCENIC DESIGN
Jo Mielziner, *The Innocents*

OUTSTANDING COSTUME DESIGN
Aline Bernstein, *Regina*

OUTSTANDING CHOREOGRAPHER
Helen Tamiris, *Touch and Go*

OUTSTANDING CONDUCTOR AND MUSICAL DIRECTOR
Maurice Abravanel, *Regina*

OUTSTANDING STAGE TECHNICIAN
Joe Lynn, master propertyman, *Miss Liberty*

SPECIAL AWARDS
Maurice Evans, for work he did in guiding the City Center Theatre Company through a highly successful season.
Philip Faversham, a volunteer worker of the American Theatre Wing's hospital program outside of New York: Eleanor Roosevelt presented a special scroll of appreciation.
Brock Pemberton, founder of awards and its original chairman (posthumous).

The producers of Outstanding Musical and Outstanding Play received scrolls, not medallions.

5th ANNUAL TONY AWARDS
PRESENTED MARCH 25, 1951
WALDORF-ASTORIA

DISTINGUISHED PERFORMANCE, DRAMATIC PLAY, FEMALE STAR
Uta Hagen, *The Country Girl*

DISTINGUISHED PERFORMANCE, DRAMATIC PLAY, MALE STAR
Claude Rains, *Darkness at Noon*

DISTINGUISHED FEATURED PERFORMANCE, DRAMATIC PLAY, FEMALE
Maureen Stapleton, *The Rose Tattoo*

DISTINGUISHED FEATURED PERFORMANCE, DRAMATIC PLAY, MALE
Eli Wallach, *The Rose Tattoo*

DISTINGUISHED PERFORMANCE, MUSICAL, FEMALE STAR
Ethel Merman, *Call Me Madam*

Ethel Merman and Irving Berlin rehearsing Call Me Madam *(1950)*

DISTINGUISHED PERFORMANCE, MUSICAL, MALE STAR
Robert Alda, *Guys and Dolls*

DISTINGUISHED FEATURED PERFORMANCE, MUSICAL, FEMALE
Isabel Bigley, *Guys and Dolls*

DISTINGUISHED FEATURED PERFORMANCE, MUSICAL, MALE
Russell Nype, *Call Me Madam*

OUTSTANDING MUSICAL
Guys and Dolls. Music and lyrics by Frank Loesser; book by Abe Burrows and Jo Swerling. Produced by Cy Feuer and Ernest Martin.

OUTSTANDING MUSICAL SCORE
Call Me Madam, by Irving Berlin

OUTSTANDING PLAY
The Rose Tattoo, by Tennessee Williams. Produced by Cheryl Crawford.

OUTSTANDING DIRECTOR
George S. Kaufman, *Guys and Dolls*

OUTSTANDING CHOREOGRAPHER
Michael Kidd, *Guys and Dolls*

OUTSTANDING SCENIC DESIGNER
Boris Aronson, *The Rose Tattoo, The Country Girl,* and *Season in the Sun*

OUTSTANDING COSTUME DESIGNER
Miles White, *Bless You All*

OUTSTANDING MUSICAL DIRECTOR
Lehman Engel, *The Consul*

OUTSTANDING STAGE TECHNICIAN
Richard Raven, master electrician, *The Autumn Garden*

SPECIAL RECOGNITION
Ruth Green, for her services as a volunteer in arranging reservations and seating for the five Antoinette Perry Awards dinners.

The producers of Outstanding Musical and Outstanding Play received scrolls, not medallions.

A special citation was presented by Major General Carl R. Gray, Jr., to the Theatre Wing for its work on behalf of veterans.

6th ANNUAL TONY AWARDS
PRESENTED MARCH 30, 1952
WALDORF-ASTORIA

DISTINGUISHED DRAMATIC ACTRESS
Julie Harris, *I Am a Camera*

DISTINGUISHED DRAMATIC ACTOR
José Ferrer, *The Shrike*

DISTINGUISHED SUPPORTING OR FEATURED ACTRESS
Marian Winters, *I Am a Camera*

DISTINGUISHED SUPPORTING OR FEATURED ACTOR
John Cromwell, *Point of No Return*

Yul Brynner in The King and I *(1951)*

DISTINGUISHED MUSICAL ACTRESS
Gertrude Lawrence, *The King and I*

DISTINGUISHED MUSICAL ACTOR
Phil Silvers, *Top Banana*

Jessica Tandy and Hume Cronyn in The Fourposter *(1951)*

DISTINGUISHED SUPPORTING OR FEATURED MUSICAL ACTRESS
Helen Gallagher, *Pal Joey*

DISTINGUISHED SUPPORTING OR FEATURED MUSICAL ACTOR
Yul Brynner, *The King and I*

OUTSTANDING MUSICAL
The King and I. Music by Richard Rodgers; book and lyrics by Oscar Hammerstein II. Produced by Richard Rodgers and Oscar Hammerstein II.

OUTSTANDING PLAY
The Fourposter, by Jan de Hartog. Produced by the Playwrights Company.

OUTSTANDING DIRECTOR
José Ferrer, *The Shrike, The Fourposter,* and *Stalag 17*

OUTSTANDING COSTUME DESIGN
Irene Sharaff, *The King and I*

OUTSTANDING SCENIC DESIGN
Jo Mielziner, *The King and I*

OUTSTANDING CHOREOGRAPHER
Robert Alton, *Pal Joey*

Outstanding Conductor and Musical Director
Max Meth, *Pal Joey*

Outstanding Stage Technician
Peter Feller, master carpenter, *Call Me Madam*

Special Awards
Judy Garland, for an important contribution to the revival of vaudeville through her recent stint at the Palace Theatre.
Edward Kook, for his contributing to and encouraging the development of stage lighting and electronics.
Charles Boyer, for distinguished performance in *Don Juan in Hell,* thereby assisting in a new theater trend.

The producers of Outstanding Musical and Outstanding Play received scrolls, not medallions.

7th ANNUAL TONY AWARDS
PRESENTED MARCH 29, 1953
WALDORF-ASTORIA

Outstanding Dramatic Actress
Shirley Booth, *Time of the Cuckoo*

Outstanding Dramatic Actor
Tom Ewell, *The Seven Year Itch*

Outstanding Supporting or Featured Dramatic Actress
Beatrice Straight, *The Crucible*

Outstanding Supporting or Featured Dramatic Actor
John Williams, *Dial M for Murder*

Outstanding Musical Actress
Rosalind Russell, *Wonderful Town*

Outstanding Musical Actor
Thomas Mitchell, *Hazel Flagg*

Outstanding Supporting or Featured Musical Actress
Sheila Bond, *Wish You Were Here*

Outstanding Supporting or Featured Musical Actor
Hiram Sherman, *Two's Company*

Outstanding Musical
Wonderful Town. Music by Leonard Bernstein; lyrics by Betty Comden and Adolph Green; book by Joseph Fields and Jerome Chodorov. Produced by Robert Fryer.

Outstanding Play
The Crucible, by Arthur Miller. Produced by Kermit Bloomgarden.

Outstanding Director
Joshua Logan, *Picnic*

Outstanding Costume Designer
Miles White, *Hazel Flagg*

Outstanding Scenic Designer
Raoul Pène du Bois, *Wonderful Town*

Outstanding Choreographer
Donald Saddler, *Wonderful Town*

Outstanding Conductor and Musical Director
Lehman Engel, *Wonderful Town,* and Gilbert and Sullivan season

Outstanding Stage Technician
Abe Kurnit, property man, *Wish You Were Here*

Contributions to the Theatre Not Covered by Regular Citations
Beatrice Lillie, for *An Evening with Beatrice Lillie*
Danny Kaye, for heading a variety bill at the Palace Theatre.
Equity Community Theatre

The producers of Outstanding Musical and Outstanding Play received scrolls, not medallions.

8th ANNUAL TONY AWARDS
PRESENTED MARCH 28, 1954
PLAZA HOTEL

Distinguished Performance in a Dramatic Play by a Female Star
Audrey Hepburn, *Ondine*

Distinguished Performance in a Dramatic Play by a Male Star
David Wayne, *The Teahouse of the August Moon*

Outstanding Supporting or Featured Dramatic Actress
Jo Van Fleet, *The Trip to Bountiful*

Outstanding Supporting or Featured Dramatic Actor
John Kerr, *Tea and Sympathy*

Outstanding Musical Actress
Dolores Gray, *Carnival in Flanders*

Outstanding Musical Actor
Alfred Drake, *Kismet*

Outstanding Supporting or Featured Musical Actress
Gwen Verdon, *Can-Can*

Outstanding Supporting or Featured Musical Actor
Harry Belafonte, *John Murray Anderson's Almanac*

Outstanding Musical
Kismet. Music by Alexander Borodin, adapted with lyrics by Robert Wright and George Forrest; book by Charles Lederer and Luther Davis. Produced by Charles Lederer.

Outstanding Play
The Teahouse of the August Moon, by John Patrick. Produced by Maurice Evans and George Schaefer.

Outstanding Director
Alfred Lunt, *Ondine*

Outstanding Costume Designer
Richard Whorf, *Ondine*

OUTSTANDING SCENIC DESIGNER
Peter Larkin, *Ondine* and *Teahouse of the August Moon*

OUTSTANDING CHOREOGRAPHER
Michael Kidd, *Can-Can*

OUTSTANDING MUSICAL CONDUCTOR
Louis Adrian, *Kismet*

OUTSTANDING STAGE TECHNICIAN
John Davis, *Picnic,* for constant good work as a theatre electrician.

The producers of Outstanding Musical and Outstanding Play received scrolls, not medallions.

OUTSTANDING DRAMATIC ACTRESS
Nancy Kelly, *The Bad Seed*

OUTSTANDING DRAMATIC ACTOR
Alfred Lunt, *Quadrille*

OUTSTANDING SUPPORTING OR FEATURED DRAMATIC ACTRESS
Patricia Jessel, *Witness for the Prosecution*

OUTSTANDING SUPPORTING OR FEATURED DRAMATIC ACTOR
Francis L. Sullivan, *Witness for the Prosecution*

OUTSTANDING MUSICAL ACTRESS
Mary Martin, *Peter Pan*

OUTSTANDING MUSICAL ACTOR
Walter Slezak, *Fanny*

OUTSTANDING SUPPORTING OR FEATURED MUSICAL ACTRESS
Carol Haney, *Pajama Game*

OUTSTANDING SUPPORTING OR FEATURED MUSICAL ACTOR
Cyril Ritchard, *Peter Pan*

OUTSTANDING MUSICAL
The Pajama Game. Music and lyrics by Richard Adler and Jerry Ross; book by George Abbott and Richard Bissell. Produced by Frederick Brisson, Robert Griffith, and Harold S. Prince.

OUTSTANDING PLAY
The Desperate Hours, by Joseph Hayes. Produced by Howard Erskine and Joseph Hayes.

OUTSTANDING DIRECTOR
Robert Montgomery, *The Desperate Hours*

OUTSTANDING COSTUME DESIGNER
Cecil Beaton, *Quadrille*

OUTSTANDING SCENIC DESIGN
Oliver Messel, *House of Flowers*

OUTSTANDING CHOREOGRAPHER
Bob Fosse, *The Pajama Game*

OUTSTANDING CONDUCTOR AND MUSICAL DIRECTOR
Thomas Schippers, *The Saint of Bleecker Street*

OUTSTANDING STAGE TECHNICIAN
Richard Rodda, *Peter Pan*

SPECIAL AWARD
Proscenium Productions, an Off-Broadway company at the Cherry Lane Theatre, for generally high quality and viewpoint shown in *The Way of the World* and *Thieves Carnival.* Presented to Warren Enters, Robert Merriman, and Sybil Trubin.

For the first time, the Theatre Wing announced the list of plays and musicals that were in the running up to the final ballot for Tony Awards as Outstanding Play and Outstanding Musical. They were the plays *Anastasia, The Bad Seed, The Desperate Hours, The Flowering Peach, The Rainmaker,* and *Witness for the Prosecution,* and the musicals *Fanny, The Golden Apple, The Pajama Game, Peter Pan, Plain and Fancy,* and *Silk Stockings.*

OUTSTANDING DRAMATIC ACTRESS
Barbara Bel Geddes, *Cat on a Hot Tin Roof*
Gladys Cooper, *The Chalk Garden*
Ruth Gordon, *The Matchmaker*
Julie Harris, *The Lark*
Siobhan McKenna, *The Chalk Garden*
Susan Strasberg, *The Diary of Anne Frank*

OUTSTANDING DRAMATIC ACTOR
Ben Gazzara, *A Hatful of Rain*
Boris Karloff, *The Lark*
Paul Muni, *Inherit the Wind*
Michael Redgrave, *Tiger at the Gates*
Edward G. Robinson, *The Middle of the Night*

OUTSTANDING SUPPORTING OR FEATURED DRAMATIC ACTRESS
Diane Cilento, *Tiger at the Gates*
Anne Jackson, *The Middle of the Night*

Andy Griffith in No Time for Sergeants *(1955)*

Una Merkel, *The Ponder Heart*
Elaine Stritch, *Bus Stop*

OUTSTANDING SUPPORTING OR FEATURED DRAMATIC ACTOR
Ed Begley, *Inherit the Wind*
Antony Franciosa, *A Hatful of Rain*
Andy Griffith, *No Time for Sergeants*
Anthony Quayle, *Tamburlaine the Great*
Fritz Weaver, *The Chalk Garden*

OUTSTANDING MUSICAL ACTRESS
Carol Channing, *The Vamp*
Gwen Verdon, *Damn Yankees*
Nancy Walker, *Phoenix '55*

OUTSTANDING MUSICAL ACTOR
Stephen Douglass, *Damn Yankees*
William Johnson, *Pipe Dream*
Ray Walston, *Damn Yankees*

OUTSTANDING SUPPORTING OR FEATURED MUSICAL ACTRESS
Rae Allen, *Damn Yankees*
Pat Carroll, *Catch a Star*
Lotte Lenya, *The Threepenny Opera* [Off-Broadway production]
Judy Tyler, *Pipe Dream*

OUTSTANDING SUPPORTING OR FEATURED MUSICAL ACTOR
Russ Brown, *Damn Yankees*
Mike Kellin, *Pipe Dream*
Will Mahoney, *Finian's Rainbow*
Scott Merrill, *The Threepenny Opera* [Off-Broadway production]

OUTSTANDING PLAY
Bus Stop, by William Inge. Produced by Robert Whitehead and Roger L. Stevens.
Cat on a Hot Tin Roof, by Tennessee Williams. Produced by the Playwrights Company.
The Chalk Garden, by Enid Bagnold. Produced by Irene Mayer Selznick.
The Diary of Anne Frank, by Frances Goodrich and Albert Hackett. Produced by Kermit Bloomgarden.

Tiger at the Gates, by Jean Giraudoux, adapted by Christopher Fry. Produced by Robert L. Joseph, the Playwrights Company, and Henry M. Margolis.

OUTSTANDING MUSICAL
Damn Yankees. Music and lyrics by Richard Adler and Jerry Ross; book by George Abbott and Douglass Wallop. Produced by Frederick Brisson, Robert Griffith, and Harold S. Prince, in association with Albert B. Taylor.
Pipe Dream. Music by Richard Rodgers; lyrics and book by Oscar Hammerstein II. Produced by Richard Rodgers and Oscar Hammerstein II.

OUTSTANDING DIRECTOR
Joseph Anthony, *The Lark*
Harold Clurman, *Bus Stop, Pipe Dream,* and *Tiger at the Gates*
Tyrone Guthrie, *The Matchmaker, Six Characters in Search of an Author,* and *Tamburlaine the Great*
Garson Kanin, *The Diary of Anne Frank*
Elia Kazan, *Cat on a Hot Tin Roof*
Albert Marre, *The Chalk Garden*
Herman Shumlin, *Inherit the Wind*

OUTSTANDING CHOREOGRAPHER
Robert Alton, *The Vamp*
Bob Fosse, *Damn Yankees*
Boris Runanin, *Phoenix '55* and *Pipe Dream*
Anna Sokolow, *Red Roses for Me*

OUTSTANDING MUSICAL DIRECTOR
Hal Hasting, *Damn Yankees*
Salvatore Dell'Isola, *Pipe Dream*
Milton Rosenstock, *The Vamp*

OUTSTANDING SCENIC DESIGN
Boris Aronson, *The Diary of Anne Frank, Bus Stop, Once Upon a Tailor,* and *A View from the Bridge*
Ben Edwards, *The Ponder Heart, Someone Waiting,* and *The Honeys*
Peter Larkin, *Inherit the Wind* and ***No Time for Sergeants***

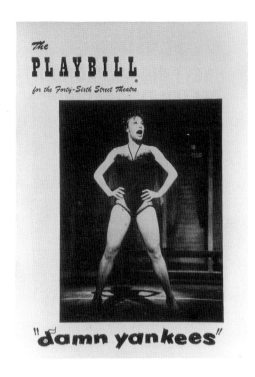

The PLAYBILL
for the Forty-Sixth Street Theatre

"damn yankees"

Jo Mielziner, *Cat on a Hot Tin Roof, The Lark, The Middle of the Night,* and *Pipe Dream*
Raymond Sovey, *The Great Sebastians*

OUTSTANDING COSTUME DESIGNER
Alvin Colt, *The Lark, Phoenix '55,* and ***Pipe Dream***
Mainbocher, *The Great Sebastians*
Helen Pons, *The Diary of Anne Frank, Heavenly Twins,* and *A View from the Bridge*

OUTSTANDING STAGE TECHNICIAN
Larry Bland, carpenter, *The Middle of the Night, The Ponder Heart,* and *Porgy and Bess.*
Harry Green, electrician and sound man, ***The Middle of the Night*** and ***Damn Yankees***

SPECIAL AWARDS
City Center
Fourth Street Chekhov Theatre
The Shakespearewrights

The Threepenny Opera, distinguished Off-Broadway production; Carmen Capalbo, Stanley Chase, producers.

The Theatre Collection of the New York Public Library, on its twenty-fifth anniversary, for its distinguished service to the theatre. George Freedley, founder and curator, accepted.

For the first time, nominations were made public and winners announced at the awards ceremony.

The producers of Outstanding Musical and Outstanding Play received scrolls, not medallions.

11th ANNUAL TONY AWARDS
PRESENTED APRIL 21, 1957
WALDORF-ASTORIA

OUTSTANDING DRAMATIC ACTRESS
Florence Eldridge, *Long Day's Journey into Night*
Margaret Leighton, *Separate Tables*
Rosalind Russell, *Auntie Mame*
Sybil Thorndike, *The Potting Shed*

OUTSTANDING DRAMATIC ACTOR
Maurice Evans, *The Apple Cart*
Wilfred Hyde-White, *The Reluctant Debutante*
Fredric March, *Long Day's Journey into Night*
Eric Porter, *Separate Tables*
Ralph Richardson, *The Waltz of the Toreadors*
Cyril Ritchard, *A Visit to a Small Planet*

OUTSTANDING SUPPORTING OR FEATURED DRAMATIC ACTRESS
Peggy Cass, *Auntie Mame*
Anna Massey, *The Reluctant Debutante*
Beryl Measor, *Separate Tables*
Mildred Natwick, *The Waltz of the Toreadors*

Phyllis Neilson-Terry, *Separate Tables*
Diana Van der Vlis, *The Happiest Millionaire*

OUTSTANDING SUPPORTING OR FEATURED DRAMATIC ACTOR
Frank Conroy, *The Potting Shed*
Eddie Mayehoff, *A Visit to a Small Planet*
William Podmore, *Separate Tables*
Jason Robards, Jr., *Long Day's Journey into Night*

OUTSTANDING MUSICAL ACTRESS
Julie Andrews, *My Fair Lady*
Judy Holliday, *Bells Are Ringing*
Ethel Merman, *Happy Hunting*

OUTSTANDING MUSICAL ACTOR
Rex Harrison, *My Fair Lady*
Fernando Lamas, *Happy Hunting*
Robert Weede, *The Most Happy Fella*

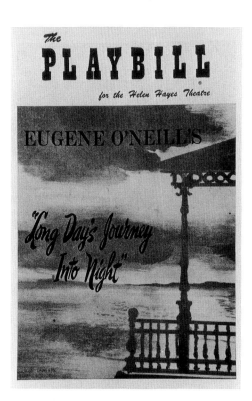

OUTSTANDING SUPPORTING OR FEATURED MUSICAL ACTRESS
Edith Adams, *Li'l Abner*
Virginia Gibson, *Happy Hunting*
Irra Petina, *Candide*
Jo Sullivan, *The Most Happy Fella*

OUTSTANDING SUPPORTING OR FEATURED MUSICAL ACTOR
Sydney Chaplin, *Bells Are Ringing*
Robert Coote, *My Fair Lady*
Stanley Holloway, *My Fair Lady*

OUTSTANDING PLAY
Long Day's Journey into Night, by Eugene O'Neill. Produced by Leigh Connell, Theodore Mann, and José Quintero.
Separate Tables, by Terence Rattigan. Produced by The Producers Theatre and Hecht-Lancaster.
The Potting Shed, by Graham Greene. Produced by Carmen Capalbo and Stanley Chase.
The Waltz of the Toreadors, by Jean Anouilh, translated by Lucienne Hill. Produced by The Producers Theatre and Robert Whitehead.

OUTSTANDING MUSICAL
Bells Are Ringing. Music by Jule Styne; book and lyrics by Betty Comden and Adolph Green. Produced by The Theatre Guild.
Candide. Music by Leonard Bernstein; lyrics by Richard Wilbur; book by Lillian Hellman. Produced by Ethel Linder Reiner, in association with Lester Osterman, Jr.
My Fair Lady. Music by Frederick Loewe; lyrics and book by Alan Jay Lerner. Produced by Herman Levin.
The Most Happy Fella. Music, lyrics, and book by Frank Loesser. Produced by Kermit Bloomgarden and Lynn Loesser.

Outstanding Director
Joseph Anthony, *A Clearing in the Woods* and *The Most Happy Fella*
Harold Clurman, *The Waltz of the Toreadors*
Peter Glenville, *Separate Tables*
Moss Hart, *My Fair Lady*
José Quintero, *Long Day's Journey into Night*

Outstanding Choreographer
Hanya Holm, *My Fair Lady*
Michael Kidd, *Li'l Abner*
Dania Krupska, *The Most Happy Fella*
Jerome Robbins and Bob Fosse, *Bells Are Ringing*

Outstanding Conductor and Musical Director
Franz Allers, *My Fair Lady*
Herbert Greene, *The Most Happy Fella*
Samuel Krachmalnick, *Candide*

Outstanding Scenic Designer
Boris Aronson, *A Hole in the Head* and *Small War on Murray Hill*
Ben Edwards, *The Waltz of the Toreadors*
George Jenkins, *The Happiest Millionaire* and *Too Late the Phalarope*
Donald Oenslager, *Major Barbara*
Oliver Smith, *A Clearing in the Woods, Candide, Auntie Mame, My Fair Lady,* and *A Visit to a Small Planet*

Outstanding Costume Designer
Cecil Beaton, *Little Glass Clock* and *My Fair Lady*
Alvin Colt, *Li'l Abner* and *The Sleeping Prince*
Dorothy Jeakins, *Major Barbara* and *Too Late the Phalarope*
Irene Sharaff, *Candide, Happy Hunting, Shangri La,* and *Small War on Murray Hill*

Outstanding Technician
Thomas Fitzgerald, sound man, *Long Day's Journey into Night*
Joseph Harbach, carpenter, *Auntie Mame*

Howard McDonald, carpenter, *Major Barbara* (posthumous)

Special Awards
American Shakespeare Festival, Stratford, Connecticut
Jean-Louis Barrault, French Repertory
Robert Russell Bennett
William Hammerstein
Paul Shyre

In some cases (e.g., Outstanding Scenic Designer), an individual was *nominated* for his or her work on several productions but actually received the award for one. In these instances, only the award-winning play appears in bold-face type.

| 12th ANNUAL TONY AWARDS |
| PRESENTED APRIL 13, 1958 |
| WALDORF-ASTORIA |

Outstanding Dramatic Actress
Helen Hayes, *Time Remembered*
Wendy Hiller, *A Moon for the Misbegotten*
Eugenie Leontovich, *The Cave Dwellers*
Siobhan McKenna, *The Rope Dancers*
Jo Van Fleet, *Look Homeward, Angel*

Outstanding Dramatic Actor
Ralph Bellamy, *Sunrise at Campobello*
Richard Burton, *Time Remembered*

Laurence Olivier in The Entertainer *(1958)*

Hugh Griffith, *Look Homeward, Angel*
Laurence Olivier, *The Entertainer*
Anthony Perkins, *Look Homeward, Angel*
Peter Ustinov, *Romanoff and Juliet*
Emlyn Williams, *A Boy Growing Up*

Outstanding Supporting or Featured Dramatic Actress
Anne Bancroft, *Two for the Seesaw*
Brenda de Banzie, *The Entertainer*
Joan Blondell, *The Rope Dancers*
Mary Fickett, *Sunrise at Campobello*
Eileen Heckart, *The Dark at the Top of the Stairs*
Joan Plowright, *The Entertainer*

Outstanding Supporting or Featured Dramatic Actor
Sig Arno, *Time Remembered*
Theodore Bikel, *The Rope Dancers*
Pat Hingle, *The Dark at the Top of the Stairs*
Henry Jones, *Sunrise at Campobello*
George Relph, *The Entertainer*

Outstanding Musical Actress
Lena Horne, *Jamaica*
Beatrice Lillie, *Ziegfeld Follies*
Thelma Ritter, *New Girl in Town*
Gwen Verdon, *New Girl in Town* [First tie in Tony Award history.]

Outstanding Musical Actor
Eddie Foy, *Rumple*
Ricardo Montalban, *Jamaica*
Tony Randall, *Oh, Captain!*
Robert Preston, *The Music Man*

Outstanding Supporting or Featured Musical Actress
Barbara Cook, *The Music Man*
Susan Johnson, *Oh, Captain!*
Carol Lawrence, *West Side Story*
Jacquelyn McKeever, *Oh, Captain!*
Josephine Premice, *Jamaica*

Outstanding Supporting or Featured Musical Actor
David Burns, *The Music Man*
Ossie Davis, *Jamaica*

Cameron Prud'homme, *New Girl in Town*
Iggie Wolfington, *The Music Man*

Robert Preston in The Music Man *(1958)*

OUTSTANDING PLAY
The Dark at the Top of the Stairs, by William Inge. Produced by Saint-Subber and Elia Kazan.
Look Back in Anger, by John Osborne. Produced by David Merrick.
Look Homeward, Angel, by Ketti Frings. Produced by Kermit Bloomgarden and Theatre 200, Inc.
Romanoff and Juliet, by Peter Ustinov. Produced by David Merrick.
Sunrise at Campobello, by Dore Schary. Produced by Lawrence Langer, Theresa Helburn, Armina Marshall, and Dore Schary.
The Rope Dancers, by Morton Wishengrad. Produced by The Playwrights Company and Gilbert Miller.

Time Remembered, by Jean Anouilh. English version by Patricia Moyes. Produced by The Playwrights Company, in association with Milton Sperling.
Two for the Seesaw, by William Gibson. Produced by Fred Coe.

OUTSTANDING MUSICAL
Jamaica. Music by Harold Arlen; lyrics by E.Y. Harburg; book by E.Y. Harburg and Fred Saidy. Produced by David Merrick.
The Music Man. Music and lyrics by Meredith Willson; book by Meredith Willson and Franklin Lacey. Produced by Kermit Bloomgarden and Herbert Greene, in association with Frank Productions.
New Girl in Town. Music and lyrics by Bob Merrill; book by George Abbott. Produced by Robert Griffiths and Harold S. Prince.
Oh, Captain! Music and lyrics by Jay Livingston and Ray Evans; book by Al Morgan and José Ferrer. Produced by Howard Merrill and Theatre Corporation of America.
West Side Story. Music by Leonard Bernstein; lyrics by Stephen Sondheim; book by Arthur Laurents. Produced by Robert Griffiths and Harold S. Prince, by arrangement with Roger L. Stevens.

OUTSTANDING DIRECTOR
Morton Da Costa, *The Music Man*
Vincent J. Donehue, *Sunrise at Campobello*
Peter Hall, *The Rope Dancers*
George Roy Hill, *Look Homeward, Angel*
Elia Kazan, *The Dark at the Top of the Stairs*
Arthur Penn, *Two for the Seesaw*

OUTSTANDING CHOREOGRAPHER
Bob Fosse, *New Girl in Town*
Jerome Robbins, *West Side Story*
Onna White, *The Music Man*

OUTSTANDING MUSICAL DIRECTOR
Herbert Green, *The Music Man*
Max Goberman, *West Side Story*

OUTSTANDING SCENIC DESIGNER
Boris Aronson, *Orpheus Descending, A Hole in the Head,* and *The Rope Dancers*
Ben Edwards, *The Dark at the Top of the Stairs*
Peter Larkin, *Compulsion, Good as Gold, Miss Isobel,* and *Blue Denim*
Jo Mielziner, *Look Homeward, Angel, Miss Lonelyhearts, The Square Root of Wonderful, Oh, Captain!,* and *The Day the Money Stopped*
Oliver Smith, *Brigadoon, Carousel, Jamaica, Nude with Violin, Time Remembered,* and ***West Side Story***

OUTSTANDING COSTUME DESIGNER
Lucinda Ballard, *Orpheus Descending*
Motley, *Look Back in Anger, Look Homeward, Angel, Shinbone Alley, The Country Wife,* and ***The First Gentleman***
Irene Sharaff, *West Side Story*
Miles White, *Jamaica, Time Remembered,* and *Oh Captain!*

OUTSTANDING STAGE TECHNICIAN
Sammy Knapp, *The Music Man*
Harry Romar, *Time Remembered*

SPECIAL AWARD
Circle in the Square
New York Shakespeare Festival, for presenting free performances in Central Park and the Hecksher Theater.
Phoenix Theatre

In some cases (e.g., Outstanding Costume Designer), an individual was *nominated* for his or her work on several productions but actually received the award for one. In these instances, only the award-winning play appears in bold-face type.

The producers of Outstanding Musical and Outstanding Play received scrolls, not medallions.

Mrs. Martin Beck received a special plaque for fifteen years of untiring dedication to the American Theatre Wing, which she served as treasurer, secretary, and chairman of the board of directors. Presented by Elaine Perry, daughter of Antoinette Perry.

Esther Hawley, American Theatre Wing executive secretary, also received a plaque for counsel and courtesy well above the call of duty, in every department including hospital services and community plays.

This year the Special Awards category included nominees as well as winners (indicated by boldface type).

13th ANNUAL TONY AWARDS
PRESENTED APRIL 12, 1959
WALDORF-ASTORIA

OUTSTANDING ACTRESS, DRAMATIC STAR
Gertrude Berg, *A Majority of One*
Claudette Colbert, *The Marriage-Go-Round*
Lynn Fontanne, *The Visit*
Kim Stanley, *A Touch of the Poet*
Maureen Stapleton, *The Cold Wind and the Warm*

OUTSTANDING ACTOR, DRAMATIC STAR
Cedric Hardwicke, *A Majority of One*
Alfred Lunt, *The Visit*
Christopher Plummer, *J.B.*
Cyril Ritchard, *The Pleasure of His Company*
Jason Robards, Jr., *The Disenchanted*
Robert Stephens, *Epitaph for George Dillon*

OUTSTANDING ACTRESS, DRAMATIC FEATURED OR SUPPORTING
Maureen Delany, *God and Kate Murphy*
Dolores Hart, *The Pleasure of His Company*
Julie Newmar, *The Marriage-Go-Round*
Nan Martin, *J.B.*
Bertice Reading, *Requiem for a Nun*

OUTSTANDING ACTOR, DRAMATIC FEATURED OR SUPPORTING
Marc Connelly, *Tall Story*
George Grizzard, *The Disenchanted*
Walter Matthau, *Once More, With Feeling*
Robert Morse, *Say Darling*
Charlie Ruggles, *The Pleasure of His Company*
George Scott, *Comes a Day*

OUTSTANDING ACTRESS, MUSICAL STAR
Miyoshi Umeki, *Flower Drum Song*
Gwen Verdon, *Redhead*

OUTSTANDING ACTOR, MUSICAL STAR
Larry Blyden, *Flower Drum Song*
Richard Kiley, *Redhead*

OUTSTANDING ACTRESS, MUSICAL FEATURED OR SUPPORTING
Julienne Marie, *Whoop-Up*
Pat Stanley, *Goldilocks*
Cast of *La Plume de Ma Tante* (Pamela Austin, Colette Brosset, Yvonne Constant, Genevieve Coulombel, Nicole Parent)

OUTSTANDING SUPPORTING OR FEATURED MUSICAL ACTOR
Russell Nype, *Goldilocks*
Leonard Stone, *Redhead*
Cast of *La Plume de Ma Tante* (Roger Caccia, Robert Dhéry, Michael Kent, Jean Lefevre, Jacques Legras, Michel Modo, Pierre Olaf, Ross Parker, Henri Pennec)

PLAY
A Touch of the Poet, by Eugene O'Neill. Produced by The Producers Theatre, Robert Whitehead, and Roger L. Stevens.
Epitaph for George Dillon, by John Osborne and Anthony Creighton. Produced by David Merrick and Joshua Logan.
J.B., by Archibald MacLeish. Produced by Alfred de Liagre, Jr.

The Disenchanted, by Budd Schulberg and Harvey Briet. Produced by William Darrid and Eleanor Saidenberg.
The Visit, by Friedrich Duerrenmatt, adapted by Maurice Valency. Produced by The Producers Theatre.

MUSICAL PLAY
Flower Drum Song. Music by Richard Rodgers; lyrics by Oscar Hammerstein II; book by Oscar Hammerstein II and Joseph Fields. Produced by Joseph Fields, Oscar Hammerstein II, and Richard Rodgers.
La Plume de Ma Tante. Music by Gerard Calvi; English lyrics by Ross Parker; written and devised by Robert Dhéry. David Merrick and Joseph Kipness present the Jack Hylton Production.
Redhead. Music by Albert Hague; lyrics by Dorothy Fields; book by Herb Fields, Dorothy Fields, Sidney Sheldon, and David Shaw. Produced by Robert Fryer and Lawrence Carr.

DIRECTOR
Peter Brook, *The Visit*
Robert Dhéry, *La Plume de Ma Tante*
William Gaskill, *Epitaph for George Dillon*
Peter Glenville, *Rashomon*
Elia Kazan, *J.B.*
Cyril Ritchard, *The Pleasure of His Company*
Dore Schary, *A Majority of One*

CHOREOGRAPHER
Agnes De Mille, *Goldilocks*
Bob Fosse, *Redhead*
Carol Haney, *Flower Drum Song*
Onna White, *Whoop-Up*

MUSICAL DIRECTOR
Jay Blackston, *Redhead*
Salvatore Dell'Isola, *Flower Drum Song*
Lehman Engel, *Goldilocks*
Gershon Kingsley, *La Plume de Ma Tante*

SCENIC DESIGNER
Boris Aronson, *J.B.*
Ballou, *The Legend of Lizzie*
Ben Edwards, *Jane Eyre*
Oliver Messel, *Rashomon*
Donald Oenslager, *A Majority of One*
Ted Otto, *The Visit*

COSTUME DESIGNER
Castillo, *Goldilocks*
Dorothy Jeakins, *The World of Suzie Wong*
Oliver Messel, *Rashomon*
Irene Sharaff, *Flower Drum Song*
Rouben Ter-Arutunian, *Redhead*

STAGE TECHNICIAN
Thomas Fitzgerald, *Who Was That Lady I Saw You With?*
Edward Flynn, *The Most Happy Fella*
Sam Knapp, *The Music Man*

SPECIAL AWARDS
John Gielgud, for contribution to theatre for his extraordinary insight into the writings of Shakespeare as demonstrated in his one-man play, *Ages of Man*.

Howard Lindsay and Russell Crouse, for a collaboration that lasted longer than Gilbert and Sullivan.
La Plume de Ma Tante (Pamela Austin, Colette Brosset, Roger Caccia, Yvonne Constant, Genevieve Coulombel, Robert Dhéry, Michael Kent, Jean Lefevre, Jacques Legras, Michel Modo, Pierre Olaf, Nicole Parent, Ross Parker, Henri Pennec), for contribution to the theatre.

Before the awards ceremony Helen Menken, American Theatre Wing President, presented an honorary medal to Dorothy Sands, an acting teacher at the Wing's school, for her devotion to the Wing's work.

14th ANNUAL TONY AWARDS
PRESENTED APRIL 24, 1960
ASTOR HOTEL

ACTRESS—DRAMATIC STAR
Anne Bancroft, *The Miracle Worker*
Margaret Leighton, *Much Ado About Nothing*
Claudia McNeil, *A Raisin in the Sun*
Geraldine Page, *Sweet Bird of Youth*
Maureen Stapleton, *Toys in the Attic*
Irene Worth, *Toys in the Attic*

ACTOR—DRAMATIC STAR
Melvyn Douglas, *The Best Man*
Jason Robards, Jr., *Toys in the Attic*
Sidney Poitier, *A Raisin in the Sun*
George C. Scott, *The Andersonville Trial*
Lee Tracy, *The Best Man*

ACTRESS—DRAMATIC FEATURED OR SUPPORTING
Leora Dana, *The Best Man*
Jane Fonda. *There Was a Little Girl*
Sarah Marshall, *Goodbye, Charlie*
Juliet Mills, *Five Finger Exercise*
Anne Revere, *Toys in the Attic*

ACTOR—DRAMATIC FEATURED OR SUPPORTING
Warren Beatty, *A Loss of Roses*
Harry Guardino, *One More River*
Roddy McDowell, *The Fighting Cock*
Rip Torn, *Sweet Bird of Youth*
Lawrence Winters, *The Long Dream*

ACTRESS—MUSICAL STAR
Carol Burnett, *Once Upon a Mattress*
Dolores Gray, *Destry Rides Again*
Eileen Herlie, *Take Me Along*
Mary Martin, *The Sound of Music*
Ethel Merman, *Gypsy*

ACTOR—MUSICAL STAR
Jackie Gleason, *Take Me Along*
Andy Griffith, *Destry Rides Again*
Robert Morse, *Take Me Along*
Anthony Perkins, *Greenwillow*
Walter Pidgeon, *Take Me Along*

ACTRESS—MUSICAL FEATURED
Sandra Church, *Gypsy*
Pert Kelton, *Greenwillow*
Patricia Neway, *The Sound of Music*
Lauri Peters and the Children [Kathy Dunn, Evanna Lien, Mary Susan Locke, Marilyn Robers, William Snowden, Joseph Stewart], *The Sound of Music*

ACTOR—MUSICAL FEATURED
Theodore Bikel, *The Sound of Music*
Tom Bosley, *Fiorello!*
Howard Da Silva, *Fiorello!*
Kurt Kaszner, *The Sound of Music*
Jack Klugman, *Gypsy*

PLAY
A Raisin in the Sun, by Lorraine Hansberry. Produced by Philip Rose and David J. Cogan.
The Best Man, by Gore Vidal. Produced by The Playwrights Company.
***The Miracle Worker*, by William Gibson. Produced by Fred Coe.**
The Tenth Man, by Paddy Chayefsky. Produced by Saint-Subber and Arthur Cantor.

Mary Martin in The Sound of Music *(1959)*

Toys in the Attic, by Lillian Hellman. Produced by Kermit Bloomgarden.

MUSICAL PLAY

Fiorello! Music by Jerry Bock; lyrics by Sheldon Harnick; book by Jerome Weidman and George Abbott. Produced by Robert E. Griffith and Harold S. Prince.

Gypsy. Music by Jule Styne; lyrics by Stephen Sondheim; book by Arthur Laurents. Produced by David Merrick and Leland Hayward.

Once Upon a Mattress. Music by Mary Rodgers; lyrics by Marshall Barer; book by Jay Thompson, Marshall Barer, and Dean Fuller. Produced by T. Edward Hambleton, Norris Houghton, William Eckart, and Jean Eckart.

The Sound of Music. Music by Richard Rodgers; lyrics by Oscar Hammerstein II; book by Howard Lindsay and Russell Crouse. Produced by Leland Hayward, Richard Halliday, Richard Rodgers, and Oscar Hammerstein II.

Take Me Along. Music and lyrics by Bob Merrill; book by Joseph Stein and Robert Russell. Produced by David Merrick.

DIRECTOR—PLAY

Joseph Anthony, *The Best Man*
Tyrone Guthrie, *The Tenth Man*
Elia Kazan, *Sweet Bird of Youth*
Arthur Penn, *The Miracle Worker*
Lloyd Richards, *Raisin in the Sun*

DIRECTOR—MUSICAL

George Abbott, *Fiorello!*
Vincent J. Donehue, *The Sound of Music*
Peter Glenville, *Take Me Along*
Michael Kidd, *Destry Rides Again*
Jerome Robbins, *Gypsy*

CHOREOGRAPHER

Peter Gennaro, *Fiorello!*
Michael Kidd, *Destry Rides Again*
Joe Layton, *Greenwillow*
Lee Scott, *Happy Town*
Onna White, *Take Me Along*

MUSICAL DIRECTOR-CONDUCTOR

Abba Bogin, *Greenwillow*
Frederick Dvonch, *The Sound of Music*
Lehman Engel, *Take Me Along*
Hal Hastings, *Fiorello!*
Milton Rosenstock, *Gypsy*

SCENIC DESIGNER—MUSICAL

Cecil Beaton, *Saratoga*
William Eckart and Jean Eckart, *Fiorello!*
Peter Larkin, *Greenwillow*
Jo Mielziner, *Gypsy*
Oliver Smith, *The Sound of Music*

SCENIC DESIGNER—PLAY

Will Steven Armstrong, *Caligula*
Howard Bay, *Toys in the Attic*
David Hays, *The Tenth Man*
George Jenkins, *The Miracle Worker*
Jo Mielziner, *The Best Man*

COSTUME DESIGNER

Cecil Beaton, *Saratoga*
Alvin Colt, *Greenwillow*
Raoul Pène du Bois, *Gypsy*
Miles White, *Take Me Along*

STAGE TECHNICIAN

Al Alloy, chief electrician, *Take Me Along*
James Orr, chief electrician, *Greenwillow*
John Walters, chief carpenter, ***The Miracle Worker***

SPECIAL AWARDS

John D. Rockefeller 3rd, for vision and leadership in creating the Lincoln Center, a landmark of theatre encompassing the performing arts.
Burgess Meredith and James Thurber, for *A Thurber Carnival.*

For the first time two awards were given for direction, one for musical productions and the other for dramatic productions; and two awards were given for scenic design, one for musical productions and the other for dramatic productions.

DRAMATIC ACTRESS
Tallulah Bankhead, *Midgie Purvis*
Barbara Baxley, *Period of Adjustment*
Barbara Bel Geddes, *Mary, Mary*
Joan Plowright, *A Taste of Honey*

DRAMATIC ACTOR
Hume Cronyn, *Big Fish, Little Fish*
Sam Levene, *The Devil's Advocate*
Zero Mostel, *Rhinoceros*
Anthony Quinn, *Becket*

DRAMATIC ACTRESS, SUPPORTING OR FEATURED
Colleen Dewhurst, *All the Way Home*
Eileen Heckart, *Invitation to a March*
Tresa Hughes, *The Devil's Advocate*
Rosemary Murphy, *Period of Adjustment*

DRAMATIC ACTOR, SUPPORTING OR FEATURED
Philip Bosco, *The Rape of the Belt*
Eduardo Ciannelli, *The Devil's Advocate*
Martin Gabel, *Big Fish, Little Fish*
George Grizzard, *Big Fish, Little Fish*

MUSICAL ACTRESS
Julie Andrews, *Camelot*
Carol Channing, *Show Girl*
Elizabeth Seal, *Irma La Douce*
Nancy Walker, *Do Re Mi*

MUSICAL ACTOR
Richard Burton, *Camelot*
Maurice Evans, *Tenderloin*
Phil Silvers, *Do Re Mi*

MUSICAL ACTRESS, SUPPORTING OR FEATURED
Nancy Dussault, *Do Re Mi*
Tammy Grimes, *The Unsinkable Molly Brown*
Chita Rivera, *Bye, Bye, Birdie*

Tammy Grimes in The Unsinkable Molly Brown *(1961)*

MUSICAL ACTOR, SUPPORTING OR FEATURED
Dick Gautier, *Bye, Bye, Birdie*
Ron Husmann, *Tenderloin*
Clive Revill, *Irma La Douce*
Dick Van Dyke, *Bye, Bye Birdie*

PLAY
All the Way Home, by Tad Mosel. Produced by Fred Coe, in association with Arthur Cantor.
Becket, by Jean Anouilh, translated by Lucienne Hill. Produced by David Merrick.
The Devil's Advocate, by Dore Schary. Produced by Dore Schary.
The Hostage, by Brendan Behan. Produced by S. Field and Caroline Burke Swann.

MUSICAL PLAY
Bye, Bye Birdie. Music by Charles Strouse; lyrics by Lee Adams; book by Michael Stewart. Produced by Edward Padula, in association with L. Slade Brown.
Do Re Mi. Music by Jule Styne; lyrics by Betty Comden and Adolph Green;

book by Garson Kanin. Produced by David Merrick.
Irma La Douce. Music by Marguerite Monnot; book and lyrics by Alexandre Breffort; English book and lyrics by Julian More, David Heneker, and Monty Norman. Produced by David Merrick, in association with Donald Albery and H. M. Tennent, Ltd.

DIRECTOR, PLAY
Joseph Anthony, *Rhinoceros*
Sir John Gielgud, *Big Fish, Little Fish*
Joan Littlewood, *The Hostage*
Arthur Penn, *All the Way Home*

DIRECTOR, MUSICAL
Peter Brook, *Irma La Douce*
Gower Champion, *Bye, Bye Birdie*
Garson Kanin, *Do Re Mi*

CHOREOGRAPHER
Gower Champion, *Bye, Bye Birdie*
Onna White, *Irma La Douce*

CONDUCTOR AND MUSICAL DIRECTOR
Franz Allers, *Camelot*
Pembroke Davenport, *13 Daughters*
Elliot Lawrence, *Bye, Bye Birdie*
Stanley Lebowsky, *Irma La Douce*

SCENIC DESIGNER, DRAMA
Roger Furse, *Duel of Angels*
David Hays, *All the Way Home*
Jo Mielziner, *The Devil's Advocate*
Oliver Smith, *Becket*
Rouben Ter-Arutunian, *Advise and Consent*

SCENIC DESIGNER, MUSICAL
George Jenkins, *13 Daughters*
Robert Randolph, *Bye, Bye Birdie*
Oliver Smith, *Camelot*

COSTUME DESIGNER, DRAMA
Theoni V. Aldredge, *The Devil's Advocate*
Motley, *Becket*
Raymond Sovey, *All the Way Home*

COSTUME DESIGNER, MUSICAL
Cecil Beaton, *Tenderloin*
Adrian and Tony Duquette, *Camelot*
Rolf Gerard, *Irma La Douce*

STAGE TECHNICIAN
Teddy Van Bemmel, *Becket*

SPECIAL AWARDS
David Merrick, in recognition of a fabulous production record over the past seven years.

The Theatre Guild, for organizing the first repertory to go abroad for the State Department. [The Theatre Guild American Repertory Company presented *The Miracle Worker, The Skin of Our Teeth,* and *The Glass Menagerie.*

For the second year, there were two awards for direction and for scenic design—one each for musical and dramatic productions.

For the first year, there were two awards for costume design—one for musical productions and one for dramatic productions.

<table>
<tr><td>

16th ANNUAL TONY AWARDS
PRESENTED APRIL 29, 1962
WALDORF-ASTORIA

</td></tr>
</table>

ACTRESS, DRAMATIC STAR
Gladys Cooper, *A Passage to India*
Colleen Dewhurst, *Great Day in the Morning*
Margaret Leighton, *Night of the Iguana*
Kim Stanley, *A Far Country*

ACTOR, DRAMATIC STAR
Fredric March, *Gideon*
John Mills, *Ross*
Donald Pleasence, *The Caretaker*
Paul Scofield, *A Man for All Seasons*

ACTRESS, DRAMATIC FEATURED OR SUPPORTING
Elizabeth Ashley, *Take Her, She's Mine*

Zohra Lampert, *Look We've Come Through*
Janet Margolin, *Daughter of Silence*
Pat Stanley, *Sunday in New York*

ACTOR, DRAMATIC FEATURED OR SUPPORTING
Godfrey M. Cambridge, *Purlie Victorious*
Joseph Campanella, *A Gift of Time*
Walter Matthau, *A Shot in the Dark*
Paul Sparer, *Ross*

ACTRESS, MUSICAL STAR
Anna Maria Alberghetti, *Carnival*
Diahann Carroll, *No Strings*
Molly Picon, *Milk and Honey*
Elaine Stritch, *Sail Away*

ACTOR, MUSICAL STAR
Ray Bolger, *All American*
Alfred Drake, *Kean*
Richard Kiley, *No Strings*
Robert Morse, *How to Succeed in Business Without Really Trying*

ACTRESS, MUSICAL FEATURED OR SUPPORTING
Elizabeth Allen, *The Gay Life*
Barbara Harris, *From the Second City*
Phyllis Newman, *Subways Are for Sleeping*
Barbra Streisand, *I Can Get It for You Wholesale*

ACTOR, MUSICAL FEATURED OR SUPPORTING
Orson Bean, *Subways Are for Sleeping*
Severn Darden, *From the Second City*
Pierre Olaf, *Carnival*
Charles Nelson Reilly, *How to Succeed in Business Without Really Trying*

OUTSTANDING PLAY
A Man for All Seasons, by Robert Bolt. Produced by Robert Whitehead and Roger L. Stevens.
Gideon, by Paddy Chayefsky. Produced by Fred Coe and Arthur Cantor.

The Caretaker, by Harold Pinter. Produced by Roger L. Stevens, Frederick Brisson, and Gilbert Miller.

Night of the Iguana, by Tennessee Williams. Produced by Charles Bowden and Viola Rubber.

OUTSTANDING DRAMATIC PRODUCER
Charles Bowden and Viola Rubber, *Night of the Iguana*
Fred Coe and Arthur Cantor, *Gideon*
David Merrick, *Ross*
Robert Whitehead and **Roger L. Stevens, *A Man for All Seasons***

OUTSTANDING MUSICAL
Carnival. Music and lyrics by Bob Merrill; book by Michael Stewart and Helen Deutsch. Produced by David Merrick.
How to Succeed in Business Without Really Trying. Music and lyrics by Frank Loesser; book by Abe Burrows, Jack Weinstock, and Willie Gilbert. Produced by Cy Feuer and Ernest Martin.
Milk and Honey. Music and lyrics by Jerry Herman; book by Don Appell. Produced by Gerald Oestreicher.
No Strings. Music and lyrics by Richard Rodgers; book by Samuel Taylor. Produced by Richard Rodgers, in association with Samuel Taylor.

OUTSTANDING COMPOSER
Richard Adler, *Kwamina*
Jerry Herman, *Milk and Honey*
Frank Loesser, *How to Succeed in Business Without Really Trying*
Richard Rodgers, *No Strings*

AUTHOR MUSICAL PLAY
Abe Burrows, Jack Weinstock, and **Willie Gilbert, *How to Succeed in Business Without Really Trying***
Michael Stewart and Helen Deutsch, *Carnival*

OUTSTANDING MUSICAL PRODUCER
Helen Bonfils, Haila Stoddard, and Charles Russell, *Sail Away*
Cy Feuer and **Ernest Martin, *How to Succeed in Business Without Really Trying***
David Merrick, *Carnival*
Gerald Oestreicher, *Milk and Honey*

OUTSTANDING DRAMATIC DIRECTOR
Tyrone Guthrie, *Gideon*
Donald McWhinnie, *The Caretaker*
José Quintero, *Great Day in the Morning*
Noel Willman, *A Man for All Seasons*

OUTSTANDING DIRECTOR OF A MUSICAL
Abe Burrows, *How to Succeed in Business Without Really Trying*

Gower Champion, *Carnival*
Joe Layton, *No Strings*
Joshua Logan, *All American*

OUTSTANDING CONDUCTOR AND MUSICAL DIRECTOR
Pembroke Davenport, *Kean*
Herbert Greene, *The Gay Life*
Elliot Lawrence, *How to Succeed in Business Without Really Trying*
Peter Matz, *No Strings*

OUTSTANDING CHOREOGRAPHER
Agnes De Mille, *Kwamina*
Michael Kidd, *Subways Are for Sleeping*
Dania Krupska, *The Happiest Girl in the World*
Joe Layton, *No Strings*

OUTSTANDING SCENIC DESIGNER
Will Steven Armstrong, *Carnival*
David Hays, *No Strings*
Oliver Smith, *The Gay Life*
Rouben Ter-Arutunian, *A Passage to India*

OUTSTANDING COSTUME DESIGNER
Lucinda Ballard, *The Gay Life*
Donald Brooks, *No Strings*
Motley, *Kwamina*
Miles White, *Milk and Honey*

OUTSTANDING STAGE TECHNICIAN
Al Alloy, *Ross*
Michael Burns, *A Man for All Seasons*

SPECIAL AWARDS
Brooks Atkinson, retired drama critic of the *New York Times.*
Franco Zeffirelli, for designs and direction of the Old Vic's *Romeo and Juliet*
Richard Rodgers, for all he has done for young people in the theatre and "for taking the men of the orchestra out of the pit and putting them on stage" in *No Strings.*

17th ANNUAL TONY AWARDS
PRESENTED APRIL 28, 1963
AMERICANA HOTEL

ACTRESS—DRAMATIC STAR
Hermione Baddeley, *The Milk Train Doesn't Stop Here Anymore*
Uta Hagen, *Who's Afraid of Virginia Woolf?*
Margaret Leighton, *Tchin-Tchin*
Claudia McNeil, *Tiger, Tiger Burning Bright*

ACTOR—DRAMATIC STAR
Charles Boyer, *Lord Pengo*
Paul Ford, *Never Too Late*
Arthur Hill, *Who's Afraid of Virginia Woolf?*
Bert Lahr, *The Beauty Part*

DRAMATIC ACTRESS—SUPPORTING OR FEATURED
Sandy Dennis, *A Thousand Clowns*
Melinda Dillon, *Who's Afraid of Virginia Woolf?*
Alice Ghostley, *The Beauty Part*
Zohra Lampert, *Mother Courage and Her Children*

Nanette Fabray and Robert Ryan in Mr. President *(1962)*

DRAMATIC ACTOR—SUPPORTING OR FEATURED
Alan Arkin, *Enter Laughing*
Barry Gordon, *A Thousand Clowns*
Paul Rogers, *Photo Finish*
Frank Silvera, *The Lady of the Camellias*

ACTRESS—MUSICAL STAR
Georgia Brown, *Oliver!*
Nanette Fabray, *Mr. President*
Sally Ann Howes, *Brigadoon*
Vivien Leigh, *Tovarich*

ACTOR—MUSICAL STAR
Sid Caesar, *Little Me*
Zero Mostel, *A Funny Thing Happened on the Way to the Forum*
Anthony Newley, *Stop the World—I Want to Get Off*
Clive Revill, *Oliver!*

MUSICAL ACTRESS—SUPPORTING OR FEATURED
Ruth Kobart, *A Funny Thing Happened on the Way to the Forum*
Virginia Martin, *Little Me*
Anna Quayle, *Stop the World—I Want to Get Off*
Louise Troy, *Tovarich*

MUSICAL ACTOR—SUPPORTING OR FEATURED
David Burns, *A Funny Thing Happened on the Way to the Forum*
Jack Gilford, *A Funny Thing Happened on the Way to the Forum*
David Jones, *Oliver!*
Swen Swenson, *Little Me*

PLAY
A Thousand Clowns, by Herb Gardner. Produced by Fred Coe and Arthur Cantor.
Mother Courage and Her Children, by Bertolt Brecht, adapted by Eric Bentley. Produced by Cheryl Crawford and Jerome Robbins.
Tchin-Tchin, by Sidney Michaels. Produced by David Merrick.

Who's Afraid of Virginia Woolf?, by Edward Albee. Produced by Theatre 1963, Richard Barr, and Clinton Wilder.

PRODUCER—PLAY
The Actors Studio Theatre, *Strange Interlude*
Richard Barr and **Clinton Wilder, *Who's Afraid of Virginia Woolf?***
Cheryl Crawford and Jerome Robbins, *Mother Courage and Her Children*
Paul Vroom, Buff Cobb, and Burry Fredrik, *Too True to Be Good*

MUSICAL PLAY
A Funny Thing Happened on the Way to the Forum. Music and lyrics by Stephen Sondheim; book by Burt Shevelove and Larry Gelbart. Produced by Harold Prince.
Little Me. Music by Cy Coleman; lyrics by Carolyn Leigh; book by Neil Simon. Produced by Cy Feuer and Ernest Martin.

Oliver! Music, lyrics, and book by Lionel Bart. Produced by David Merrick and Donald Albery.

Stop the World—I Want to Get Off. Music, lyrics, and book by Leslie Bricusse and Anthony Newley. Produced by David Merrick, in association with Bernard Delfont.

COMPOSER AND LYRICIST—MUSICAL PLAY
Lionel Bart, *Oliver!*
Leslie Bricusse and Anthony Newley, *Stop the World—I Want to Get Off*
Cy Coleman and Carolyn Leigh, *Little Me*
Milton Shafer and Ronny Graham, *Bravo Giovanni*

AUTHOR—MUSICAL PLAY
Lionel Bart, *Oliver!*
Leslie Bricusse and Anthony Newley, *Stop the World—I Want to Get Off*
Burt Shevelove and **Larry Gelbart, *A Funny Thing Happened on the Way to the Forum***
Neil Simon, *Little Me*

PRODUCER—MUSICAL PLAY
Cy Feuer and Ernest Martin, *Little Me*
David Merrick and Donald Albery, *Oliver!*
Harold Prince, *A Funny Thing Happened on the Way to the Forum*

DIRECTOR—PLAY
George Abbott, *Never Too Late*
John Gielgud, *The School for Scandal*
Peter Glenville, *Tchin-Tchin*
Alan Schneider, *Who's Afraid of Virginia Woolf?*

DIRECTOR—MUSICAL PLAY
George Abbott, *A Funny Thing Happened on the Way to the Forum*
Peter Coe, *Oliver!*
John Fearnley, *Brigadoon*
Cy Feuer and Bob Fosse, *Little Me*

MUSICAL DIRECTOR-CONDUCTOR
Jay Blackton, *Mr. President*

Anton Coppola, *Bravo Giovanni*
Donald Pippin, *Oliver!*
Julius Rudel, *Brigadoon*

CHOREOGRAPHER
Bob Fosse, *Little Me*
Carol Haney, *Bravo Giovanni*

SCENIC DESIGNER
Will Steven Armstrong, *Tchin-Tchin*
Sean Kenny, *Oliver!*
Anthony Powell, *The School for Scandal*
Franco Zeffirelli, *The Lady of the Camellias*

COSTUME DESIGNER
Marcel Escoffier, *The Lady of the Camellias*
Robert Fletcher, *Little Me*
Motley, *Mother Courage and Her Children*
Anthony Powell, *The School for Scandal*

STAGE TECHNICIAN
Solly Pernick, *Mr. President*
Milton Smith, *Beyond the Fringe*

SPECIAL AWARDS
Irving Berlin, for his distinguished contribution to the musical theatre for these many years.
W. McNeil Lowry, on behalf of the Ford Foundation, for his and their distinguished support of the American Theatre.
Alan Bennett, Peter Cook, Jonathan Miller, and Dudley Moore, for *Beyond the Fringe,* for their brilliance which has shattered all the old concepts of comedy.

18th ANNUAL TONY AWARDS
PRESENTED MAY 24, 1964
NEW YORK HILTON

ACTRESS—DRAMATIC STAR
Elizabeth Ashley, *Barefoot in the Park*
Sandy Dennis, *Any Wednesday*

Richard Burton and Eileen Herlie in Hamlet *(1964)*

Colleen Dewhurst, *The Ballad of the Sad Cafe*
Julie Harris, *Marathon '33*

ACTOR—DRAMATIC STAR
Richard Burton, *Hamlet*
Albert Finney, *Luther*
Alec Guinness, *Dylan*
Jason Robards, Jr., *After the Fall*

DRAMATIC ACTRESS—SUPPORTING OR FEATURED
Barbara Loden, *After the Fall*
Rosemary Murphy, *Any Wednesday*
Kate Reid, *Dylan*
Diana Sands, *Blues for Mister Charlie*

DRAMATIC ACTOR—SUPPORTING OR FEATURED
Lee Allen, *Marathon '33*
Hume Cronyn, *Hamlet*
Michael Dunn, *The Ballad of the Sad Cafe*
Larry Gates, *A Case of Libel*

ACTRESS—MUSICAL STAR
Carol Channing, *Hello, Dolly!*

Beatrice Lillie, *High Spirits*
Barbra Streisand, *Funny Girl*
Inga Swenson, *110 in the Shade*

ACTOR—MUSICAL STAR
Sydney Chaplin, *Funny Girl*
Bob Fosse, *Pal Joey*
Bert Lahr, *Foxy*
Steve Lawrence, *What Makes Sammy Run?*

MUSICAL ACTRESS—SUPPORTING OR FEATURED
Julienne Marie, *Foxy*
Kay Medford, *Funny Girl*
Tessie O'Shea, *The Girl Who Came to Supper*
Louise Troy, *High Spirits*

MUSICAL ACTOR—SUPPORTING OR FEATURED
Jack Cassidy, *She Loves Me*
Will Geer, *110 in the Shade*
Danny Meehan, *Funny Girl*
Charles Nelson Reilly, *Hello, Dolly!*

PLAY
The Ballad of the Sad Cafe, by Edward Albee. Produced by Lewis Allen and Ben Edwards.

Daniel Massey and Barbara Cook in
She Loves Me *(1964)*

Barefoot in the Park, by Neil Simon. Produced by Saint-Subber.
Dylan, by Sidney Michaels. Produced by George W. George and Frank Granat.
Luther, by John Osborne. Produced by David Merrick.

PRODUCER—PLAY
Lewis Allen and Ben Edwards, *The Ballad of the Sad Cafe*
George W. George and Frank Granat, *Dylan*
Saint-Subber, *Barefoot in the Park*
Herman Shumlin, *The Deputy*

MUSICAL
Funny Girl. Music by Jule Styne; lyrics by Bob Merrill; book by Isobel Lennert. Produced by Ray Stark.
Hello, Dolly! Music and lyrics by Jerry Herman; book by Michael Stewart. Produced by David Merrick.
High Spirits. Music, lyrics, and book by Hugh Martin and Timothy Gray. Produced by Lester Osterman, Robert Fletcher, and Richard Horner.
She Loves Me. Music by Jerry Bock; lyrics by Sheldon Harnick; book by Joe Masteroff. Produced by Harold Prince, in association with Lawrence N. Kasha and Philip C. McKenna.

COMPOSER AND LYRICIST—MUSICAL PLAY
Jerry Herman, *Hello, Dolly!*
Hugh Martin and Timothy Gray, *High Spirits*
Harvey Schmidt and Tom Jones, *110 in the Shade*
Jule Styne and Bob Merrill, *Funny Girl*

AUTHOR—MUSICAL
Noel Coward and Harry Kurnitz, *The Girl Who Came to Supper*
Hugh Martin and Timothy Gray, *High Spirits*
Joe Masteroff, *She Loves Me*
Michael Stewart, *Hello, Dolly!*

PRODUCER—MUSICAL PLAY
City Center Light Opera Company, *West Side Story*
David Merrick, *Hello, Dolly!*
Harold Prince, *She Loves Me*
Ray Stark, *Funny Girl*

DIRECTOR—PLAY
June Havoc, *Marathon '33*
Mike Nichols, *Barefoot in the Park*
Alan Schneider, *The Ballad of the Sad Cafe*
Herman Shumlin, *The Deputy*

DIRECTOR—MUSICAL PLAY
Joseph Anthony, *110 in the Shade*
Gower Champion, *Hello, Dolly!*
Noel Coward, *High Spirits*
Harold Prince, *She Loves Me*

MUSICAL DIRECTOR-CONDUCTOR
Shepard Coleman, *Hello, Dolly!*
Lehman Engel, *What Makes Sammy Run?*
Charles Jaffe, *West Side Story*
Fred Werner, *High Spirits*

CHOREOGRAPHER
Gower Champion, *Hello, Dolly!*
Danny Daniels, *High Spirits*
Carol Haney, *Funny Girl*
Herbert Ross, *Anyone Can Whistle*

SCENIC DESIGNER
Raoul Pène du Bois, *The Student Gypsy*
Ben Edwards, *The Ballad of the Sad
　Cafe*
David Hays, *Marco Millions*
Oliver Smith, *Hello, Dolly!*

COSTUME DESIGNER
Beni Montresor, *Marco Millions*
Irene Sharaff, *The Girl Who Came to
　Supper*
Rouben Ter-Arutunian, *Arturo Ui*
Freddy Wittop, *Hello, Dolly!*

SPECIAL AWARD
Eva Le Gallienne, celebrating her 50th
　year as an actress, honored for her
　work with the National Repertory
　Theater.

19th ANNUAL TONY AWARDS
PRESENTED JUNE 13, 1965
ASTOR HOTEL

ACTRESS—DRAMATIC STAR
Marjorie Rhodes, *All in Good Time*
Beah Richards, *The Amen Corner*
Diana Sands, *The Owl and the Pussycat*
Irene Worth, *Tiny Alice*

ACTOR—DRAMATIC STAR
John Gielgud, *Tiny Alice*
Walter Matthau, *The Odd Couple*
Donald Pleasence, *Poor Bitos*
Jason Robards, *Hughie*

**ACTRESS—DRAMATIC FEATURED OR
SUPPORTING**
Rae Allen, *Traveller Without Luggage*
Alexandra Berlin, *All in Good Time*
Carolan Daniels, *Slow Dance on the
　Killing Ground*
**Alice Ghostley, *The Sign in Sidney
　Brustein's Window***

**ACTOR—DRAMATIC FEATURED OR
SUPPORTING**
Jack Albertson, *The Subject Was Roses*
Murray Hamilton, *Absence of a Cello*
Martin Sheen, *The Subject Was Roses*
Clarence Williams III, *Slow Dance on
　the Killing Ground*

ACTRESS—MUSICAL STAR
Elizabeth Allen, *Do I Hear a Waltz?*
Nancy Dussault, *Bajour*
Liza Minnelli, *Flora, the Red Menace*
Inga Swenson, *Baker Street*

ACTOR—MUSICAL STAR
Sammy Davis, *Golden Boy*
Zero Mostel, *Fiddler on the Roof*
Cyril Ritchard, *The Roar of the Grease-
　paint—The Smell of the Crowd*
Tommy Steele, *Half a Sixpence*

**ACTRESS—MUSICAL FEATURED OR
SUPPORTING**
Maria Karnilova, *Fiddler on the Roof*
Luba Lisa, *I Had a Ball*

Carrie Nye, *Half a Sixpence*
Barabara Windsor, *Oh What a Lovely
　War*

**ACTOR—MUSICAL FEATURED OR
SUPPORTING**
Jack Cassidy, *Fade Out—Fade In*
James Grout, *Half a Sixpence*
Jerry Orbach, *Guys and Dolls*
Victor Spinetti, *Oh What a Lovely War*

PLAY
Luv, by Murray Schisgal. Produced by
　Claire Nichtern.
The Odd Couple, by Neil Simon. Pro-
　duced by Saint-Subber.
***The Subject Was Roses,* by Frank Gilroy.
　Produced by Edgar Lansbury.**
Tiny Alice, by Edward Albee. Produced
　by Theatre 1965, Richard Barr, and
　Clinton Wilder.

AUTHOR—PLAY
Edward Albee, *Tiny Alice*
Frank Gilroy, *The Subject Was Roses*
Murray Schisgal, *Luv*
Neil Simon, *The Odd Couple*

PRODUCER—PLAY
Hume Cronyn–Allen Hodgdon, Inc.,
　Stevens Productions, Inc., and Bon-
　fils-Seawell Enterprises, *Slow Dance
　on the Killing Ground*
Claire Nichtern, *Luv*
Theatre 1965, Richard Barr, and Clinton
　Wilder, *Tiny Alice*
Robert Whitehead, *Tartuffe*

MUSICAL PLAY
Fiddler on the Roof. Music by Jerry
　Bock; lyrics by Sheldon Harnick;
　book by Joseph Stein. Produced by
　Harold Prince.
Golden Boy. Music by Charles Strouse;
　lyrics by Lee Adams; book by Clif-
　ford Odets and William Gibson. Pro-
　duced by Hillard Ekins.
Half a Sixpence. Music and lyrics by
　David Heneker; book by Beverly
　Cross. Produced by Allen Hodgdon,
　Stevens Productions, and Harold
　Fielding.

Oh What a Lovely War. Devised by Joan Littlewood for Theatre Workshop, Charles Chilton, and members of the cast. Produced by David Merrick and Gerry Raffles.

COMPOSER AND LYRICIST—MUSICAL PLAY

Jerry Bock and **Sheldon Harnick,** *Fiddler on the Roof*

Leslie Bricusse and Anthony Newley, *The Roar of the Greasepaint—The Smell of the Crowd*

David Heneker, *Half a Sixpence*

Richard Rodgers and Stephen Sondheim, *Do I Hear a Waltz?*

AUTHOR—MUSICAL PLAY

Jerome Coopersmith, *Baker Street*

Beverly Cross, *Half a Sixpence*

Sidney Michaels, *Ben Franklin in Paris*

Joseph Stein, *Fiddler on the Roof*

PRODUCER—MUSICAL PLAY

Hillard Elkins, *Golden Boy*

Allen Hodgdon, Stevens Productions, and Harold Fielding, *Half a Sixpence*

David Merrick, *The Roar of the Greasepaint—The Smell of the Crowd*

Harold Prince, *Fiddler on the Roof*

Jack Cassidy in Fade Out/Fade In *(1964)*

DIRECTOR—PLAY

William Ball, *Tartuffe*

Ulu Grosbard, *The Subject Was Roses*

Mike Nichols, *Luv* and *The Odd Couple*

Alan Schneider, *Tiny Alice*

DIRECTOR—MUSICAL PLAY

Joan Littlewood, *Oh What a Lovely War*

Anthony Newley, *The Roar of the Greasepaint—The Smell of the Crowd*

Jerome Robbins, *Fiddler on the Roof*

Gene Saks, *Half a Sixpence*

CHOREOGRAPHER

Peter Gennaro, *Bajour*

Donald McKayle, *Golden Boy*

Jerome Robbins, *Fiddler on the Roof*

Onna White, *Half a Sixpence*

SCENIC DESIGNER

Boris Aronson, *Fiddler on the Roof* and *Incident at Vichy*

Sean Kenny, *The Roar of the Greasepaint—The Smell of the Crowd*

Beni Montresor, *Do I Hear a Waltz?*

Oliver Smith, *Baker Street, Luv,* and *The Odd Couple*

COSTUME DESIGNER

Jane Greenwood, *Tartuffe*

Motley, *Baker Street*

Freddy Wittop, *The Roar of the Greasepaint—The Smell of the Crowd*

Patricia Zipprodt, *Fiddler on the Roof*

SPECIAL AWARDS

Gilbert Miller, for having produced 88 plays and musicals, and for his perseverance which has helped to keep New York and theatre alive.

Oliver Smith

In some cases (eg., Outstanding Scenic Designer), an individual was *nominated* for his or her work on several productions but actually received the award for one. In these instances, only the award-winning play appears in bold-face type.

OUTSTANDING DRAMATIC ACTRESS

Sheila Hancock, *Entertaining Mr. Sloane*

Rosemary Harris, *The Lion in Winter*

Kate Reid, *Slapstick Tragedy*

Lee Remick, *Wait Until Dark*

OUTSTANDING DRAMATIC ACTOR

Roland Culver, *Ivanov*

Donal Donnelly and Patrick Bedford, *Philadelphia, Here I Come!*

Hal Holbrook, *Mark Twain Tonight!*

Nicol Williamson, *Inadmissible Evidence*

OUTSTANDING DRAMATIC ACTRESS, SUPPORTING OR FEATURED

Zoe Caldwell, *Slapstick Tragedy*

Glenda Jackson, *The Persecution and Assassination of Jean-Paul Marat as Performed by the Inmates of the Asylum of Charenton Under the Direction of the Marquis de Sade*

Mairin D. O'Sullivan, *Philadelphia, Here I Come!*

Brenda Vaccaro, *Cactus Flower*

OUTSTANDING DRAMATIC ACTOR, SUPPORTING OR FEATURED

Burt Brinckerhoff, *Cactus Flower*

A. Larry Haines, *Generation*

Eamon Kelly, *Philadelphia, Here I Come!*

Patrick Magee, *The Persecution and Assassination of Jean-Paul Marat as Performed by the Inmates of the Asylum of Charenton Under the Direction of the Marquis de Sade*

OUTSTANDING MUSICAL ACTRESS

Barbara Harris, *On a Clear Day You Can See Forever*

Julie Harris, *Skyscraper*

Angela Lansbury, *Mame*

Gwen Verdon, *Sweet Charity*

Robert Preston and Rosemary Harris in The Lion in Winter *(1966)*

OUTSTANDING MUSICAL ACTOR
Jack Cassidy, *It's a Bird . . . It's a Plane . . . It's Superman*
John Cullum, *On a Clear Day You Can See Forever*
Richard Kiley, *Man of La Mancha*
Harry Secombe, *Pickwick*

OUTSTANDING MUSICAL ACTRESS, SUPPORTING OR FEATURED
Beatrice Arthur, *Mame*
Helen Gallagher, *Sweet Charity*
Patricia Marand, *It's a Bird . . . It's a Plane . . . It's Superman*
Carlotte Rae, *Pickwick*

OUTSTANDING MUSICAL ACTOR, SUPPORTING OR FEATURED
Roy Castle, *Pickwick*
John McMartin, *Sweet Charity*
Frankie Michaels, *Mame*
Michael O'Sullivan, *It's a Bird . . . It's a Plane . . . It's Superman*

OUTSTANDING PLAY
Inadmissible Evidence, by John Osborne. Produced by The David Merrick Arts Foundation.
***The Persecution and Assassination of Jean-Paul Marat as Performed by the Inmates of the Asylum of Charenton Under the Direction of the Marquis de Sade,* by Peter Weiss, English version by Geoffrey Skelton. Produced by The David Merrick Arts Foundation.**
Philadelphia, Here I Come!, by Brian Friel. Produced by The David Merrick Arts Foundation.
The Right Honourable Gentleman, by Michael Dyne. Produced by Peter Cookson, Amy Lynn, and Walter Schwimmer.

OUTSTANDING MUSICAL
Mame. Music and lyrics by Jerry Herman; book by Jerome Lawrence and Robert E. Lee. Produced by Sylvia and Joseph Harris, Robert Fryer, and Lawrence Carr.
***Man of La Mancha.* Music by Mitch Leigh; lyrics by Joe Darion; book by Dale Wasserman. Produced by Albert W. Seldon and Hal James.**
Skyscraper. Music by James Van Heusen; lyrics by Sammy Cahn; book by Peter Stone. Produced by Cy Feuer and Ernest Martin.
Sweet Charity. Music by Cy Coleman; lyrics by Dorothy Fields; book by Neil Simon. Produced by Sylvia and Joseph Harris, Robert Fryer, and Lawrence Carr.

OUTSTANDING COMPOSER AND LYRICIST
Cy Coleman and Dorothy Fields, *Sweet Charity*
Jerry Herman, *Mame*
Burton Lane and Alan Jay Lerner, *On a Clear Day You Can See Forever*
Mitch Leigh and Joe Darion, *Man of La Mancha*

OUTSTANDING DIRECTOR OF A PLAY
Peter Brook, *The Persecution and Assassination of Jean-Paul Marat as Performed by the Inmates of the Asylum of Charenton Under the Direction of the Marquis de Sade*
Hilton Edwards, *Philadelphia, Here I Come!*
Ellis Rabb, *You Can't Take It with You*
Noel Willman, *The Lion in Winter*

OUTSTANDING DIRECTOR OF A MUSICAL
Cy Feuer, *Skyscraper*
Bob Fosse, *Sweet Charity*
Albert Marre, *Man of La Mancha*
Gene Saks, *Mame*

OUTSTANDING CHOREOGRAPHER
Jack Cole, *Man of La Mancha*
Bob Fosse, *Sweet Charity*
Michael Kidd, *Skyscraper*
Onna White, *Mame*

OUTSTANDING SCENIC DESIGNER
Howard Bay, *Man of La Mancha*
William and Jean Eckart, *Mame*
David Hays, *Drat! The Cat!*
Robert Randolph, *Anya, Skyscraper,* and *Sweet Charity*

OUTSTANDING COSTUME DESIGNER
Howard Bay and Patton Campbell, *Man of La Mancha*
Gunilla Palmstierna-Weiss, *The Persecution and Assassination of Jean-Paul Marat as Performed by the Inmates of the Asylum of Charenton Under the Direction of the Marquis de Sade*
Loudon Sainthill, *The Right Honourable Gentleman*
Irene Sharaff, *Sweet Charity*

SPECIAL AWARD
Helen Mencken, for a lifetime of devotion and dedicated service to the Broadway theatre (posthumous).

Owing to the recent death of Helen Mencken, the president of the American Theatre Wing, the awards ceremony featured no entertainment and was held, for the only time, during the afternoon.

For the first time the awards were not voted on by the membership of the American Theatre Wing, but the vote was given over to members of the first- and second-night press lists, and the governing boards of Actors Equity, the Dramatists Guild, and the Society of Stage Directors and Choreographers.

21st ANNUAL TONY AWARDS
PRESENTED MARCH 26, 1967
SAM S. SHUBERT THEATRE

BEST ACTRESS IN A DRAMATIC PLAY
Eileen Atkins, *The Killing of Sister George*
Vivien Merchant, *The Homecoming*
Rosemary Murphy, *A Delicate Balance*
Beryl Reid, *The Killing of Sister George*

BEST ACTOR IN A DRAMATIC PLAY
Hume Cronyn, *A Delicate Balance*
Donald Madden, *Black Comedy*
Donald Moffat, *Right You Are* and *The Wild Duck*
Paul Rogers, *The Homecoming*

BEST SUPPORTING ACTRESS IN A DRAMATIC PLAY
Camila Ashland, *Black Comedy*
Brenda Forbes, *The Loves of Cass McGuire*
Marian Seldes, *A Delicate Balance*
Maria Tucci, *The Rose Tattoo*

BEST SUPPORTING ACTOR IN A DRAMATIC PLAY
Clayton Corzatte, *The School for Scandal*
Stephen Elliott, *Marat/Sade*
Ian Holm, *The Homecoming*
Sydney Walker, *The Wild Duck*

BEST ACTRESS IN A MUSICAL PLAY
Barbara Harris, *The Apple Tree*
Lotte Lenya, *Cabaret*
Mary Martin, *I Do! I Do!*
Louise Troy, *Walking Happy*

BEST ACTOR IN A MUSICAL PLAY
Alan Alda, *The Apple Tree*
Jack Gilford, *Cabaret*
Robert Preston, *I Do! I Do!*
Norman Wisdom, *Walking Happy*

THE APPLE TREE

BEST SUPPORTING ACTRESS IN A MUSICAL PLAY
Peg Murray, *Cabaret*
Leland Palmer, *A Joyful Noise*
Josephine Premice, *A Hand Is on the Gate*
Susan Watson, *A Joyful Noise*

BEST SUPPORTING ACTOR IN A MUSICAL PLAY
Leon Bibb, *A Hand Is on the Gate*
Gordon Dilworth, *Walking Happy*
Joel Grey, *Cabaret*
Edward Winter, *Cabaret*

BEST DRAMATIC PLAY
A Delicate Balance, by Edward Albee. Produced by Theatre 1967, Richard Barr, and Clinton Wilder.

Black Comedy, by Peter Shaffer. Produced by Alexander Cohen.
The Homecoming, by Harold Pinter. Produced by Alexander Cohen.
The Killing of Sister George, by Frank Marcus. Produced by Helen Bonfils and Morton Gottlieb.

BEST MUSICAL PLAY
Cabaret. Music by John Kander; lyrics by Fred Ebb; book by Joseph Masteroff. Produced by Harold Prince, in association with Ruth Mitchell.
I Do! I Do! Music by Harvey Schmidt; lyrics and book by Tom Jones. Produced by David Merrick.
The Apple Tree. Music by Jerry Bock; lyrics by Sheldon Harnick; book by Jerry Bock and Sheldon Harnick. Produced by Stuart Ostrow.
Walking Happy. Music by James Van Heusen; lyrics by Sammy Cahn; book by Roger O. Hirson and Ketti Frings. Produced by Cy Feuer and Ernest M. Martin.

BEST COMPOSER AND LYRICIST
Jerry Bock and Sheldon Harnick, *The Apple Tree*
Sammy Cahn and James Van Heusen, *Walking Happy*
Tom Jones and Harvey Schmidt, *I Do! I Do!*
John Kander and **Fred Ebb, *Cabaret***

BEST DIRECTOR OF A DRAMATIC PLAY
John Dexter, *Black Comedy*
Donald Driver, *Marat/Sade*
Peter Hall, *The Homecoming*
Alan Schneider, *A Delicate Balance*

BEST DIRECTOR OF A MUSICAL PLAY
Gower Champion, *I Do! I Do!*
Mike Nichols, *The Apple Tree*
Harold Prince, *Cabaret*
Jack Sydow, *Annie Get Your Gun*

BEST CHOREOGRAPHER
Michael Bennett, *A Joyful Noise*
Danny Daniels, *Walking Happy* and *Annie Get Your Gun*

Ronald Field, *Cabaret*
Lee Theodore, *The Apple Tree*

BEST SCENE DESIGNER
Boris Aronson, *Cabaret*
John Bury, *The Homecoming*
Oliver Smith, *I Do! I Do!*
Alan Tagg, *Black Comedy*

BEST COSTUME DESIGNER
Nancy Potts, *The Wild Duck* and *The School for Scandal*
Tony Walton, *The Apple Tree*
Freddy Wittop, *I Do! I Do!*
Patricia Zipprodt, *Cabaret*

First nationwide telecast of the Tony Award ceremony.

Peter Weiss's *The Persecution and Assassination of Jean-Paul Marat as Performed by the Inmates of the Asylum of Charenton Under the Direction of the Marquis de Sade,* under the shortened title of *Marat/Sade,* was revived on Broadway in this completely new production eight months after the original Royal Shakespeare Company production closed. The original production ran for 145 performances; *Marat/Sade* ran fifty-five performances on Broadway and then toured the United States.

22nd ANNUAL TONY AWARDS
PRESENTED APRIL 21, 1968
SAM S. SHUBERT THEATRE

BEST ACTRESS IN A DRAMATIC PLAY
Zoe Caldwell, *The Prime of Miss Jean Brodie*
Colleen Dewhurst, *More Stately Mansions*
Maureen Stapleton, *Plaza Suite*
Dorothy Tutin, *Portrait of a Queen*

BEST ACTOR IN A DRAMATIC PLAY
Martin Balsam, *You Know I Can't Hear You When the Water's Running*
Albert Finney, *A Day in the Death of Joe Egg*

Milo O'Shea, *Staircase*
Alan Webb, *I Never Sang for My Father*

BEST SUPPORTING ACTRESS IN A DRAMATIC PLAY
Pert Kelton, *Spofford*
Zena Walker, *A Day in the Death of Joe Egg*
Ruth White, *The Birthday Party*
Eleanor Wilson, *Weekend*

BEST SUPPORTING ACTOR IN A DRAMATIC PLAY
Paul Hecht, *Rosencrantz and Guildenstern Are Dead*
Brian Murray, *Rosencrantz and Guildenstern Are Dead*
James Patterson, *The Birthday Party*
John Wood, *Rosencrantz and Guildenstern Are Dead*

BEST ACTRESS IN A MUSICAL PLAY
Melina Mercouri, *Illya Darling*
Patricia Routledge, *Darling of the Day*
Leslie Uggams, *Hallelujah, Baby!*
Brenda Vaccaro, *How Now, Dow Jones*

BEST ACTOR IN A MUSICAL PLAY
Robert Goulet, *The Happy Time*
Robert Hooks, *Hallelujah, Baby!*
Anthony Robert, *How Now, Dow Jones*
David Wayne, *The Happy Time*

BEST SUPPORTING ACTRESS IN A MUSICAL PLAY
Geula Gill, *The Grand Music Hall of Israel*
Julie Gregg, *The Happy Time*
Lillian Hayman, *Hallelujah, Baby!*
Alice Playten, *Henry, Sweet Henry*

BEST SUPPORTING ACTOR IN A MUSICAL PLAY
Scott Jacoby, *Golden Rainbows*
Nikos Kourkoulos, *Illya Darling*
Mike Rupert, *The Happy Time*
Hiram Sherman, *How Now, Dow Jones*

BEST DRAMATIC PLAY
A Day in the Death of Joe Egg, by Peter Nichols. Produced by Joseph Cates and Henry Fownes.

Plaza Suite, by Neil Simon. Produced by Saint-Subber.
Rosencrantz and Guildenstern Are Dead, by Tom Stoppard. Produced by The David Merrick Arts Foundation.
The Price, by Arthur Miller. Produced by Robert Whitehead.

BEST MUSICAL PLAY
Hallelujah, Baby! Music by Jule Styne; lyrics by Betty Comden and Adolph Green; book by Arthur Laurents. Produced by Albert Selden, Hal James, Jane C. Nusbaum, and Harry Rigby.
The Happy Time. Music by John Kander; lyrics by Fred Ebb; book by N. Richard Nash. Produced by David Merrick.
How Now, Dow Jones. Music by Elmer Bernstein; lyrics by Carolyn Leigh; book by Max Shulman. Produced by David Merrick.
Illya, Darling. Music by Manos Hadjidakis; lyrics by Joe Darion; book by Jules Dassin. Produced by Kermit Bloomgarden.

BEST COMPOSER AND LYRICIST
Elmer Bernstein and Carolyn Leigh, *How Now, Dow Jones*
Manos Hadjidakis and Joe Darion, *Illya Darling*
John Kander and Fred Ebb, *The Happy Time*
Jule Styne, Betty Comden, and Adolph Green, *Hallelujah, Baby!*

BEST DIRECTOR OF A DRAMATIC PLAY
Michael Blakemore, *A Day in the Death of Joe Egg*
Derek Goldby, *Rosencrantz and Guildenstern Are Dead*
Mike Nichols, *Plaza Suite*
Alan Schneider, *You Know I Can't Hear You When the Water's Running*

BEST DIRECTOR OF A MUSICAL PLAY
George Abbott, *How Now, Dow Jones*
Gower Champion, *The Happy Time*

Jules Dassin, *Illya Darling*
Burt Shevelove, *Hallelujah, Baby!*

BEST CHOREOGRAPHER
Michael Bennett, *Henry, Sweet Henry*
Kevin Carlisle, *Hallelujah, Baby!*
Gower Champion, *The Happy Time*
Onna White, *Illya Darling*

BEST SCENIC DESIGNER
Boris Aronson, *The Price*
Desmond Heeley, *Rosencrantz and Guildenstern Are Dead*
Robert Randolph, *Golden Rainbow*
Peter Wexler, *The Happy Time*

BEST COSTUME DESIGNER
Jane Greenwood, *More Stately Mansions*
Desmond Heeley, *Rosencrantz and Guildenstern Are Dead*
Irene Sharaff, *Hallelujah, Baby!*
Freddy Wittop, *The Happy Time*

SPECIAL AWARDS
APA-Phoenix Theatre
Pearl Bailey
Carol Channing
Maurice Chevalier
Marlene Dietrich
Audrey Hepburn
David Merrick

Pearl Bailey in Hello, Dolly! *(1967)*

23rd ANNUAL TONY AWARDS
PRESENTED APRIL 20, 1969
MARK HELLINGER THEATRE

BEST ACTRESS IN A DRAMATIC PLAY
Julie Harris, *Forty Carats*
Estelle Parsons, *The Seven Descents of Myrtle*
Charlotte Rae, *Morning, Noon, and Night*
Brenda Vaccaro, *The Goodbye People*

BEST ACTOR IN A DRAMATIC PLAY
Art Carney, *Lovers*
James Earl Jones, *The Great White Hope*
Alec McCowen, *Hadrian VII*
Donald Pleasence, *The Man in the Glass Booth*

BEST SUPPORTING ACTRESS IN A DRAMATIC PLAY
Jane Alexander, *The Great White Hope*
Diane Keaton, *Play It Again, Sam*
Lauren Jones, *Does a Tiger Wear a Necktie?*
Anna Manahan, *Lovers*

BEST SUPPORTING ACTOR IN A DRAMATIC PLAY
Richard Castellano, *Lovers and Other Strangers*
Al Pacino, *Does a Tiger Wear a Necktie?*
Anthony Roberts, *Play It Again, Sam*
Louis Zorich, *Hadrian VII*

BEST ACTRESS IN A MUSICAL PLAY
Maria Karnilova, *Zorba*
Angela Lansbury, *Dear World*
Dorothy Loudon, *The Fig Leaves Are Falling*
Jill O'Hara, *Promises, Promises*

BEST ACTOR IN A MUSICAL PLAY
Herschel Bernardi, *Zorba*
Jack Cassidy, *Maggie Flynn*
Joel Grey, *George M!*
Jerry Orbach, *Promises, Promises*

BEST SUPPORTING ACTRESS IN A MUSICAL PLAY
Sandy Duncan, *Canterbury Tales*

Marian Mercer, *Promises, Promises*
Lorraine Serabian, *Zorba*
Virginia Vestoff, *1776*

BEST SUPPORTING ACTOR IN A MUSICAL PLAY
William Daniels, *1776*
A. Larry Haines, *Promises, Promises*
Ronald Holgate, *1776*
Edward Winter, *Promises, Promises*

BEST DRAMATIC PLAY
***The Great White Hope*, by Howard Sackler. Produced by Herman Levin.**
Hadrian VII, by Peter Luke. Produced by Lester Osterman Productions, Bill Freedman, and Charles Kasher.
Lovers, by Brian Friel. Produced by Helen Bonfils and Morton Gottlieb.
The Man in the Glass Booth, by Robert Shaw. Produced by Glasshouse Productions and Peter Bridge, Ivor David Balding & Associates, Ltd., and Edward M. Meyers with Leslie Ogden.

BEST MUSICAL PLAY
Hair. Music by Galt MacDermot; lyrics by James Rado; book by Gerome Ragni and James Rado. Produced by Michael Butler.
Promises, Promises. Music by Burt Bacharach; lyrics by Hal David; book by Neil Simon. Produced by David Merrick.
1776. Music and lyrics by Sherman Edwards; book by Peter Stone. Produced by Stuart Ostrow.
Zorba. Music by John Kander; lyrics by Fred Ebb; book by Joseph Stein. Produced by Harold Prince.

BEST DIRECTOR OF A DRAMATIC PLAY
Peter Dews, *Hadrian VII*
Joseph Hardy, *Play It Again, Sam*
Harold Pinter, *The Man in the Glass Booth*
Michael A. Schultz, *Does a Tiger Wear a Necktie?*

Carol Burnett in Fade Out/Fade In *(1964)*

BEST DIRECTOR OF A MUSICAL PLAY
Peter Hunt, *1776*
Robert Moore, *Promises, Promises*
Tom O'Horgan, *Hair*
Harold Prince, *Zorba*

BEST CHOREOGRAPHER
Sammy Bayes, *Canterbury Tales*
Michael Bennett, *Promises, Promises*
Ronald Field, *Zorba*
Joe Layton, *George M!*

BEST SCENIC DESIGNER
Boris Aronson, *Zorba*
Derek Cousins, *Canterbury Tales*
Jo Mielziner, *1776*
Oliver Smith, *Dear World*

BEST COSTUME DESIGNER
Michael Annals, *Morning, Noon, and Night*
Robert Fletcher, *Hadrian VII*
Louden Sainthill, *Canterbury Tales*
Patricia Zipprodt, *Zorba*

SPECIAL AWARDS
The National Theatre Company of Great Britain
The Negro Ensemble Company
Rex Harrison

Leonard Bernstein
Carol Burnett

William Daniels refused to accept the nomination as Best Supporting Actor *(1776)*, feeling that his role was not supporting, but leading. His name was removed from the voting ballot.

24th ANNUAL TONY AWARDS
PRESENTED APRIL 19, 1970
MARK HELLINGER THEATRE

BEST ACTRESS IN A DRAMATIC PLAY
Geraldine Brooks, *Brightower*
Tammy Grimes, *Private Lives*
Helen Hayes, *Harvey*

BEST ACTOR IN A DRAMATIC PLAY
James Coco, *Last of the Red Hot Lovers*
Frank Grimes, *Borstal Boy*
Stacy Keach, *Indians*
Fritz Weaver, *Child's Play*

BEST SUPPORTING ACTRESS IN A DRAMATIC PLAY
Blythe Danner, *Butterflies Are Free*
Alice Drummond, *The Chinese and Dr. Fish*
Eileen Heckart, *Butterflies Are Free*
Linda Lavin, *Last of the Red Hot Lovers*

BEST SUPPORTING ACTOR IN A DRAMATIC PLAY
Joseph Bova, *The Chinese and Dr. Fish*
Ken Howard, *Child's Play*
Dennis King, *A Patriot for Me*

BEST ACTRESS IN A MUSICAL PLAY
Lauren Bacall, *Applause*
Katharine Hepburn, *Coco*
Dilys Watling, *Georgy*

BEST ACTOR IN A MUSICAL PLAY
Len Cariou, *Applause*
Cleavon Little, *Purlie*
Robert Weede, *Cry for Us All*

BEST SUPPORTING ACTRESS IN A MUSICAL PLAY
Bonnie Franklin, *Applause*
Penny Fuller, *Applause*
Melissa Hart, *Georgy*
Melba Moore, *Purlie*

BEST SUPPORTING ACTOR IN A MUSICAL PLAY
Rene Auberjonois, *Coco*
Brandon Maggart, *Applause*
George Rose, *Coco*

BEST DRAMATIC PLAY
Borstal Boy, by Frank McMahon. Produced by Michael McAloney and Burton C. Kaiser.
Child's Play, by Robert Marasco. Produced by David Merrick.
Indians, by Arthur Kopit. Produced by Lyn Austin, Oliver Smith, Joel Schenker, and Roger L. Stevens.
Last of the Red Hot Lovers, by Neil Simon. Produced by Saint-Subber.

BEST MUSICAL PLAY
Applause. Music by Charles Strouse; lyrics by Lee Adams; book by Betty Comden and Adolph Green. Produced by Joseph Kipness and Lawrence Kasha.
Coco. Music by André Previn; lyrics and book by Alan Jay Lerner. Produced by Frederick Brisson.
Purlie. Music by Gary Geld; lyrics by Peter Udell; book by Ossie Davis, Philip Rose, and Peter Udell. Produced by Philip Rose.

BEST DIRECTOR OF A DRAMATIC PLAY
Joseph Hardy, *Child's Play*
Milton Katselas, *Butterflies Are Free*
Tomas MacAnna, *Borstal Boy*
Robert Moore, *Last of the Red Hot Lovers*

BEST DIRECTOR OF A MUSICAL
Michael Benthall, *Coco*
Ron Field, *Applause*
Philip Rose, *Purlie*

BEST CHOREOGRAPHER
Michael Bennett, *Coco*
Grover Dale, *Billy*
Ron Field, *Applause*
Louis Johnson, *Purlie*

BEST SCENIC DESIGNER
Howard Bay, *Cry for Us All*
Ming Cho Lee, *Billy*
Jo Mielziner, *Child's Play*
Robert Randolph, *Applause*

BEST COSTUME DESIGNER
Ray Aghayan, *Applause*
Cecil Beaton, *Coco*
W. Robert Lavine, *Jimmy*
Freddy Wittop, *A Patriot for Me*

BEST LIGHTING DESIGNER
Jo Mielziner, *Child's Play*
Tharon Musser, *Applause*
Thomas Skelton, *Indians*

Noel Coward

SPECIAL AWARDS
New York Shakespeare Festival Public
   Theatre, for pioneering efforts on
   behalf of new plays.
Sir Noel Coward, for his multiple and
   immortal contributions to the theatre.
Lynn Fontanne
Alfred Lunt
Barbra Streisand

Awards for Best Lighting Designer were first
given this year.

25th ANNUAL TONY AWARDS
PRESENTED MARCH 28, 1971
PALACE THEATRE

BEST ACTRESS IN A PLAY
Estelle Parsons, *And Miss Reardon
   Drinks a Little*
Diana Rigg, *Abelard and Heloise*
Marian Seldes, *Father's Day*
**Maureen Stapleton, *The Gingerbread
   Lady***

BEST ACTOR IN A PLAY
Brian Bedford, *The School for Wives*
John Gielgud, *Home*
Alec McCowen, *The Philanthropist*
Ralph Richardson, *Home*

BEST SUPPORTING ACTRESS IN A PLAY
**Rae Allen, *And Miss Reardon Drinks a
   Little***
Lili Darvas, *Les Blancs*
Joan Van Ark, *The School for Wives*
Mona Washbourne, *Home*

BEST SUPPORTING ACTOR IN A PLAY
Ronald Radd, *Abelard and Heloise*
Donald Pickering, *Conduct
   Unbecoming*
Paul Sand, *Story Theatre*
Ed Zimmermann, *The Philanthropist*

BEST ACTRESS IN A MUSICAL PLAY
Susan Browning, *Company*
Sandy Duncan, *The Boy Friend*

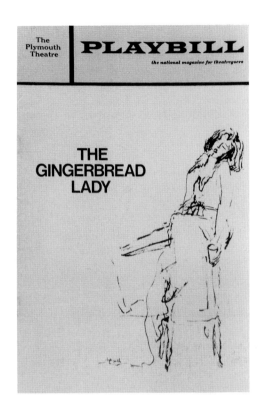

Helen Gallagher, *No, No, Nanette*
Elaine Stritch, *Company*

BEST ACTOR IN A MUSICAL PLAY
David Burns, *Lovely Ladies, Kind
   Gentlemen*
Larry Kert, *Company*
Hal Linden, *The Rothschilds*
Bobby Van, *No, No, Nanette*

**BEST SUPPORTING ACTRESS IN A
MUSICAL PLAY**
Barbara Barrie, *Company*
Patsy Kelly, *No, No, Nanette*
Pamela Myers, *Company*

**BEST SUPPORTING ACTOR IN A MUSICAL
PLAY**
Keene Curtis, *The Rothschilds*
Charles Kimbrough, *Company*
Walter Willison, *Two by Two*

BEST PLAY
Home, by David Storey. Produced by Alexander Cohen.
Sleuth, by Anthony Shaffer. Produced by Helen Bonfils, Morton Gottlieb, and Michael White.
Story Theatre, by Paul Sills. Produced by Zev Bufman.
The Philanthropist, by Christopher Hampton. Produced by David Merrick and Byron Goldman.

BEST MUSICAL PLAY
Company. Produced by Harold Prince.
The Me Nobody Knows. Produced by Jeff Britton.
The Rothschilds. Produced by Hillard Elkins and Lester Osterman.

BEST MUSIC OF A MUSICAL PLAY
Jerry Bock, *The Rothschilds*
Gary William Friedman, *The Me Nobody Knows*
Stephen Sondheim, *Company*

BEST LYRICS OF A MUSICAL PLAY
Sheldon Harnick, *The Rothschilds*
William Holt, *The Me Nobody Knows*
Stephen Sondheim, *Company*

BEST BOOK OF A MUSICAL PLAY
George Furth, *Company*
Robert H. Livingston and Herb Schapiro, *The Me Nobody Knows*
Sherman Yellen, *The Rothschilds*

BEST DIRECTOR OF A DRAMATIC PLAY
Lindsay Anderson, *Home*
Peter Brook, *A Midsummer Night's Dream*
Stephen Porter, *The School for Wives*
Clifford Williams, *Sleuth*

BEST DIRECTOR OF A MUSICAL PLAY
Michael Kidd, *The Rothschilds*
Robert H. Livingston, *The Me Nobody Knows*
Harold Prince, *Company*
Burt Shevelove, *No, No, Nanette*

BEST CHOREOGRAPHER
Michael Bennett, *Company*
Michael Kidd, *The Rothschilds*
Donald Saddler, *No, No, Nanette*

BEST SCENIC DESIGNER
Boris Aronson, *Company*
John Bury, *The Rothschilds*
Sally Jacobs, *A Midsummer Night's Dream*
Jo Mielziner, *Father's Day*

BEST COSTUME DESIGNER
Raoul Pène du Bois, *No, No, Nanette*
Jane Greenwood, *Hay Fever*
Jane Greenwood, *Les Blancs*
Freddy Wittop, *Lovely Ladies, Kind Gentlemen*

BEST LIGHTING DESIGNER
Robert Ornbo, *Company*
H. R. Poindexter, *Story Theatre*
William Ritman, *Sleuth*

SPECIAL AWARDS
Ingram Ash, president of Blaine-Thompson Advertising, for decades of devoted service to the theatre.
Elliot Norton, drama critic, for distinguished theatrical commentary.
Roger L. Stevens of Kennedy Center, for helping to focus government attention on the arts.
Playbill, for chronicling Broadway through the years.

26th ANNUAL TONY AWARDS
PRESENTED APRIL 23, 1972
BROADWAY THEATRE

BEST ACTRESS IN A PLAY
Eileen Atkins, *Vivat! Vivat Regina!*
Colleen Dewhurst, *All Over*
Rosemary Harris, *Old Times*
Sada Thompson, *Twigs*

BEST ACTOR IN A PLAY
Tom Aldredge, *Sticks and Bones*
Cliff Gorman, *Lenny*
Donald Pleasence, *Wise Child*
Jason Robards, *The Country Girl*

BEST SUPPORTING ACTRESS IN A PLAY
Cara Duff-MacCormick, *Moonchildren*
Mercedes McCambridge, *The Love Suicide at Schofield Barracks*
Frances Sternhagen, *The Sign in Sidney Brustein's Window*
Elizabeth Wilson, *Sticks and Bones*

BEST SUPPORTING ACTOR IN A PLAY
Vincent Gardenia, *The Prisoner of Second Avenue*
Douglas Rain, *Vivat! Vivat Regina!*
Lee Richardson, *Vivat! Vivat Regina!*
Joe Silver, *Lenny*

BEST ACTRESS IN A MUSICAL PLAY
Jonelle Allen, *Two Gentlemen of Verona*
Dorothy Collins, *Follies*
Mildred Natwick, *70 Girls 70*
Alexis Smith, *Follies*

BEST ACTOR IN A MUSICAL PLAY
Clifton Davis, *Two Gentlemen of Verona*
Barry Bostwick, *Grease*
Raul Julia, *Two Gentlemen of Verona*
Phil Silvers, *A Funny Thing Happened on the Way to the Forum*

BEST SUPPORTING ACTRESS IN A MUSICAL PLAY
Adrienne Barbeau, *Grease*
Linda Hopkins, *Inner City*
Bernadette Peters, *On the Town*
Beatrice Winde, *Ain't Supposed to Die a Natural Death*

BEST SUPPORTING ACTOR IN A MUSICAL PLAY
Larry Blyden, *A Funny Thing Happened on the Way to the Forum*
Timothy Meyers, *Grease*
Gene Nelson, *Follies*
Ben Vereen, *Jesus Christ Superstar*

BEST PLAY
Old Times, by Harold Pinter. Produced by Roger L. Stevens.
The Prisoner of Second Avenue, by Neil Simon. Produced by Saint-Subber.

Sticks and Bones, by David Rabe. Produced by The New York Shakespeare Festival/Joseph Papp.

Vivat! Vivat Regina!, by Robert Bolt. Produced by David Merrick and Arthur Cantor.

BEST MUSICAL PLAY

Ain't Supposed to Die a Natural Death. Produced by Eugene V. Wolsk, Charles Blackwell, Emanuel Azenberg, and Robert Malina.

Follies. Produced by Harold Prince.

Two Gentlemen of Verona. Produced by The New York Shakespeare Festival/ Joseph Papp.

Grease. Produced by Kenneth Waissman and Maxine Fox.

BEST SCORE OF A MUSICAL

Ain't Supposed to Die a Natural Death, music and lyrics by Melvin Van Peebles.

Follies, music and lyrics by Stephen Sondheim.

Jesus Christ Superstar, music by Andrew Lloyd Webber; lyrics by Tim Rice.

Two Gentlemen of Verona, music by Galt McDermot; lyrics by John Guare.

BEST BOOK OF A MUSICAL

Ain't Supposed to Die a Natural Death, by Melvin Van Peebles

Follies, by James Goldman

Grease, by Jim Jacobs and Warren Casey

Two Gentlemen of Verona, by John Guare and Mel Shapiro

BEST DIRECTOR OF A PLAY

Jeff Bleckner, *Sticks and Bones*

Gordon Davidson, *The Trial of the Catonsville Nine*

Peter Hall, *Old Times*

Mike Nichols, *The Prisoner of Second Avenue*

BEST DIRECTOR OF A MUSICAL PLAY

Gilbert Moses, *Ain't Supposed to Die a Natural Death*

Harold Prince and **Michael Bennett, *Follies***

Mel Shapiro, *Two Gentlemen of Verona*

Burt Shevelove, *A Funny Thing Happened on the Way to the Forum*

BEST CHOREOGRAPHER

Michael Bennett, *Follies*

Patricia Birch, *Grease*

Jean Erdman, *Two Gentlemen of Verona*

BEST SCENIC DESIGNER

Boris Aronson, *Follies*

John Bury, *Old Times*

Kert Lundell, *Ain't Supposed to Die a Natural Death*

Robin Wagner, *Jesus Christ Superstar*

BEST COSTUME DESIGNER

Theoni V. Aldredge, *Two Gentlemen of Verona*

Randy Barcelo, *Jesus Christ Superstar*

Florence Klotz, *Follies*

Carrie F. Robbins, *Grease*

BEST LIGHTING DESIGNER

Martin Aronstein, *Ain't Supposed to Die a Natural Death*

John Bury, *Old Times*

Jules Fisher, *Jesus Christ Superstar*

Tharon Musser, *Follies*

SPECIAL AWARDS

Fiddler on the Roof, on becoming the longest-running musical in Broadway history.

The Theatre Guild/American Theatre Society, for its many years of service to audiences for touring shows.

Ethel Merman

Richard Rodgers

BEST ACTRESS IN A PLAY

Jane Alexander, *6 Rms Riv Vu*

Colleen Dewhurst, *Mourning Becomes Electra*

Julie Harris, *The Last of Mrs. Lincoln*

Kathleen Widdoes, *Much Ado About Nothing*

BEST ACTOR IN A PLAY

Jack Albertson, *The Sunshine Boys*

Alan Bates, *Butley*

Wilifred Hyde-White, *The Jockey Club Stakes*

Paul Sorvino, *That Championship Season*

BEST SUPPORTING ACTRESS IN A PLAY

Maya Angelou, *Look Away*

Leora Dana, *The Last of Mrs. Lincoln*

Katherine Helmond, *The Great God Brown*

Penelope Windust, *Elizabeth I*

BEST SUPPORTING ACTOR IN A PLAY

Barnard Hughes, *Much Ado About Nothing*

John Lithgow, *The Changing Room*

John McMartin, *Don Juan*

Hayward Morse, *Butley*

BEST ACTRESS IN A MUSICAL PLAY

Glynis Johns, *A Little Night Music*

Leland Palmer, *Pippin*

Debbie Reynolds, *Irene*

Marcia Rodd, *Shelter*

BEST ACTOR IN A MUSICAL PLAY

Len Cariou, *A Little Night Music*

Robert Morse, *Sugar*

Brock Peters, *Lost in the Stars*

Ben Vereen, *Pippin*

BEST SUPPORTING ACTRESS IN A MUSICAL PLAY

Patricia Elliott, *A Little Night Music*

Hermione Gingold, *A Little Night Music*
Patsy Kelly, *Irene*
Irene Ryan, *Pippin*

BEST SUPPORTING ACTOR IN A MUSICAL PLAY
Laurence Guittard, *A Little Night Music*
George S. Irving, *Irene*
Avon Long, *Don't Play Us Cheap*
Gilbert Price, *Lost in the Stars*

BEST PLAY
Butley, by Simon Gray. Produced by Lester Osterman and Richard Horner.
That Championship Season, by Jason Miller. Produced by The New York Shakespeare Festival/Joseph Papp.
The Changing Room, by David Storey. Produced by Charles Bowden, Lee Reynolds, and Isobel Robins.
The Sunshine Boys, by Neil Simon. Produced by Emanuel Azenberg and Eugene V. Wolsk.

BEST MUSICAL
A Little Night Music. Produced by Harold Prince.
Don't Bother Me, I Can't Cope. Produced by Edward Padula and Arch Lustberg.
Pippin. Produced by Stuart Ostrow.
Sugar. Produced by David Merrick.

BEST SCORE OF A MUSICAL
A Little Night Music, music and lyrics by Stephen Sondheim.
Don't Bother Me, I Can't Cope, music and lyrics by Micki Grant.
Much Ado About Nothing, music by Peter Link.
Pippin, music and lyrics by Stephen Schwartz.

BEST BOOK OF A MUSICAL
A Little Night Music, by Hugh Wheeler.
Don't Bother Me, I Can't Cope, by Micki Grant.

Don't Play Us Cheap, by Melvin Van Peebles.
Pippin, by Roger O. Hirson.

BEST DIRECTOR OF A PLAY
A. J. Antoon, *That Championship Season*
A. J. Antoon, Much Ado About Nothing
Alan Arkin, *The Sunshine Boys*
Michael Rudman, *The Changing Room*

BEST DIRECTOR OF A MUSICAL PLAY
Vinnette Carroll, *Don't Bother Me, I Can't Cope*
Gower Champion, *Sugar*
Bob Fosse, *Pippin*
Harold Prince, *A Little Night Music*

BEST CHOREOGRAPHER
Gower Champion, *Sugar*
Bob Fosse, *Pippin*
Peter Gennaro, *Irene*
Donald Saddler, *Much Ado About Nothing*

BEST SCENIC DESIGNER
Boris Aronson, *A Little Night Music*
David Jenkins, *The Changing Room*
Santo Loquasto, *That Championship Season*
Tony Walton, *Pippin*

BEST COSTUME DESIGNER
Theoni V. Aldredge, *Much Ado About Nothing*
Florence Klotz, *A Little Night Music*
Miles White, *Tricks*
Patricia Zipprodt, *Pippin*

BEST LIGHTING DESIGNER
Martin Aronstein, *Much Ado About Nothing*
Ian Calderon, *That Championship Season*
Jules Fisher, *Pippin*
Tharon Musser, *A Little Night Music*

SPECIAL AWARDS
The Shubert Organization
Actors Fund of America
John V. Lindsay, Mayor of New York City

BEST ACTRESS IN A PLAY
Jane Alexander, *Find Your Way Home*
Colleen Dewhurst, *A Moon for the Misbegotten*
Julie Harris, *The Au Pair Man*
Madeline Kahn, *Boom Boom Room*
Rachel Roberts, *Chemin de Fer* and *The Visit*

BEST ACTOR IN A PLAY
Michael Moriarty, *Find Your Way Home*
Zero Mostel, *Ulysses in Nighttown*
Jason Robards, *A Moon for the Misbegotten*
George C. Scott, *Uncle Vanya*
Nicol Williamson, *Uncle Vanya*

BEST SUPPORTING ACTRESS IN A PLAY
Regina Baff, *Veronica's Room*
Fionnuala Flanagan, *Ulysses in Nighttown*
Charlotte Moore, *Chemin de Fer*
Roxie Roker, *The River Niger*
Frances Sternhagen, *The Good Doctor*

BEST SUPPORTING ACTOR IN A PLAY
Rene Auberjonois, *The Good Doctor*
Ed Flanders, *A Moon for the Misbegotten*
Douglas Turner Ward, *The River Niger*
Dick A. Williams, *What the Wine-Sellers Buy*

BEST ACTRESS IN A MUSICAL PLAY
Virginia Capers, *Raisin*
Carol Channing, *Lorelei*
Michele Lee, *Seesaw*

BEST ACTOR IN A MUSICAL PLAY
Alfred Drake, *Gigi*
Joe Morton, *Raisin*
Christopher Plummer, *Cyrano*
Lewis J. Stadlen, *Candide*

BEST SUPPORTING ACTRESS IN A MUSICAL PLAY
Leigh Beery, *Cyrano*
Maureen Brennan, *Candide*

June Gable, *Candide*
Ernestine Jackson, *Raisin*
Janie Sell, *Over Here!*

BEST SUPPORTING ACTOR IN A MUSICAL PLAY
Mark Baker, *Candide*
Ralph Carter, *Raisin*
Tommy Tune, *Seesaw*

BEST PLAY
Boom Boom Room, by David Rabe. Produced by Joseph Papp.
The Au Pair Man, by Hugh Leonard. Produced by Joseph Papp.
The River Niger, by Joseph A. Walker. Produced by The Negro Ensemble Company.
Ulysses in Nighttown, by Marjorie Barkentin. Produced by Alexander Cohen and Bernard Delfont.

Patti and Maxene Andrews in Over Here *(1974)*

BEST MUSICAL
Over Here! Produced by Kenneth Waissman and Maxine Fox.
Raisin. Produced by Robert Nemiroff.
Seesaw. Produced by Joseph Kipness, Lawrence Kasha, James Nederlander, George M. Steinbrenner III, and Lorin E. Price.

BEST SCORE OF A MUSICAL
Gigi, music by Frederick Loewe; lyrics by Alan Jay Lerner.

The Good Doctor, music by Peter Link; lyrics by Neil Simon.
Raisin, music by Judd Woldin; lyrics by Robert Brittan.
Seesaw, music by Cy Coleman; lyrics by Dorothy Fields.

BEST BOOK OF A MUSICAL PLAY
Candide, by Hugh Wheeler.
Raisin, by Robert Nemiroff and Charlotte Zaltzberg.
Seesaw, by Michael Bennett.

BEST DIRECTOR OF A PLAY
Burgess Meredith, *Ulysses in Nighttown*
Mike Nichols, *Uncle Vanya*
Stephen Porter, *Chemin de Fer*
José Quintero, *A Moon for the Misbegotten*
Edwin Sherin, *Find Your Way Home*

BEST DIRECTOR OF A MUSICAL PLAY
Michael Bennett, *Seesaw*
Donald McKayle, *Raisin*
Tom Moore, *Over Here!*
Harold Prince, *Candide*

BEST CHOREOGRAPHER
Michael Bennett, *Seesaw*
Patricia Birch, *Over Here!*
Donald McKayle, *Raisin*

BEST SCENIC DESIGNER
John Conklin, *The Au Pair Man*
Franne Lee and **Eugene Lee, *Candide***
Santo Loquasto, *What the Wine-Sellers Buy*
Oliver Smith, *Gigi*
Ed Wittstein, *Ulysses in Nighttown*

BEST COSTUME DESIGNER
Theoni V. Aldredge, *The Au Pair Man*
Finlay James, *Crown Matrimonial*
Franne Lee, *Candide*
Oliver Messel, *Gigi*
Carrie F. Robbins, *Over Here!*

BEST LIGHTING DESIGNER
Martin Aronstein, *Boom Boom Room*
Ken Billington, *The Visit*

Dudley Moore and Peter Cook in Good Evening *(1973)*

Ben Edwards, *A Moon for the Misbegotten*
Jules Fisher, *Ulysses in Nighttown*
Tharon Musser, *The Good Doctor*

SPECIAL AWARDS
A Moon for the Misbegotten, an outstanding dramatic revival of an American classic.
Candide, an outstanding contribution to the artistic development of the musical theatre.
Peter Cook and Dudley Moore, costars and authors of *Good Evening.*
Bette Midler, for adding lustre to the Broadway season.
Liza Minnelli, for adding lustre to the Broadway season.

THEATRE AWARD '74
John F. Wharton, veteran theatrical attorney
Harold Friedlander, the industry's foremost printing expert

Actors Equity Association, on the occasion of its sixtieth anniversary of diligent and tireless effort on behalf of American actors and actresses.

Theatre Development Fund, for its imaginative and energetic array of programs, which nurture and enlarge the audiences for the living theatre.

The Theatre Award '74, instituted this year, was given by the American Theatre Wing. It was not accompanied by a Tony Award medallion, but honorees were given plaques.

Douglas Turner refused to accept the nomination as Best Supporting Actor *(The River Niger)*, feeling that his role was not supporting, but leading. His name was removed from the voting ballot.

29th ANNUAL TONY AWARDS
PRESENTED APRIL 20, 1975
WINTER GARDEN THEATRE

BEST ACTRESS IN A BROADWAY PLAY
Elizabeth Ashley, *Cat on a Hot Tin Roof*
Ellen Burstyn, *Same Time, Next Year*
Diana Rigg, *The Misanthrope*
Maggie Smith, *Private Lives*
Liv Ullmann, *A Doll's House*

BEST ACTOR IN A BROADWAY PLAY
Jim Dale, *Scapino!*
Peter Firth, *Equus*
Henry Fonda, *Clarence Darrow*
Ben Gazzara, *Hughie* and *Duet* [two one-act plays presented in a single performance]
John Kani and **Winston Ntshona,** *Sizwe Banzi Is Dead* and *The Island* [two one-act plays presented in a single performance]
John Wood, *Sherlock Holmes*

BEST SUPPORTING ACTRESS IN A BROADWAY PLAY
Linda Miller, *Black Picture Show*
Rita Moreno, *The Ritz*

Geraldine Page, *Absurd Person Singular*
Carole Shelley, *Absurd Person Singular*
Elizabeth Spriggs, *London Assurance*
Frances Sternhagen, *Equus*

BEST SUPPORTING ACTOR IN A BROADWAY PLAY
Larry Blyden, *Absurd Person Singular*
Leonard Frey, *The National Health*
Frank Langella, *Seascape*
Philip Locke, *Sherlock Holmes*
George Rose, *My Fat Friend*
Dick Anthony Williams, *Black Picture Show*

BEST ACTRESS IN A BROADWAY MUSICAL
Lola Falana, *Doctor Jazz*
Angela Lansbury, *Gypsy*
Bernadette Peters, *Mack and Mabel*
Ann Reinking, *Goodtime Charley*

BEST ACTOR IN A BROADWAY MUSICAL
John Cullum, *Shenandoah*
Joel Grey, *Goodtime Charley*
Raul Julia, *Where's Charley?*
Eddie Mekka, *The Lieutenant*
Robert Preston, *Mack and Mabel*

BEST SUPPORTING ACTRESS IN A BROADWAY MUSICAL
Dee Dee Bridgewater, *The Wiz*
Susan Browning, *Goodtime Charley*
Zan Charisse, *Gypsy*
Taina Elg, *Where's Charley?*
Kelly Garrett, *The Night That Made America Famous*
Donna Theodore, *Shenandoah*

BEST SUPPORTING ACTOR IN A BROADWAY MUSICAL
Tom Aldredge, *Where's Charley?*
John Bottoms, *Dance with Me*
Doug Henning, *The Magic Show*
Gilbert Price, *The Night That Made America Famous*
Ted Ross, *The Wiz*
Richard B. Shull, *Goodtime Charley*

BEST BROADWAY PLAY
Equus, by Peter Shaffer. Produced by Kermit Bloomgarden and Doris Cole Abrahams.
Same Time, Next Year, by Bernard Slade. Produced by Morton Gottlieb.
Seascape, by Edward Albee. Produced by Richard Barr, Charles Woodward, and Clinton Wilder.
Short Eyes, by Miguel Piñero. Produced by The New York Shakespeare Festival/Joseph Papp.
Sizwe Banzi Is Dead and *The Island,* by Athol Fugard, John Kani, and Winston Ntshona. Produced by Hillard Elkins, Lester Osterman Productions, Bernard Delfont, and Michael White.
The National Health, by Peter Nichols. Produced by Circle in the Square, Inc.

BEST BROADWAY MUSICAL
Mack and Mabel. Produced by David Merrick.
The Lieutenant. Produced by Joseph Kutrzeba and Spofford Beadle.
Shenandoah. Produced by Philip Rose, Gloria Sher, and Louis K. Sher.
The Wiz. Produced by Ken Harper.

BEST SCORE OF A BROADWAY MUSICAL
Letter for Queen Victoria, music and lyrics by Alan Lloyd.
Shenandoah, music by Gary Geld; lyrics by Peter Udell.
The Lieutenant, music and lyrics by Gene Curty, Nitra Scharfman, and Chuck Strand.
The Wiz, music and lyrics by Charlie Smalls.

BEST BOOK OF A BROADWAY MUSICAL
Mack and Mabel, by Michael Stewart
Shenandoah, by James Lee Barrett, Peter Udell, and Philip Rose
The Lieutenant, by Gene Curty, Nitra Scharfman, and Chuck Strand
The Wiz, by William F. Brown

BEST DIRECTOR OF A BROADWAY PLAY
Arvin Brown, *The National Health*
John Dexter, *Equus*

Frank Dunlop, *Scapino!*
Ronald Eyre, *London Assurance*
Athol Fugard, *Sizwe Banzi Is Dead* and *The Island*
Gene Saks, *Same Time, Next Year*

BEST DIRECTOR OF A BROADWAY MUSICAL
Gower Champion, *Mack and Mabel*
Grover Dale, *The Magic Show*
Geoffrey Holder, *The Wiz*
Arthur Laurents, *Gypsy*

BEST CHOREOGRAPHER
Gower Champion, *Mack and Mabel*
George Faison, *The Wiz*
Donald McKayle, *Doctor Jazz*
Margo Sappington, *Where's Charley?*
Robert Tucker, *Shenandoah*
Joel Zwick, *Dance with Me*

BEST SCENIC DESIGNER
Scott Johnson, *Dance with Me*
Tanya Moiseiwitsch, *The Misanthrope*
William Ritman, *God's Favorite*
Rouben Ter-Arutunian, *Goodtime Charley*
Carl Toms, *Sherlock Holmes*
Robin Wagner, *Mack and Mabel*

BEST COSTUME DESIGNER
Arthur Boccia, *Where's Charley?*
Raoul Pène du Bois, *Doctor Jazz*
Geoffrey Holder, *The Wiz*
Willa Kim, *Goodtime Charley*
Tanya Moiseiwitsch, *The Misanthrope*
Patricia Zipprodt, *Mack and Mabel*

BEST LIGHTING DESIGNER
Chipmonck, *The Rocky Horror Show*
Feder, *Goodtime Charley*
Neil Peter Jampolis, *Sherlock Holmes*
Andy Phillips, *Equus*
Thomas Shelton, *All God's Chillun Got Wings*
James Tilton, *Seascape*

SPECIAL AWARD
Neil Simon

THEATRE AWARD '75
Al Hirschfeld

BEST ACTRESS IN A BROADWAY PLAY
Tovah Feldshuh, *Yentl*
Rosemary Harris, *The Royal Family*
Lynn Redgrave, *Mrs. Warren's Profession*
Irene Worth, *Sweet Bird of Youth*

BEST ACTOR IN A BROADWAY PLAY
Moses Gunn, *The Poison Tree*
George C. Scott, *Death of a Salesman*
Donald Sinden, *Habeas Corpus*
John Wood, *Travesties*

BEST ACTRESS IN A FEATURED ROLE IN A BROADWAY PLAY
Marybeth Hurt, *Trelawny of the "Wells"*
Shirley Knight, *Kennedy's Children*
Lois Nettleton, *They Knew What They Wanted*
Meryl Streep, *27 Wagons Full of Cotton*

BEST ACTOR IN A FEATURED ROLE IN A BROADWAY PLAY
Barry Bostwick, *They Knew What They Wanted*
Gabriel Dell, *Lamppost Reunion*
Edward Herrmann, *Mrs. Warren's Profession*
Daniel Seltzer, *Knock, Knock*

BEST ACTRESS IN A BROADWAY MUSICAL
Donna McKechnie, *A Chorus Line*
Vivian Reed, *Bubbling Brown Sugar*
Chita Rivera, *Chicago*
Gwen Verdon, *Chicago*

BEST ACTOR IN A BROADWAY MUSICAL
Mako, *Pacific Overtures*
Jerry Orbach, *Chicago*
Ian Richardson, *My Fair Lady*
George Rose, *My Fair Lady*

BEST ACTRESS IN A FEATURED ROLE IN A BROADWAY MUSICAL
Carole Bishop, *A Chorus Line*
Priscilla Lopez, *A Chorus Line*

Patti LuPone, *The Robber Bridegroom*
Virginia Seidel, *Very Good Eddie*

BEST ACTOR IN A FEATURED ROLE IN A BROADWAY MUSICAL
Robert LuPone, *A Chorus Line*
Charles Repole, *Very Good Eddie*
Isao Sato, *Pacific Overtures*
Sammy Williams, *A Chorus Line*

BEST BROADWAY PLAY
The First Breeze of Summer, by Leslie Lee. Produced by The Negro Ensemble Company.
Knock, Knock, by Jules Feiffer. Produced by Harry Rigby and Terry Allen Kramer.
Lamppost Reunion, by Louis LaRusso II. Produced by Joe Garofalo.
Travesties, by Tom Stoppard. Produced by David Merrick, Doris Cole Abrahams, and Burry Frederik, in association with S. Spencer Davids and Eddie Kulukundis.

BEST BROADWAY MUSICAL
A Chorus Line. Produced by The New York Shakespeare Festival/Joseph Papp
Bubbling Brown Sugar. Produced by J. Lloyd Grant, Richard Bell, Robert M. Cooper, and Ashton Springer, in association with Moe Septee, Inc.
Chicago. Produced by Robert Fryer and James Cresson.
Pacific Overtures. Produced by Harold Prince, in association with Ruth Mitchell.

BEST SCORE OF A BROADWAY MUSICAL
A Chorus Line, music by Marvin Hamlisch; lyrics by Edward Kleban
Chicago, music by John Kander; lyrics by Fred Ebb
Pacific Overtures, music and lyrics by Stephen Sondheim
Treemonisha, music and lyrics by Scott Joplin

BEST BOOK OF A BROADWAY MUSICAL

A Chorus Line, by James Kirkwood and Nicholas Dante

Chicago, by Fred Ebb and Bob Fosse

Pacific Overtures, by John Weidman

The Robber Bridegroom, by Alfred Uhry

BEST DIRECTOR OF A BROADWAY PLAY

Arvin Brown, *Ah, Wilderness!*

Marshall W. Mason, *Knock, Knock*

Ellis Rabb, *The Royal Family*

Peter Wood, *Travesties*

BEST DIRECTOR OF A BROADWAY MUSICAL

Michael Bennett, *A Chorus Line*

Bob Fosse, *Chicago*

Bill Gile, *Very Good Eddie*

Harold Prince, *Pacific Overtures*

BEST CHOREOGRAPHER OF A BROADWAY MUSICAL

Michael Bennett and **Bob Avian, *A Chorus Line***

Patricia Birch, *Pacific Overtures*

Bob Fosse, *Chicago*

Billy Wilson, *Bubbling Brown Sugar*

BEST SCENIC DESIGNER OF A BROADWAY PLAY

Boris Aronson, *Pacific Overtures*

Ben Edwards, *A Matter of Gravity*

David Mitchell, *Trelawny of the "Wells"*

Tony Walton, *Chicago*

BEST COSTUME DESIGNER OF A BROADWAY PLAY

Theoni V. Aldredge, *A Chorus Line*

Florence Klotz, *Pacific Overtures*

Ann Roth, *The Royal Family*

Patricia Zipprodt, *Chicago*

BEST LIGHTING DESIGNER OF A BROADWAY PLAY

Ian Calderon, *Trelawney of the "Wells"*

Jules Fisher, *Chicago*

Tharon Musser, *A Chorus Line*

Tharon Musser, *Pacific Overtures*

SPECIAL AWARDS

Mathilde Pincus, for outstanding service to the Broadway musical theatre.

Thomas H. Fitzgerald, to the gifted lighting technician of countless Broadway shows and many Tony telecasts (posthumous).

Arena Stage, Washington, D.C.—this award takes note of the company's balanced program of distinguished revivals and a broad spectrum of new works and American premieres of important foreign plays.

Circle in the Square, for twenty-five continuous years of quality productions.

Richard Burton

LAWRENCE LANGNER AWARD

George Abbott

Named after the co-founder of the Theatre Guild, a major Broadway production group of the thirties and forties, the Lawrence Langner Award is given for "distinguished lifetime achievement" in the theater.

31st ANNUAL TONY AWARDS
PRESENTED JUNE 5, 1977
SAM S. SHUBERT THEATRE

BEST ACTRESS IN A BROADWAY PLAY

Colleen Dewhurst, *Who's Afraid of Virginia Woolf?*

Julie Harris, *The Belle of Amherst*

Liv Ullmann, *Anna Christie*

Irene Worth, *The Cherry Orchard*

BEST ACTOR IN A BROADWAY PLAY

Tom Courtenay, *Otherwise Engaged*

Ben Gazzara, *Who's Afraid of Virginia Woolf?*

Al Pacino, *The Basic Training of Pavlo Hummel*

Ralph Richardson, *No Man's Land*

BEST ACTRESS IN A FEATURED ROLE IN A BROADWAY PLAY

Trazana Beverley, *For Colored Girls Who Have Considered Suicide/When the Rainbow Is Enuf*

Patricia Elliott, *The Shadow Box*

Rose Gregorio, *The Shadow Box*

Mary McCarty, *Anna Christie*

BEST ACTOR IN A FEATURED ROLE IN A BROADWAY PLAY

Bob Dishy, *Sly Fox*

Joe Fields, *The Basic Training of Pavlo Hummel*

Laurence Luckinbill, *The Shadow Box*

Jonathan Pryce, *Comedians*

BEST ACTRESS IN A BROADWAY MUSICAL

Clamma Dale, *Porgy and Bess*

Ernestine Jackson, *Guys and Dolls*

Dorothy Loudon, *Annie*

Andrea McArdle, *Annie*

BEST ACTOR IN A BROADWAY MUSICAL
Barry Bostwick, *The Robber Bridegroom*
Robert Guillaume, *Guys and Dolls*
Raul Julia, *Threepenny Opera*
Reid Shelton, *Annie*

BEST ACTRESS IN A FEATURED ROLE IN A BROADWAY MUSICAL
Ellen Greene, *Threepenny Opera*
Delores Hall, *Your Arm's Too Short to Box with God*
Julie N. McKenzie, *Side by Side by Sondheim*
Millicent Martin, *Side by Side by Sondheim*

BEST ACTOR IN A FEATURED ROLE IN A BROADWAY MUSICAL
Lenny Baker, *I Love My Wife*
David Kernan, *Side by Side by Sondheim*
Larry Marshall, *Porgy and Bess*
Ned Sherrin, *Side by Side by Sondheim*

BEST BROADWAY PLAY
For Colored Girls Who Have Considered Suicide/When The Rainbow Is Enuf, by Ntozake Shange. Produced by Joseph Papp.
Otherwise Engaged, by Simon Gray. Produced by Michael Codron, Frank Milton, and James M. Nederlander.
Streamers, by David Rabe. Produced by Joseph Papp.
The Shadow Box, by Michael Cristofer. Produced by Allan Francis, Ken Marsolais, Lester Osterman, and Leonard Soloway.

BEST BROADWAY MUSICAL
Annie. Produced by Lewis Allen, Mike Nichols, Irwin Meyer, and Stephen R. Friedman.
Happy End. Produced by Michael Harvey and the Chelsea Theatre Center.
I Love My Wife. Produced by Terry Allen Kramer and Harry Rigby, in association with Joseph Kipness.

Side by Side by Sondheim. Produced by Harold Prince, in association with Ruth Mitchell.

BEST SCORE OF A BROADWAY MUSICAL
Annie, music by Charles Strouse; lyrics by Martin Charnin
Godspell, music and lyrics by Stephen Schwartz
Happy End, music by Kurt Weill; lyrics by Bertolt Brecht; lyrics adapted by Michael Feingold
I Love My Wife, music by Cy Coleman; lyrics by Michael Stewart

BEST BOOK OF A BROADWAY MUSICAL
Annie, by Thomas Meehan
Happy End, by Elizabeth Hauptmann, adapted by Michael Feingold
I Love My Wife, by Michael Stewart
Your Arm's Too Short to Box with God, by Vinnette Carroll

BEST DIRECTOR OF A BROADWAY PLAY
Gordon Davidson, *The Shadow Box*
Ulu Grosbard, *American Buffalo*
Mike Nichols, *Streamers*
Mike Nichols, *Comedians*

BEST DIRECTOR OF A BROADWAY MUSICAL
Vinnette Carroll, *Your Arm's Too Short to Box with God*
Martin Charnin, *Annie*
Jack O'Brien, *Porgy and Bess*
Gene Saks, *I Love My Wife*

BEST CHOREOGRAPHER
Talley Beatty, *Your Arm's Too Short to Box with God*
Patricia Birch, *Music Is*
Peter Gennaro, *Annie*
Onna White, *I Love My Wife*

BEST SCENIC DESIGNER OF A BROADWAY PLAY
Santo Loquasto, *American Buffalo* and *Threepenny Opera*
David Mitchell, *Annie*
Robert Randolph, *Porgy and Bess*

The Cherry Orchard *(1977)*

BEST COSTUME DESIGNER OF A BROADWAY PLAY
Theoni V. Aldredge, *Annie* and *Threepenny Opera*
Santo Loquasto, *The Cherry Orchard*
Nancy Potts, *Porgy and Bess*

BEST LIGHTING DESIGNER OF A BROADWAY PLAY
John Bury, *No Man's Land*
Pat Collins, *Threepenny Opera*
Neil Peter Jampolis, *The Innocents*
Jennifer Tipton, *The Cherry Orchard*

MOST INNOVATIVE PRODUCTION OF A REVIVAL
Guys and Dolls. Produced by Moe Septee, in association with Victor H. Potamkin, Carmen F. Zollo, and Ashton Springer.
Porgy and Bess. Produced by Sherwin M. Goldman and the Houston Grand Opera.
The Cherry Orchard. Produced by Joseph Papp.
Threepenny Opera. Produced by Joseph Papp.

SPECIAL AWARDS
Equity Library Theatre
The National Theatre of the Deaf
Center Theatre Group/Mark Taper Forum, Los Angeles, California
Barry Manilow
Diana Ross
Lily Tomlin

LAWRENCE LANGNER AWARD
Cheryl Crawford

In some cases (e.g., Best Costume Designer of a Broadway Play), an individual was *nominated* for his or her work on several productions but actually received the award for one. In these instances, only the award-winning play appears in boldface type.

32nd ANNUAL TONY AWARDS
PRESENTED JUNE 4, 1978
SAM S. SHUBERT THEATRE

OUTSTANDING PERFORMANCE BY AN ACTRESS IN A BROADWAY PLAY
Anne Bancroft, *Golda*
Anita Gillette, *Chapter Two*
Estelle Parsons, *Miss Margarida's Way*
Jessica Tandy, *The Gin Game*

OUTSTANDING PERFORMANCE BY AN ACTOR IN A BROADWAY PLAY
Hume Cronyn, *The Gin Game*
Barnard Hughes, *Da*
Frank Langella, *Dracula*
Jason Robards, *A Touch of the Poet*

OUTSTANDING PERFORMANCE BY AN ACTRESS IN A FEATURED ROLE IN A BROADWAY PLAY
Starletta DuPois, *The Mighty Gents*
Swoosie Kurtz, *Tartuffe*
Marian Seldes, *Deathtrap*
Ann Wedgeworth, *Chapter Two*

OUTSTANDING PERFORMANCE BY AN ACTOR IN A FEATURED ROLE IN A BROADWAY PLAY
Morgan Freeman, *The Mighty Gents*
Victor Garber, *Deathtrap*
Cliff Gorman, *Chapter Two*
Lester Rawlins, *Da*

OUTSTANDING PERFORMANCE BY AN ACTRESS IN A BROADWAY MUSICAL
Madeline Kahn, *On the Twentieth Century*
Eartha Kitt, *Timbuktu!*
Liza Minnelli, *The Act*
Frances Sternhagen, *Angel*

OUTSTANDING PERFORMANCE BY AN ACTOR IN A BROADWAY MUSICAL
Eddie Bracken, *Hello, Dolly!*
John Cullum, *On the Twentieth Century*
Barry Nelson, *The Act*
Gilbert Price, *Timbuktu!*

OUTSTANDING PERFORMANCE BY AN ACTRESS IN A FEATURED ROLE IN A BROADWAY MUSICAL
Nell Carter, *Ain't Misbehavin'*
Imogene Coca, *On the Twentieth Century*
Ann Reinking, *Dancin'*
Charlaine Woodard, *Ain't Misbehavin'*

OUTSTANDING PERFORMANCE BY AN ACTOR IN A FEATURED ROLE IN A BROADWAY PLAY
Steven Boockvor, *Working*

Wayne Cilento, *Dancin'*
Rex Everhart, *Working*
Kevin Kline, *On the Twentieth Century*

BEST BROADWAY PLAY
Chapter Two, by Neil Simon. Produced by Emanuel Azenberg.
Da, by Hugh Leonard. Produced by Lester Osterman, Marilyn Strauss, and Marc Howard.
Deathtrap, by Ira Levin. Produced by Alfred de Liagre, Jr., and Roger L. Stevens.
The Gin Game, by D. L. Coburn. Produced by The Shubert Organization, Hume Cronyn, and Mike Nichols.

BEST BROADWAY MUSICAL
Ain't Misbehavin'. Produced by Emanuel Azenberg, Dasha Epstein, The Shubert Organization, Jane Gaynor, and Ron Dante.
Dancin'. Produced by Jules Fisher, The Shubert Organization, and Columbia Pictures.
On The Twentieth Century. Produced by The Producers Circle 2, Inc. (Robert Fryer, Mary Lea Johnson, James Cresson, Martin Richards), Joseph Harris, and Ira Bernstein.
Runaways. Produced by Joseph Papp.

BEST SCORE OF A BROADWAY MUSICAL
The Act, music by John Kander; lyrics by Fred Ebb
On the Twentieth Century, music by Cy Coleman; lyrics by Betty Comden and Adolph Green
Runaways, music and lyrics by Elizabeth Swados
Working, music and lyrics by Craig Carnelia, Micki Grant, Mary Rodgers/Susan Birkenhead, Stephen Schwartz, and James Taylor

BEST BOOK OF A BROADWAY MUSICAL
A History of the American Film, by Christopher Durang
On the Twentieth Century, by Betty Comden and Adolph Green

Runaways, by Elizabeth Swados
Working, by Stephen Schwartz

OUTSTANDING DIRECTOR OF A BROADWAY PLAY
Melvin Bernhardt, *Da*
Robert Moore, *Deathtrap*
Mike Nichols, *The Gin Game*
Dennis Rosa, *Dracula*

OUTSTANDING DIRECTOR OF A BROADWAY MUSICAL
Bob Fosse, *Dancin'*
Richard Maltby, Jr., *Ain't Misbehavin'*
Harold Prince, *On the Twentieth Century*
Elizabeth Swados, *Runaways*

OUTSTANDING CHOREOGRAPHER OF A BROADWAY MUSICAL
Arthur Faria, *Ain't Misbehavin'*
Bob Fosse, *Dancin'*
Ron Lewis, *The Act*
Elizabeth Swados, *Runaways*

OUTSTANDING SCENIC DESIGNER OF A BROADWAY PLAY
Zack Brown, *The Importance of Being Earnest*
Edward Gorey, *Dracula*
David Mitchell, *Working*
Robin Wagner, *On the Twentieth Century*

OUTSTANDING COSTUME DESIGNER OF A BROADWAY PLAY
Edward Gorey, *Dracula*
Halston, *The Act*
Geoffrey Holder, *Timbuktu!*
Willa Kim, *Dancin'*

OUTSTANDING LIGHTING DESIGNER OF A BROADWAY PLAY
Ken Billington, *Working*
Jules Fisher, *Beatlemania*
Jules Fisher, *Dancin'*
Tharon Musser, *The Act*

MOST INNOVATIVE PRODUCTION OF A REVIVAL
Dracula. Produced by Jujamcyn Theatre, Elizabeth I. McCann, John Wulp, Victor Lurie, Nelle Nugent, and Max Weitzenhoffer.
Tartuffe. Produced by Circle in the Square.
Timbuktu! Produced by Luther Davis.
A Touch of the Poet. Produced by Elliot Martin.

SPECIAL AWARDS
Long Wharf Theatre, New Haven, Connecticut

THEATRE AWARD '78
To the creators, Charles Moss and Stan Dragoti (of Wells, Rich, Greene, Inc.), of the "I Love New York Broadway Show Tours," and its sponsor, The New York State Department of Commerce.

LAWRENCE LANGNER MEMORIAL AWARD FOR DISTINGUISHED LIFETIME ACHIEVEMENT IN THE AMERICAN THEATRE
Irving Berlin

33rd ANNUAL TONY AWARDS
PRESENTED JUNE 3, 1979
SAM S. SHUBERT THEATRE

OUTSTANDING PERFORMANCE BY AN ACTRESS IN A BROADWAY PLAY
Jane Alexander, *First Monday in October*
Constance Cummings, *Wings*
Carole Shelley, *The Elephant Man*
Frances Sternhagen, *On Golden Pond*

OUTSTANDING PERFORMANCE BY AN ACTOR IN A BROADWAY PLAY
Philip Anglim, *The Elephant Man*
Tom Conti, *Whose Life Is It Anyway?*
Jack Lemmon, *Tribute*
Alec McCowen, *St. Mark's Gospel*

OUTSTANDING PERFORMANCE BY A FEATURED ACTRESS IN A BROADWAY PLAY
Joan Hickson, *Bedroom Farce*
Laurie Kennedy, *Man and Superman*
Susan Littler, *Bedroom Farce*
Mary-Joan Negro, *Wings*

OUTSTANDING PERFORMANCE BY A FEATURED ACTOR IN A BROADWAY PLAY
Bob Balaban, *The Inspector General*
Michael Gough, *Bedroom Farce*
Joseph Maher, *Spokesong*
Edward James Olmos, *Zoot Suit*

OUTSTANDING PERFORMANCE BY AN ACTRESS IN A BROADWAY MUSICAL
Tovah Feldshuh, *Sarava*
Angela Lansbury, *Sweeney Todd*
Dorothy Loudon, *Ballroom*
Alexis Smith, *Platinum*

OUTSTANDING PERFORMANCE BY AN ACTOR IN A BROADWAY MUSICAL
Len Cariou, *Sweeney Todd*
Vincent Gardenia, *Ballroom*
Joel Grey, *The Grand Tour*
Robert Klein, *They're Playing Our Song*

OUTSTANDING PERFORMANCE BY A FEATURED ACTRESS IN A BROADWAY MUSICAL
Joan Ellis, *The Best Little Whorehouse in Texas*
Carlin Glynn, *The Best Little Whorehouse in Texas*
Millicent Martin, *King of Hearts*
Maxine Sullivan, *My Old Friends*

OUTSTANDING PERFORMANCE BY A FEATURED ACTOR IN A BROADWAY MUSICAL
Richard Cox, *Platinum*
Henderson Forsythe, *The Best Little Whorehouse in Texas*
Gregory Hines, *Eubie!*
Ron Holgate, *The Grand Tour*

Michael Gough and Joan Hickson in Bedroom Farce *(1979)*

BEST BROADWAY PLAY
Bedroom Farce, by Alan Ayckbourn. Produced by Robert Whitehead, Roger L. Stevens, George W. George, and Frank Milton.
The Elephant Man, by Bernard Pomerance. Produced by Richmond Crinkley, Elizabeth I. McCann, and Nelle Nugent.
Whose Life Is It Anyway?, by Brian Clark. Produced by Emanuel Azenberg, James Nederlander, and Ray Cooney.
Wings, by Arthur Kopit. Produced by the Kennedy Center.

BEST BROADWAY MUSICAL
Ballroom. Produced by Michael Bennett, Bob Avian, Bernard Gersten, and Susan MacNair.
Sweeney Todd. Produced by Richard Barr, Charles Woodward, Robert Fryer, Mary Lea Johnson, and Martin Richards.
The Best Little Whorehouse in Texas. Produced by Universal Pictures.
They're Playing Our Song. Produced by Emanuel Azenberg.

BEST SCORE OF A MUSICAL
Carmelina, music by Burton Lane; lyrics by Alan Jay Lerner
Eubie!, music by Eubie Blake; lyrics by Noble Sissle, Andy Razaf, F. E. Miller, Johnny Brandon, and Jim Europe
Sweeney Todd, music and lyrics by Stephen Sondheim
The Grand Tour, music and lyrics by Jerry Herman

BEST BOOK OF A BROADWAY MUSICAL
Ballroom, by Jerome Kass
Sweeney Todd, by Hugh Wheeler
The Best Little Whorehouse in Texas, by Larry L. King and Peter Masterson
They're Playing Our Song, by Neil Simon

OUTSTANDING DIRECTION OF A BROADWAY PLAY
Alan Ayckbourn and Peter Hall, *Bedroom Farce*
Paul Giovanni, *The Crucifer of Blood*
Jack Hofsiss, *The Elephant Man*
Michael Lindsay-Hogg, *Whose Life Is It Anyway?*

OUTSTANDING DIRECTION OF A BROADWAY MUSICAL
Michael Bennett, *Ballroom*
Peter Masterson and Tommy Tune, *The Best Little Whorehouse in Texas*

Robert Moore, *They're Playing Our Song*
Harold Prince, *Sweeney Todd*

OUTSTANDING CHOREOGRAPHY OF A BROADWAY PRODUCTION
Michael Bennett and **Bob Avian, *Ballroom***
Henry LeTang and Billy Wilson, *Eubie!*
Dan Siretta, *Whoopee!*
Tommy Tune, *The Best Little Whorehouse in Texas*

OUTSTANDING SCENIC DESIGN OF A BROADWAY PRODUCTION
Karl Eigsti, *Knockout*
David Jenkins, *The Elephant Man*
Eugene Lee, *Sweeney Todd*
John Wulp, *The Crucifer of Blood*

OUTSTANDING COSTUME DESIGN OF A BROADWAY PRODUCTION
Theoni V. Aldredge, *Ballroom*
Franne Lee, *Sweeney Todd*
Ann Roth, *The Crucifer of Blood*
Julie Weiss, *The Elephant Man*

OUTSTANDING LIGHTING DESIGN OF A BROADWAY PRODUCTION
Ken Billington, *Sweeney Todd*
Beverly Emmons, *The Elephant Man*
Roger Morgan, *The Crucifer of Blood*
Tharon Musser, *Ballroom*

SPECIAL AWARDS
American Conservatory Theater, San Francisco, California
Eugene O'Neill Theatre Center, Waterford, Connecticut
Henry Fonda
Walter F. Diehl, International President of the International Alliance of Theatrical Stage Employees and Moving Picture Operators, has been an active force in advancing the well-being of the Broadway theatre and of theatre nationally.

LAWRENCE LANGNER AWARD FOR DISTINGUISHED LIFETIME ACHIEVEMENT IN THE THEATRE
Richard Rodgers

34th ANNUAL TONY AWARDS
PRESENTED JUNE 8, 1980
MARK HELLINGER THEATRE

OUTSTANDING PERFORMANCE BY AN ACTRESS IN A BROADWAY PLAY
Blythe Danner, *Betrayal*
Phyllis Frelich, *Children of a Lesser God*
Maggie Smith, *Night and Day*
Anne Twomey, *Nuts*

OUTSTANDING PERFORMANCE BY AN ACTOR IN A BROADWAY PLAY
Charles Brown, *Home*
Gerald Kiken, *Strider*
Judd Hirsch, *Talley's Folly*
John Rubinstein, *Children of a Lesser God*

OUTSTANDING PERFORMANCE BY A FEATURED ACTRESS IN A BROADWAY PLAY
Maureen Anderman, *The Lady from Dubuque*
Pamela Burrell, *Strider*
Lois deBanzie, *Morning's at Seven*
Dinah Manoff, *I Ought to Be in Pictures*

OUTSTANDING PERFORMANCE BY A FEATURED ACTOR IN A BROADWAY PLAY
David Dukes, *Bent*
George Hearn, *Watch on the Rhine*
Earle Hyman, *The Lady from Dubuque*
Joseph Maher, *Night and Day*
David Rounds, *Morning's at Seven*

OUTSTANDING PERFORMANCE BY AN ACTRESS IN A BROADWAY MUSICAL
Christine Andreas, *Oklahoma!*
Sandy Duncan, *Peter Pan*
Patti LuPone, *Evita*
Ann Miller, *Sugar Babies*

OUTSTANDING PERFORMANCE BY AN ACTOR IN A BROADWAY MUSICAL
Jim Dale, *Barnum*
Gregory Hines, *Comin' Uptown*
Mickey Rooney, *Sugar Babies*
Giorgio Tozzi, *The Most Happy Fella*

OUTSTANDING PERFORMANCE BY A FEATURED ACTRESS IN A BROADWAY MUSICAL
Debbie Allen, *West Side Story*
Glenn Close, *Barnum*
Jossie DeGuzman, *West Side Story*
Priscilla Lopez, *A Day in Hollywood/A Night in the Ukraine*

OUTSTANDING PERFORMANCE BY A FEATURED ACTOR IN A BROADWAY MUSICAL
David Garrison, *A Day in Hollywood/A Night in the Ukraine*
Harry Groener, *Oklahoma!*
Bob Gunton, *Evita*
Mandy Patinkin, *Evita*

BEST BROADWAY PLAY
Bent, by Martin Sherman. Produced by Jack Schlissel and Steven Steinlauf.
Children of a Lesser God, by Mark Medoff. Produced by Emanuel Azenberg, the Shubert Organization, Dasha Epstein, and Ron Dante.

Home, by Samm-Art Williams. Produced by Elizabeth I. McCann, Nelle Nugent, Gerald S. Krone, and Ray Larsen.
Talley's Folly, by Lanford Wilson. Produced by Nancy Cooperstein, Porter Van Zandt, and Marc Howard.

BEST BROADWAY MUSICAL
A Day in Hollywood/A Night in the Ukraine. Produced by Alexander Cohen and Hildy Parks.
Barnum. Produced by Cy Coleman, Judy Gordon, Maurice Rosenfeld, and Lois Rosenfeld.
Evita. Produced by Robert Stigwood.
Sugar Babies. Produced by Terry Allen Kramer and Harry Rigby.

BEST SCORE OF A BROADWAY MUSICAL
A Day in Hollywood/A Night in the Ukraine, music by Frank Lazarus; lyrics by Dick Vosburgh.
Barnum, music by Cy Coleman; lyrics by Michael Stewart.
Evita, music by Andrew Lloyd Webber; lyrics by Tim Rice.
Sugar Babies, music and lyrics by Arthur Malvin.

BEST BOOK OF A BROADWAY MUSICAL
A Day in Hollywood/A Night in the Ukraine, by Dick Vosburgh
Barnum, by Mark Bramble
Evita, by Tim Rice
Sugar Babies, by Ralph G. Allen and Harry Rigby

OUTSTANDING DIRECTION OF A BROADWAY PLAY
Gordon Davidson, *Children of a Lesser God*
Peter Hall, *Betrayal*
Marshall W. Mason, *Talley's Folly*
Vivian Matalon, *Morning's at Seven*

OUTSTANDING DIRECTION OF A BROADWAY MUSICAL
Ernest Flatt and Rudy Tronto, *Sugar Babies*

Joe Layton, *Barnum*
Hal Prince, *Evita*
Tommy Tune, *A Day in Hollywood/A Night in the Ukraine*

OUTSTANDING CHOREOGRAPHY OF A BROADWAY PRODUCTION
Ernest Flatt, *Sugar Babies*
Larry Fuller, *Evita*
Joe Layton, *Barnum*
Tommy Tune and **Thommie Walsh, *A Day in Hollywood/A Night in the Ukraine***

OUTSTANDING SCENIC DESIGN OF A BROADWAY PRODUCTION
John Lee Beatty, *Talley's Folly*
David Mitchell, *Barnum*
Timothy O'Brien and Tazeena Firth, *Evita*
Tony Walton, *A Day in Hollywood/A Night in the Ukraine*

OUTSTANDING COSTUME DESIGN OF A BROADWAY PRODUCTION
Theoni V. Aldredge, *Barnum*
Pierre Balmain, *Happy New Year*
Timothy O'Brien and Tazeena Firth, *Evita*
Raoul Pène Du Bois, *Sugar Babies*

OUTSTANDING LIGHTING DESIGN OF A BROADWAY PRODUCTION
Beverly Emmons, *A Day in Hollywood/A Night in the Ukraine*
David Hersey, *Evita*
Craig Miller, *Barnum*
Dennis Parichy, *Talley's Folly*

OUTSTANDING REPRODUCTION OF A BROADWAY PLAY OR MUSICAL
Major Barbara. Produced by Circle in the Square.
Morning's at Seven. Produced by Elizabeth I. McCann, Nelle Nugent, and Ray Larson.
Peter Pan. Produced by Zev Bufman and James M. Nederlander.

West Side Story. Produced by Gladys Rackmil, the John F. Kennedy Center, James M. Nederlander, and Ruth Mitchell.

SPECIAL AWARDS
Actors Theatre of Louisville, Kentucky
Goodspeed Opera House, East Haddam, Connecticut
Mary Tyler Moore, *Whose Life Is It Anyway?*

THEATER AWARD '80
Richard Fitzgerald, honored for his installing the infrared system in Broadway theaters, thus bringing the compassion and dedication of making theatergoing for those with impaired hearing, rewarding, stimulating, and enjoyable.
Hobe Morrison, theater editor of *Variety.*

LAWRENCE LANGNER AWARD FOR DISTINGUISHED LIFETIME ACHIEVEMENT IN THE THEATRE
Helen Hayes

OUTSTANDING PERFORMANCE BY AN ACTRESS IN A PLAY
Glenda Jackson, *Rose*
Jane Lapotaire, *Piaf*
Eva Le Gallienne, *To Grandmother's House We Go*
Elizabeth Taylor, *The Little Foxes*

OUTSTANDING PERFORMANCE BY AN ACTOR IN A PLAY
Tim Curry, *Amadeus*
Roy Dotrice, *A Life*
Ian McKellen, *Amadeus*
Jack Weston, *The Floating Light Bulb*

OUTSTANDING PERFORMANCE BY A FEATURED ACTRESS IN A PLAY
Swoosie Kurtz, *Fifth of July*

Maureen Stapleton, *The Little Foxes*
Jessica Tandy, *Rose*
Zoe Wanamaker, *Piaf*

OUTSTANDING PERFORMANCE BY A FEATURED ACTOR IN A PLAY
Tom Aldredge, *The Little Foxes*
Brian Backer, *The Floating Light Bulb*
Adam Redfield, *A Life*
Shepperd Strudwick, *To Grandmother's House We Go*

OUTSTANDING PERFORMANCE BY AN ACTRESS IN A MUSICAL
Lauren Bacall, *Woman of the Year*
Meg Bussert, *Brigadoon*
Chita Rivera, *Bring Back Birdie*
Linda Ronstadt, *The Pirates of Penzance*

OUTSTANDING PERFORMANCE BY AN ACTOR IN A MUSICAL
Gregory Hines, *Sophisticated Ladies*
Keven Kline, *The Pirates of Penzance*
George Rose, *The Pirates of Penzance*
Martin Vidnovic, *Brigadoon*

OUTSTANDING PERFORMANCE BY A FEATURED ACTRESS IN A MUSICAL
Marilyn Cooper, *Woman of the Year*
Phillis Hyman, *Sophisticated Ladies*
Wanda Richert, *42nd Street*
Lynne Thigpen, *Tintypes*

OUTSTANDING PERFORMANCE BY A FEATURED ACTOR IN A MUSICAL
Tony Azito, *The Pirates of Penzance*
Hinton Battle, *Sophisticated Ladies*
Lee Roy Reams, *42nd Street*
Paxton Whitehead, *Camelot*

BEST PLAY
A Lesson from Aloes, by Athol Fugard. Produced by Jay J. Cohen, Richard Press, Louis Bush Hager Associates, and Yale Repertory Theater.
A Life, by Hugh Leonard. Produced by Lester Osterman, Richard Horner, Hinks Shimberg, and Freydberg Cutler-Diamond Productions.

Amadeus, by Peter Shaffer. Produced by The Shubert Organization, Elizabeth I. McCann, Nelle Nugent, and Roger S. Berlind.

Fifth of July, by Lanford Wilson. Produced by Robert Lussier and Warner Theatre Productions, Inc.

BEST MUSICAL

42nd Street. Produced by David Merrick.

Sophisticated Ladies. Produced by Roger S. Berlind, Manheim Fox, Sondra Gilman, Burton L. Litwin, Louise Westergaard, Belwin Mills Publishing Corp., and Norzar Productions, Inc.

Tintypes. Produced by Richmond Crinkley, Royal Pardon Productions, Ivan Bloch, Larry J. Silva, Eve Skina, and Joan F. Tobin.

Woman of the Year. Produced by Lawrence Kasha, David S. Landay, James M. Nederlander, Warner Theatre Productions, Claire Nichtern, Carole J. Shorenstein, and Stewart F. Lane.

BEST SCORE OF A MUSICAL

Charlie and Algernon, music by Charles Strouse; lyrics by David Rogers

Copperfield, music and lyrics by Al Kasha and Joel Hirschhorn

Shakespeare's Cabaret, music by Lance Mulcahy

Woman of the Year, music by John Kander; lyrics by Fred Ebb

BEST BOOK OF A MUSICAL

42nd Street, by Michael Stewart and Mark Bramble

The Mooney Shapiro Songbook, by Monty Norman and Julian More

Tintypes, by Mary Kyte

Woman of the Year, by Peter Stone

OUSTANDING DIRECTOR OF A PLAY

Peter Coe, *A Life*

Peter Hall, *Amadeus*

Marshall W. Mason, *Fifth of July*

Austin Pendleton, *The Little Foxes*

OUTSTANDING DIRECTOR OF A MUSICAL

Gower Champion, *42nd Street*

Wilford Leach, *The Pirates of Penzance*

Robert Moore, *Woman of the Year*

Michael Smuin, *Sophisticated Ladies*

OUTSTANDING CHOREOGRAPHY

Gower Champion, *42nd Street*

Graciela Daniele, *The Pirates of Penzance*

Henry LeTang, Donald McKayle, and Michael Smuin, *Sophisticated Ladies*

Roland Petit, *Can-Can*

OUTSTANDING SCENIC DESIGNER

John Lee Beatty, *Fifth of July*

John Bury, *Amadeus*

Santo Loquasto, *The Suicide*

David Mitchell, *Can-Can*

OUTSTANDING COSTUME DESIGNER

Theoni V. Aldredge, *42nd Street*

John Bury, *Amadeus*

Willa Kim, *Sophisticated Ladies*

Franca Squarciapino, *Can-Can*

OUTSTANDING LIGHTING DESIGNER

John Bury, *Amadeus*

Tharon Musser, *42nd Street*

Dennis Parichy, *Fifth of July*

Jennifer Tipton, *Sophisticated Ladies*

OUTSTANDING REPRODUCTION OF A PLAY OR MUSICAL

Brigadoon. Produced by Zev Bufman and The Shubert Organization.

Camelot. Produced by Mike Merrick and Don Gregory.

The Little Foxes. Produced by Zev Bufman, Donald C. Carter, and Jon Cutler.

The Pirates of Penzance. Produced by Joseph Papp and The New York Shakespeare Festival.

SPECIAL AWARDS

Trinity Square Repertory Company, Providence, Rhode Island

Lena Horne, for *Lena Horne: A Lady and Her Music*

OUTSTANDING PERFORMANCE BY AN ACTRESS IN A PLAY

Zoe Caldwell, *Medea*

Katharine Hepburn, *The West Side Waltz*

Geraldine Page, *Agnes of God*

Amanda Plummer, *A Taste of Honey*

OUTSTANDING PERFORMANCE BY AN ACTOR IN A PLAY

Tom Courtenay, *The Dresser*

Milo O'Shea, *Mass Appeal*

Christopher Plummer, *Othello*

Roger Rees, *The Life and Adventures of Nicholas Nickleby*

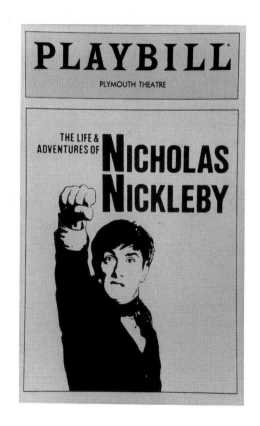

OUTSTANDING PERFORMANCE BY A FEATURED ACTRESS IN A PLAY
Judith Anderson, *Medea*
Mia Dillon, *Crimes of the Heart*
Mary Beth Hurt, *Crimes of the Heart*
Amanda Plummer, *Agnes of God*

OUTSTANDING PERFORMANCE BY A FEATURED ACTOR IN A PLAY
Richard Kavanaugh, *The Hothouse*
Zakes Mokae, *'Master Harold' . . . and the boys*
Edward Petherbridge, *The Life and Adventures of Nicholas Nickleby*
David Threlfall, *The Life and Adventures of Nicholas Nickleby*

OUTSTANDING PERFORMANCE BY AN ACTRESS IN A MUSICAL
Jennifer Holliday, *Dreamgirls*
Lisa Mordente, *Marlowe*
Mary Gordon Murray, *Little Me*
Sheryl Lee Ralph, *Dreamgirls*

OUTSTANDING PERFORMANCE BY AN ACTOR IN A MUSICAL
Herschel Bernardi, *Fiddler on the Roof*
Victor Garber, *Little Me*
Ben Harney, *Dreamgirls*
Raul Julia, *Nine*

OUTSTANDING PERFORMANCE BY A FEATURED ACTRESS IN A MUSICAL
Karen Akers, *Nine*
Laurie Beechman, *Joseph and the Amazing Technicolor Dreamcoat*
Liliane Montevecchi, *Nine*
Anita Morris, *Nine*

OUTSTANDING PERFORMANCE BY A FEATURED ACTOR IN A MUSICAL
Obba Babatunde, *Dreamgirls*
Cleavant Derricks, *Dreamgirls*
David Alan Grier, *The First*
Bill Hutton, *Joseph and the Amazing Technicolor Dreamcoat*

BEST PLAY
Crimes of the Heart, by Beth Henley. Produced by Warner Theatre Productions, Inc., Claire Nichtern, Mary

Lea Johnson, Martin Richards, and Francine LeFrak.
The Dresser, by Ronald Harwood. Produced by James M. Nederlander, Elizabeth I. McCann, Nelle Nugent, Warner Theatre Productions, Inc., and Michael Codron.
***The Life and Adventures of Nicholas Nickleby,* by David Edgar.** Produced by James M. Nederlander, The Shubert Organization, Elizabeth I. McCann, and Nelle Nugent.
'Master Harold' . . . and the boys, by Athol Fugard. Produced by The Shubert Organization, Freydberg/Block Productions, Dasha Epstein, Emanuel Azenberg, and David Geffen.

BEST MUSICAL
Dreamgirls. Produced by Michael Bennett, Bob Avian, Geffen Records, and The Shubert Organization.
Joseph and the Amazing Technicolor Dreamcoat. Produced by Zev Bufman, Susan R. Rose, Melvin J. Estrin, Sidney Schlenker, and Gail Berman.
Nine. Produced by Michel Stuart, Harvey J. Klaris, Roger S. Berlind, James M. Nederlander, Francine LeFrak, and Kenneth D. Greenblatt.
Pump Boys and Dinettes. Produced by Dodger Productions, Louis Busch Hager, Marilyn Strauss, Kate Studley, Warner Theater Productions, Inc., and Max Weitzenhoffer.

BEST SCORE OF A MUSICAL
Dreamgirls, music by Henry Krieger; lyrics by Tom Eyen
Joseph and the Amazing Technicolor Dreamcoat, music by Andrew Lloyd Webber; lyrics by Tim Rice
Merrily We Roll Along, music and lyrics by Stephen Sondheim
***Nine,* music and lyrics by Maury Yeston**

BEST BOOK OF A MUSICAL
***Dreamgirls,* by Tom Eyen**
Joseph and the Amazing Technicolor Dreamcoat, by Tim Rice
Nine, by Arthur Kopit
The First, by Joel Siegel and Martin Charnin

BEST DIRECTOR OF A DRAMATIC PLAY
Melvyn Bernhardt, *Crimes of the Heart*
Geraldine Fitzgerald, *Mass Appeal*
Athol Fugard, *'Master Harold' . . . and the boys*
Trevor Nunn and **John Caird, *The Life and Adventures of Nicholas Nickleby***

OUTSTANDING DIRECTION OF A MUSICAL
Michael Bennett, *Dreamgirls*
Martin Charnin, *The First*
Tony Tanner, *Joseph and the Amazing Technicolor Dreamcoat*
Tommy Tune, *Nine*

OUTSTANDING CHOREOGRAPHY
Michael Bennett and **Michael Peters, *Dreamgirls***
Peter Gennaro, *Little Me*
Tony Tanner, *Joseph and the Amazing Technicolor Dreamcoat*
Tommy Tune, *Nine*

OUTSTANDING SCENIC DESIGN
Ben Edwards, *Medea*
Lawrence Miller, *Nine*
John Napier and **Dermot Hayes, *The Life and Adventures of Nicholas Nickleby***
Robin Wagner, *Dreamgirls*

OUTSTANDING COSTUME DESIGN
Theoni V. Aldredge, *Dreamgirls*
Jane Greenwood, *Medea*
William Ivey Long, *Nine*
John Napier, *The Life and Adventures of Nicholas Nickleby*

OUTSTANDING LIGHTING DESIGN
Martin Aronstein, *Medea*
David Hersey, *The Life and Adventures of Nicholas Nickleby*
Marcia Madeira, *Nine*
Tharon Musser, *Dreamgirls*

OUTSTANDING REPRODUCTION OF A PLAY OR MUSICAL

A Taste of Honey. Produced by Roundabout Theatre Co., Gene Feist, and Michael Fried.

Medea. Produced by Barry and Fran Weissler, The Kennedy Center, and Bunny and Warren Austin.

My Fair Lady. Produced by Mike Merrick and Don Gregory.

Othello. Produced by Barry and Fran Weissler and CBS Video Enterprises.

SPECIAL AWARDS

The Guthrie Theater, Minneapolis, Minnesota

The Actors' Fund of America

THEATRE AWARD '82

Warner Communications

Radio City Music Hall

37th ANNUAL TONY AWARDS
PRESENTED JUNE 5, 1983
GERSHWIN THEATRE

OUTSTANDING PERFORMANCE BY AN ACTRESS IN A PLAY

Kathy Bates, *'night, Mother*

Kate Nelligan, *Plenty*

Anne Pitoniak, *'night, Mother*

Jessica Tandy, *Foxfire*

OUTSTANDING PERFORMANCE BY AN ACTOR IN A PLAY

Jeffrey DeMunn, *K2*

Harvey Fierstein, *Torch Song Trilogy*

Edward Herrmann, *Plenty*

Tony LoBianco, *A View from the Bridge*

OUTSTANDING PERFORMANCE BY A FEATURED ACTRESS IN A PLAY

Elizabeth Franz, *Brighton Beach Memoirs*

Roxanne Hart, *Passion*

Judith Ivey, *Steaming*

Margaret Tyzack, *All's Well That Ends Well*

OUTSTANDING PERFORMANCE BY A FEATURED ACTOR IN A PLAY

Matthew Broderick, *Brighton Beach Memoirs*

Željko Ivanek, *Brighton Beach Memoirs*

George N. Martin, *Plenty*

Stephen Moore, *All's Well That Ends Well*

OUTSTANDING PERFORMANCE BY AN ACTRESS IN A MUSICAL

Lonette McKee, *Show Boat*

Natalia Makarova, *On Your Toes*

Chita Rivera, *Merlin*

Twiggy, *My One and Only*

OUTSTANDING PERFORMANCE BY AN ACTOR IN A MUSICAL

Al Green, *Your Arm's Too Short to Box with God*

George Hearn, *A Doll's Life*

Michael V. Smartt, *Porgy and Bess*

Tommy Tune, *My One and Only*

OUTSTANDING PERFORMANCE BY A FEATURED ACTRESS IN A MUSICAL

Christine Andreas, *On Your Toes*

Betty Buckley, *Cats*

Karla Burns, *Show Boat*

Denny Dillon, *My One and Only*

OUTSTANDING PERFORMANCE BY A FEATURED ACTOR IN A MUSICAL

Charles "Honi" Coles, *My One and Only*

Harry Groener, *Cats*

Stephen Hanan, *Cats*

Lara Teeter, *On Your Toes*

BEST PLAY

Angels Fall, by Landord Wilson. Produced by Elliot Martin, Circle Repertory Company, Lucille Lortel, The Shubert Organization, and The Kennedy Center.

'night, Mother, by Marsha Norman. Produced by Dann Byck, Wendell Cherry, The Shubert Organization, and Frederick M. Zollo.

Plenty, by David Hare. Produced by Joseph Papp.

Torch Song Trilogy, by Harvey Fierstein. Produced by Kenneth Waissman, Martin Markinson, Lawrence Lane, John Glines, BetMar, and Donald Tick.

BEST MUSICAL

Blues in the Night. Produced by Mitchell Maxwell, Alan J. Schuster, Fred H. Krones, and M2 Entertainment, Inc.

Cats. Produced by Cameron Mackintosh, The Really Useful Company, Ltd., David Geffen, and The Shubert Organization.

Merlin. Produced by Ivan Reitman, Columbia Pictures Stage Productions, Inc., Marvin A. Krauss, and James M. Nederlander.

My One and Only. Produced by Paramount Theatre Productions, Francine LeFrak, and Kenneth-Mark Productions

BEST SCORE OF A MUSICAL
A Doll's Life, music by Larry Grossman; lyrics by Betty Comden and Adolph Green
Cats, music by Andrew Lloyd Webber; lyrics by T. S. Eliot
Merlin, music by Elmer Bernstein; lyrics by Don Black
Seven Brides for Seven Brothers, music by Gene de Paul, Al Kasha, and Joel Hirshhorn; lyrics by Johnny Mercer, Al Kasha, and Joel Hirshhorn.

BEST BOOK OF A MUSICAL
A Doll's Life, by Betty Comden and Adolph Green
Cats, by T. S. Eliot
Merlin, by Richard Levinson and William Link
My One and Only, by Peter Stone and Timothy S. Mayer

OUTSTANDING DIRECTION OF A PLAY
Marshall W. Mason, *Angels Fall*
Tom Moore, *'night, Mother*
Trevor Nunn, *All's Well That Ends Well*
Gene Saks, *Brighton Beach Memoirs*

OUTSTANDING DIRECTOR OF A MUSICAL
Michael Kahn, *Show Boat*
Trevor Nunn, *Cats*
Ivan Reitman, *Merlin*
Tommy Tune and Thommie Walsh, *My One and Only*

OUTSTANDING CHOREOGRAPHY
George Faison, *Porgy and Bess*
Gillian Lynne, *Cats*
Donald Saddler, *On Your Toes*
Tommy Tune and **Thommie Walsh,** *My One and Only*

OUTSTANDING SCENIC DESIGN
John Gunter, *All's Well That Ends Well*
Ming Cho Lee, *K2*
David Mitchell, *Foxfire*
John Napier, *Cats*

OUTSTANDING COSTUME DESIGN
Linda Hemmings, *All's Well That Ends Well*

John Napier, *Cats*
Rita Ryack, *My One and Only*
Patricia Zipprodt, *Alice in Wonderland*

OUTSTANDING LIGHTING DESIGN
Ken Billington, *Foxfire*
Robert Bryan and Beverly Emmons, *All's Well That Ends Well*
David Hersey, *Cats*
Allen Lee Hughes, *K2*

OUTSTANDING REPRODUCTION OF A PLAY OR MUSICAL
All's Well That Ends Well. Produced by the Royal Shakespeare Company.
A View from the Bridge. Produced by Zev Bufman and Sidney Schlenker
The Caine Mutiny Court-Martial. Produced by Circle in the Square Theatre and The Kennedy Center.
On Your Toes. Produced by Alfred De Liagre, Jr., Roger L. Stevens, John Mauceri, Donald R. Seawell, and Andre Pastoria

SPECIAL AWARDS
Oregon Shakespeare Festival Association, Ashland, Oregon

THEATRE AWARD '83
The Theatre Collection, Museum of the City of New York

The awards ceremony began at the Uris Theatre and ended at the Gershwin Theatre. The theatre was renamed during the Tony Award telecast.

38th ANNUAL TONY AWARDS
PRESENTED JUNE 3, 1984
GERSHWIN THEATRE

ACTRESS IN A PLAY
Glenn Close, *The Real Thing*
Rosemary Harris, *Heartbreak House*
Linda Hunt, *End of the World*
Kate Nelligan, *A Moon for the Misbegotten*

ACTOR IN A PLAY
Rex Harrison, *Heartbreak House*
Jeremy Irons, *The Real Thing*
Calvin Levels, *Open Admissions*
Ian McKellen, *Ian McKellen Acting Shakespeare*

FEATURED ACTRESS IN A PLAY
Christine Baranski, *The Real Thing*
Jo Henderson, *Play Memory*
Dana Ivey, *Heartbreak House*
Deborah Rush, *Noises Off*

FEATURED ACTOR IN A PLAY
Philip Bosco, *Heartbreak House*
Joe Mantegna, *Glengarry Glen Ross*
Robert Prosky, *Glengarry Glen Ross*
Douglas Seale, *Noises Off*

ACTRESS IN A MUSICAL
Rhetta Hughes, *The Amen Corner*
Liza Minnelli, *The Rink*
Bernadette Peters, *Sunday in the Park with George*
Chita Rivera, *The Rink*

ACTOR IN A MUSICAL
Gene Barry, *La Cage Aux Folles*
George Hearn, *La Cage Aux Folles*
Ron Moody, *Oliver!*
Mandy Patinkin, *Sunday in the Park with George*

FEATURED ACTRESS IN A MUSICAL
Martine Allard, *The Tap Dance Kid*
Liz Callaway, *Baby*
Dana Ivey, *Sunday in the Park with George*
Lila Kedrova, *Zorba*

FEATURED ACTOR IN A MUSICAL
Hinton Battle, *The Tap Dance Kid*
Stephen Geoffreys, *The Human Comedy*
Todd Graff, *Baby*
Samuel E. Wright, *The Tap Dance Kid*

PLAY
Glengarry Glen Ross, by David Mammet. Produced by Elliot Martin, The Shubert Organization, Arnold Bernhard, and The Goodman Theatre.
Noises Off, by Michael Frayn. Produced by James M. Nederlander, Robert Fryer, Jerome Minskoff, The Kennedy Center, Michael Codron, Jonathan Farkas, and MTM Enterprises.
Play Memory, by Joanna Glass. Produced by Alexander H. Cohen and Hildy Parks
The Real Thing, by Tom Stoppard. Produced by Emanuel Azenberg, The Shubert Organization, Icarus Productions, Byron Goldman, Ivan Bloch, Roger Berlind, and Michael Codron.

MUSICAL
Baby. Produced by James B. Freydberg, Ivan Bloch, Kenneth-John Productions, Suzanne J. Schwartz, and Manuscript Productions.
La Cage Aux Folles. Produced by Allan Carr, Kenneth D. Greenblatt, Marvin A. Kruass, Stewart F. Lane, James M. Nederlander, Martin Richards, Barry Brown, and Fritz Holt.

Sunday in the Park with George. Produced by The Shubert Organization and Emanuel Azenberg.
The Tap Dance Kid. Produced by Stanley White, Evelyn Barron, Harvey J. Klaris, and Michel Stuart.

SCORE OF A MUSICAL
Baby, music by David Shire; lyrics by Richard Maltby, Jr.
La Cage Aux Folles, music and lyrics by Jerry Herman
The Rink, music by John Kander; lyrics by Fred Ebb
Sunday in the Park with George, music and lyrics by Stephen Sondheim

BOOK OF A MUSICAL
Baby, by Sybille Pearson
La Cage Aux Folles, by Harvey Fierstein
Sunday in the Park with George, by James Lapine
The Tap Dance Kid, by Charles Blackwell

DIRECTOR OF A PLAY
Michael Blakemore, *Noises Off*
David Leveaux, A Moon for the Misbegotten
Gregory Mosher, *Glengarry Glen Ross*
Mike Nichols, *The Real Thing*

DIRECTOR OF A MUSICAL
James Lapine, *Sunday in the Park with George*
Arthur Laurents, *La Cage Aux Folles*
Richard Maltby, Jr., *Baby*
Vivian Matalon, *The Tap Dance Kid*

CHOREOGRAPHER
Wayne Cilento, *Baby*
Graciela Daniele, *The Rink*
Danny Daniels, *The Tap Dance Kid*
Scott Salmon, *La Cage Aux Folles*

SCENIC DESIGN
Clarke Dunham, *End of the World*
Peter Larkin, *The Rink*
Tony Straiges, *Sunday in the Park with George*
Tony Walton, *The Real Thing*

COSTUME DESIGN
Theoni V. Aldredge, *La Cage Aux Folles*
Jane Greenwood, *Heartbreak House*
Anthea Sylbert, *The Real Thing*
Patricia Zipprodt and Ann Hould-Ward, *Sunday in the Park with George*

LIGHTING DESIGN
Ken Billington, *End of the World*
Jules Fisher, *La Cage aux Folles*
Richard Nelson, *Sunday in the Park with George*
Marc B. Weiss, *A Moon for the Misbegotten*

REPRODUCTION OF A PLAY OR MUSICAL
American Buffalo. Produced by Elliot Martin and Arnold Bernhard.
Death of a Salesman. Produced by Robert Whitehead and Roger L. Stevens.
Heartbreak House. Produced by Circle in the Square.

A Moon for the Misbegotten. Produced by The Shubert Organization and Emanuel Azenberg.

SPECIAL AWARDS
Old Globe Theatre, San Diego, California
La Tragedie de Carmen, for outstanding achievement in musical theatre.
Peter Feller, a master craftsman who has devoted forty years to theatre stagecraft and magic.
A Chorus Line—a special gold Tony Award was presented to honor the longest-running Broadway show.

BROOKS ATKINSON AWARD (awarded this year only)
Al Hirschfeld, for sixty years of extraordinary service to the theatre.

39th ANNUAL TONY AWARDS
PRESENTED JUNE 2, 1985
SAM S. SHUBERT THEATER

OUTSTANDING ACTRESS IN A PLAY
Stockard Channing, *Joe Egg*
Sinead Cusack, *Much Ado About Nothing*
Rosemary Harris, *Pack of Lies*
Glenda Jackson, *Strange Interlude*

OUTSTANDING ACTOR IN A PLAY
Jim Dale, *Joe Egg*
Jonathan Hogan, *As Is*
Derek Jacobi, *Much Ado About Nothing*
John Lithgow, *Requiem for a Heavyweight*

OUTSTANDING FEATURED ACTRESS IN A PLAY
Joanna Gleason, *Joe Egg*
Judith Ivey, *Hurlyburly*
Theresa Merritt, *Ma Rainey's Black Bottom*
Sigourney Weaver, *Hurlyburly*

OUTSTANDING FEATURED ACTOR IN A PLAY
Charles S. Dutton, *Ma Rainey's Black Bottom*
William Hurt, *Hurlyburly*
Barry Miller, *Biloxi Blues*
Edward Petherbridge, *Strange Interlude*

OUTSTANDING FEATURED ACTRESS IN A MUSICAL
Evalyn Baron, *Quilters*
Leilani Jones, *Grind*
Mary Beth Peil, *The King and I*
Lenka Peterson, *Quilters*

OUTSTANDING FEATURED ACTOR IN A MUSICAL
Rene Auberjonois, *Big River*
Daniel H. Jenkins, *Big River*
Kurt Knudson, *Take Me Along*
Ron Richardson, *Big River*

OUTSTANDING PLAY
As Is, by William M. Hoffman. Produced by John Glines, Lawrence Lane, Lucille Lortel, and *The Shubert Organization.*

Biloxi Blues, by Neil Simon. Produced by Emanuel Azenberg and Center Theatre Group/Ahmanson Theatre, Los Angeles.
Hurlyburly, by David Rabe. Produced by Icarus Productions, Frederick M. Zollo, Ivan Bloch, and ERB Productions.
Ma Rainey's Black Bottom, by August Wilson. Produced by Ivan Bloch, Robert Cole, and Frederick M. Zollo.

OUTSTANDING MUSICAL
Big River. Produced by Rocco Landesman, Heidi Landesman, Rick Steiner, M. Anthony Fisher, and Dodger Productions.
Grind. Produced by Kenneth D. Greenblatt, John J. Pomerantz, Mary Lea Johnson, Martin Richards, James M. Nederlander, Harold Prince, Michael Frazier, Susan Madden Samson, and Jonathan Farkas.
Leader of the Pack. Produced by Elizabeth I. McCann, Nelle Nugent, Francine LeFrank, Clive Davis, John Hart Associates, Inc., Rodger Hess, and Richard Kagen.
Quilters. Produced by the Denver Center for the Performing Arts, The John F. Kennedy Center for the Performing Arts, The American National Theatre and Academy, and Brockman Seawell.

OUTSTANDING ORIGINAL SCORE
Big River, music and lyrics by Roger Miller
Grind, music by Larry Grossman; lyrics by Ellen Fitzhugh
Quilters, music and lyrics by Barbara Damashek

OUTSTANDING BOOK OF A MUSICAL
Big River, by William Hauptman
Grind, by Fay Kanin
Harrigan 'n Hart, by Michael Stewart
Quilters, by Molly Newman and Barbara Damashek

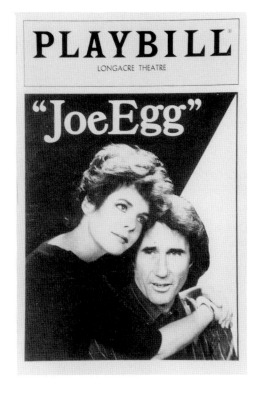

OUTSTANDING DIRECTION OF A PLAY
Keith Hack, *Strange Interlude*
Terry Hands, *Much Ado About Nothing*
Marshall W. Mason, *As Is*
Gene Saks, *Biloxi Blues*

OUTSTANDING DIRECTION OF A MUSICAL
Barbara Damashek, *Quilters*
Mitch Leigh, *The King and I*
Des McAnuff, *Big River*
Harold Prince, *Grind*

OUTSTANDING SCENIC DESIGN
Clarke Dunham, *Grind*
Ralph Koltai, *Much Ado About Nothing*
Heidi Landesman, *Big River*
Voytek and Michael Levine, *Strange Interlude*

OUTSTANDING COSTUME DESIGN
Florence Klotz, *Grind*
Patricia McGourty, *Big River*
Alexander Reid, *Cyrano de Bergerac*
Alexander Reid, *Much Ado About Nothing*

OUTSTANDING LIGHTING DESIGN
Terry Hands, *Cyrano de Bergerac*
Terry Hands, *Much Ado About Nothing*
Allen Lee Hughes, *Strange Interlude*
Richard Riddell, *Big River*

OUTSTANDING REPRODUCTION OF A PLAY OR MUSICAL
Cyrano de Bergerac. Produced by James M. Nederlander, Elizabeth I. McCann, Nelle Nugent, Cynthia Wood, Dale Duffy, and Allan Carr.
Joe Egg. Produced by The Shubert Organization, Emanuel Azenberg, Roger Berlind, Ivan Bloch, and MTM Enterprises, Inc.
Much Ado About Nothing. Produced by James M. Nederlander, Elizabeth I. McCann, Nelle Nugent, Cynthia Wood, Dale Duffy, and Allan Carr.
Strange Interlude. Produced by Robert Michael Geisler, John Roberdeau, Douglas Urbanski, James M. Nederlander, Duncan C. Weldon, Paul

Gregg, Lionel Becker, and Jerome Minskoff.

SPECIAL AWARDS
Steppenwolf Theater Company, Chicago, Illinois
New York State Council for the Arts
Yul Brynner, honoring his 4,525 performances in *The King and I*.

THE LAWRENCE LANGNER AWARD FOR LIFETIME ACHIEVEMENT IN THE THEATRE
Edwin Lester, Founder and General Manager for forty years of the Los Angeles Civic Light Opera

Three categories—Outstanding Actress in a Musical, Outstanding Actor in a Musical, and Outstanding Choreographer—were not awarded because the Tony Award nominating committee did not feel suitable candidates were available.

40th ANNUAL TONY AWARDS
PRESENTED JUNE 1, 1986
MINSKOFF THEATRE

ACTRESS IN A PLAY
Rosemary Harris, *Hay Fever*
Mary Beth Hurt, *Benefactors*
Jessica Tandy, *The Petition*
Lily Tomlin, *The Search for Signs of Intelligent Life in the Universe*

ACTOR IN A PLAY
Hume Cronyn, *The Petition*
Ed Harris, *Precious Sons*
Judd Hirsch, *I'm Not Rappaport*
Jack Lemmon, *Long Day's Journey into Night*

FEATURED ACTRESS IN A PLAY
Stockard Channing, *The House of Blue Leaves*
Swoosie Kurtz, *The House of Blue Leaves*
Bethel Leslie, *Long Day's Journey into Night*
Zoe Wanamaker, *Loot*

FEATURED ACTOR IN A PLAY
Peter Gallagher, *Long Day's Journey into Night*
Charles Keating, *Loot*
Joseph Maher, *Loot*
John Mahoney, *The House of Blue Leaves*

ACTRESS IN A MUSICAL
Debbie Allen, *Sweet Charity*
Cleo Laine, *The Mystery of Edwin Drood*
Bernadette Peters, *Song & Dance*
Chita Rivera, *Jerry's Girls*

ACTOR IN A MUSICAL
Don Correia, *Singin' in the Rain*
Cleavant Derricks, *Big Deal*
Maurice Hines, *Uptown . . . It's Hot!*
George Rose, *The Mystery of Edwin Drood*

FEATURED ACTRESS IN A MUSICAL
Patti Cohenour, *The Mystery of Edwin Drood*
Bebe Neuwirth, *Sweet Charity*
Jana Schneider, *The Mystery of Edwin Drood*
Elisabeth Welch, *Jerome Kern Goes to Hollywood*

FEATURED ACTOR IN A MUSICAL
Christopher d'Amboise, *Song & Dance*
John Herrera, *The Mystery of Edwin Drood*
Howard McGillin, *The Mystery of Edwin Drood*
Michael Rupert, *Sweet Charity*

PLAY
Benefactors, by Michael Frayn, Produced by James M. Nederlander, Robert Fryer, Douglas Urbanski, Michael Codron, MTM Enterprises, and CBS Productions.
Blood Knot, by Athol Fugard. Produced by James B. Freydberg, Max Weizenhoffer, Lucille Lortel, Estrin Rose Berman Productions, and FWM Producing Group.

The House of Blue Leaves, by John Guare. Produced by Lincoln Center Theatre, Gregory Mosher, and Bernard Gersten.
I'm Not Rappaport, by Herb Gardner. Produced by James Walsh, Lewis Allen, and Martin Heinfling.

MUSICAL
Big Deal. Produced by The Shubert Organization, Roger Berlind, Jerome Minskoff, and Jonathan Farkas.
The Mystery of Edwin Drood. Produced by Joseph Papp.
Song & Dance. Produced by Cameron MacKintoch, The Shubert Organization, FWM Producing Group, and The Really Useful Co.
Tango Argentino. Produced by Mel Howard and Donald K. Donald.

ORIGINAL SCORE
The Mystery of Edwin Drood, music and lyrics by Rupert Holmes
The News, music and lyrics by Paul Schierhorn
Song & Dance, music by Andrew Lloyd Webber; lyrics by Don Black and Richard Maltby, Jr.
Wind in the Willows, music by William Perry; lyrics by Roger McGough and William Perry

BOOK OF A MUSICAL
Big Deal, by Bob Fosse
The Mystery of Edwin Drood, by Rupert Holmes
Singin' In the Rain, by Betty Comden and Adolph Green
Wind in the Willows, by Jane Ireland

DIRECTION OF A PLAY
Jonathan Miller, *Long Day's Journey into Night*
José Quintero, *The Iceman Cometh*
John Tillinger, *Loot*
Jerry Zaks, *The House of Blue Leaves*

DIRECTION OF A MUSICAL
Bob Fosse, *Big Deal*

Wilford Leach, *The Mystery of Edwin Drood*
Richard Maltby, Jr., *Song & Dance*
Claudio Segovia and Hector Orezzoli, *Tango Argentino*

CHOREOGRAPHY
Graciela Daniele, *The Mystery of Edwin Drood*
Bob Fosse, *Big Deal*
Peter Martins, *Song & Dance*
Tango Argentino Dancers, *Tango Argentino*

SCENIC DESIGN
Ben Edwards, *The Iceman Cometh*
David Mitchell, *The Boys of Winter*
Beni Montressor, *The Marriage of Figaro*
Tony Walton, *The House of Blue Leaves*

COSTUME DESIGN
Willa Kim, *Song & Dance*
Beni Montressor, *The Marriage of Figaro*

Ann Roth, *The House of Blue Leaves*
Patricia Zipprodt, *Sweet Charity*

LIGHTING DESIGN
Pat Collins, *I'm Not Rappaport*
Jules Fisher, *Song and Dance*
Paul Gallo, *The House of Blue Leaves*
Thomas R. Skelton, *The Iceman Cometh*

REPRODUCTION OF A PLAY OR MUSICAL
Hay Fever. Produced by Roger Peters and MBS Co.
The Iceman Cometh. Produced by Lewis Allen, James M. Nederlander, Stephen Graham, and Ben Edwards.
Loot. Produced by The David Merrick Arts Foundation, Charles P. Kopelman, and Mark Simon.
Sweet Charity. Produced by Jerome Minskoff, James M. Nederlander, Arthur Rubin, and Joseph Harris.

SPECIAL AWARDS
American Repertory Theatre, Cambridge, Massachusetts

41st ANNUAL TONY AWARDS
PRESENTED JUNE 7, 1987
MARK HELLINGER THEATRE

ACTRESS IN A PLAY
Lindsay Duncan, *Les Liaisons Dangereuses*
Linda Lavin, *Broadway Bound*
Geraldine Page, *Blithe Spirit*
Amanda Plummer, *Pygmalion*

ACTOR IN A PLAY
Philip Bosco, *You Never Can Tell*
James Earl Jones, *Fences*
Richard Kiley, *All My Sons*
Alan Rickman, *Les Liaisons Dangereuses*

FEATURED ACTRESS IN A PLAY
Mary Alice, *Fences*
Annette Bening, *Coastal Disturbances*

Phyllis Newman, *Broadway Bound*
Carole Shelley, *Stepping Out*

FEATURED ACTOR IN A PLAY
Frankie R. Faison, *Fences*
John Randolph, *Broadway Bound*
Jamey Sheridan, *All My Sons*
Courtney B. Vance, *Fences*

ACTRESS IN A MUSICAL
Catherine Cox, *Oh Coward!*
Maryann Plunkett, *Me and My Girl*
Teresa Stratas, *Rags*

ACTOR IN A MUSICAL
Roderick Cook, *Oh Coward!*
Robert Lindsay, *Me and My Girl*
Terrence Mann, *Les Misérables*
Colm Wilkinson, *Les Misérables*

FEATURED ACTRESS IN A MUSICAL
Jane Connell, *Me and My Girl*
Judy Kuhn, *Les Misérables*
Frances Ruffelle, *Les Misérables*
Jane Summerhays, *Me and My Girl*

FEATURED ACTOR IN A MUSICAL
George S. Irving, *Me and My Girl*
Timothy Jerome, *Me and My Girl*
Michael Maguire, *Les Misérables*
Robert Torti, *Starlight Express*

PLAY
Broadway Bound, by Neil Simon. Produced by Emanuel Azenberg.
Coastal Disturbances, by Tina Howe. Produced by Circle in the Square, Theodore Mann, and Paul Libin.
***Fences,* by August Wilson. Produced by Carole Shorenstein Hays and the Yale Repertory Theatre.**
Les Liaisons Dangereuses, by Christopher Hampton. Produced by James M. Nederlander, the Shubert Organization, Jerome Minskoff, Elizabeth I. McCann, Stephen Graham, and Jonathan Farkas.

MUSICAL
***Les Misérables.* Produced by Cameron Mackintosh.**

PLAYBILL
MARK HELLINGER THEATRE

The League of American Theatres and Producers and The American Theatre Wing present the 41st Annual Antoinette Perry Awards

Me and My Girl. Produced by Richard Armitage, Terry Allen Kramer, James M. Nederlander, and Stage Promotions Limited & Company.
Rags. Produced by Lee Guber, Martin Heinfling, and Marvin A. Krauss.
Starlight Express. Produced by Martin Starger and Lord Lew Grade.

ORIGINAL SCORE
***Les Misérables,* music and lyrics by Claude-Michel Schönberg, Herbert Kretzmer, and Alain Boublil.**
Me and My Girl, music by Noel Gay; lyrics by L. Arthur Rose, Douglas Furber, Stephen Fry, and Mike Ockrent.
Rags, music by Charles Strouse; lyrics by Stephen Schwartz.
Starlight Express, music by Andrew Lloyd Webber; lyrics by Richard Stilgoe.

BOOK OF A MUSICAL
Les Misérables, **by Alain Boublil and Claude-Michel Schönberg.**
Me and My Girl, by L. Arthur Rose, Douglas Furber, Stephen Fry, and Mike Ockrent.
Rags, by Joseph Stein.
Smile, by Howard Ashman.

DIRECTION OF A PLAY
Howard Davies, *Les Liaisons Dangereuses*
Mbongeni Ngema, *Asinamali!*
Lloyd Richards, *Fences*
Carole Rothman, *Coastal Disturbances*

DIRECTION OF A MUSICAL
Brian Macdonald, *The Mikado*
Trevor Nunn and John Caird, *Les Misérables*
Trevor Nunn, *Starlight Express*
Mike Ockrent, *Me and My Girl*

CHOREOGRAPHY
Ron Field, *Rags*

Gillian Gregory, *Me and My Girl*
Brian Macdonald, *The Mikado*
Arlene Phillips, *Starlight Express*

SCENIC DESIGN
Bob Crowley, *Les Liaisons Dangereuses*
Martin Jones, *Me and My Girl*
John Napier, *Les Misérables*
Tony Walton, *The Front Page*

COSTUME DESIGN
Bob Crowley, *Les Liaisons Dangereuses*
Ann Curtis, *Me and My Girl*
John Napier, *Starlight Express*
Andreane Neofitou, *Les Misérables*

LIGHTING DESIGN
Martin Aronstein, *Wild Honey*
David Hersey, *Les Misérables*
David Hersey, *Starlight Express*
Chris Parry and Beverly Emmons, *Les Liaisons Dangereuses*

REPRODUCTION OF A PLAY OR MUSICAL
All My Sons. **Produced by Jay H. Fuchs,** Steven Warnick, and Charles Patsos.
The Front Page. Produced by Lincoln Center Theater, Gregory Mosher, and Bernard Gerstein.
The Life and Adventures of Nicholas Nickleby. Produced by the Shubert Organization, Three Knights, Ltd., and Robert Fox, Ltd.
Pygmalion. Produced by the Shubert Organization, Jerome Minskoff, and Duncan C. Weldon.

SPECIAL AWARDS
George Abbott, on the occasion of his 100th birthday.
Jackie Mason, for *The World According to Me.*
The San Francisco Mime Troupe

LAWRENCE LANGNER MEMORIAL AWARD FOR DISTINGUISHED LIFETIME ACHIEVEMENT IN THE AMERICAN THEATRE
Robert Preston (posthumous)

INDEX

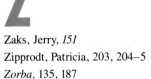

PICTURE CREDITS